AMYTHIA

LOYAL D. RUE

AMYTHIA

Crisis in the Natural History of Western Culture

with a Foreword by
William G. Doty

The University of Alabama Press
Tuscaloosa and London

Library of Congress Cataloging-in-Publication Data

Rue, Loyal D.
Amythia : crisis in the natural history of western culture.

Bibliography: p.
Includes index
1. Myth. 2. Civilization, Modern—20th century.
I. Title.
BL304.R84 1989   291.1'3   88-27846
ISBN 0–8173–0428–2

British Library Cataloguing-in-Publication Data available.

With all my love,
for

Carl Anders Boonsong
Anna Christine Sirikit
Elena Marso Surin

Contents

Foreword

It would be simplistic to suppose that anyone today might easily resolve the question that Friedrich Nietzsche posed around the turn of the century:

> And now the myth-less man remains eternally hungering among all the bygones, and digs and grubs for roots, though he have to dig for them even among the remotest antiquities. The stupendous historical exigency of the unsatisfied modern culture, the gathering around one of the countless other cultures, the consuming desire for knowledge—what does all this point to, if not to the loss of myth, the loss of the mythical home, the mythical source?[1]

As recently as 1972, William Barrett could conclude only that "the emancipation from myth leaves us neurotic."[2]

But Loyal Rue attempts a resolution: he does so by naming "amythia" as a root problem of Nietzschean proportions, a problem that leaves our culture unlikely to "survive very far into the twenty-first century" unless we find ways of countering its influence. The mythology we have inherited is no longer serviceable and may even be damaging—including the established mythico-theological perspectives founded upon the metaphor that Deity is Person.

Rue minces few words: "There is no longer any point in being mealymouthed about it; the personal metaphor of God is dead," and today it may even be the cause of alienation. Such a metaphor requires one to deny the scientific worldview according to which I have my illnesses treated by a physician or according to which my automobile functions as well as it does.

Amythia results when cosmology and morality are not effectively integrated by a root metaphor, and the only possibility for the future is to transpose the old Christian notion of God as Person to a root metaphor that is even older in origin, the concept of the Covenant tradition inherited from Israel but understood now in a nonsupernaturalist manner.

This is a most provocative analysis of the ways our culture suffers amythia: we now lack a coherent mythological basis for our highly developed Western civilization, and intellectual freedom has given way to the most extreme sort of moral pluralism, with consequent loss of any innate connection between rights and responsibilities. (Here Rue pursues many of the problematics identified recently in various acclaimed books: Robert Bellah and others, *Habits of the Heart*; Alastair MacIntyre, *After Virtue*; and Allan Bloom, *The Closing of the American Mind*.)

Rue seeks to commission a new mythopoesis, a new artistic realization of the basic metaphor of Covenant—which he interprets not as modeling a deity:human relationship as much as a quality of intensity of human experience. In myth "we encounter the integrity of cosmology and morality," and there—according to Rue—we might come to appreciate the continuity of what much of the Christian world has considered polar opposites: nature and culture.

Rue works for a reintegration of the realms of the biological and the cultural, if not indeed for the recognition that theology is a way of charting the "natural history of culture." Perhaps the first contemporary work to argue that biological findings are as normative for a contemporary worldview as the theological or mythological views of our received traditions, Rue's book posits *evolution* as the metaphor which might replace the myth of God as person that has led us into such straits in which subjectivity has become a burden, a superplus symptom of amythia. When God "died," we turned to the Self as the new absolute, a turning which leaves us no less repressively tyrannized than did any Law of the past. In such a situation God-Talk has disappeared from the discourse of routine intelligent conversation—the only holdout being the brief worship hours of the various religious bodies. Philosophy's vocation—that of countervailing amythia—is lost in a pluralistic age that is "overwhelmed with meaning."

You will soon learn that basic cultural critque happens in this volume—but also the attempts of a sympathetic writer to deal with some of the most painful and awkward junctures of our times: the tone of the last chapter suggests that there are ways in which a contemporary person might address amythia, particularly by going back into "the churches" armed with the metaphor of evolution and the hermeneutics of adaptivity.

"Ooh, heaven is a place on earth," intones the singing group on the radio as I write these words, and I suspect few of us who work regularly with public audiences can shirk any longer the necessity of acknowledging the loss of religious/mythic centers in our own audiences' experiences. More than once I have had students yawn at the suggestion that existentialist literature named something crucially absent and yet painfully everpresent: the naming of that absence has become part of the rock music that surrounds them, while they see only options such as apartheid or the bomb offering realistic counters to such apathy. However, Rue is not so ready to call it quits; he writes as a person of commitment ready to readapt and readjust his own religious traditions, and he calls upon readers to do likewise.

A state university press's willingness to publish a work that does not blink the fact that it engages theological concerns is a sign of our times: first, because theology need not equal propaganda for a particular religious tradition but can quite legitimately develop within the collegiate academy that also supports theoretical sociologists, Marxian economists, or political scientists and business specialists whose works are crucial to regional and national policy.

Moreover, we saw the academic discipline of religious studies move to the university (away from the religious sponsorship of seminaries and professional schools), and the first wave of its work was oh, so terribly noncommital and free of values. A second wave is now beginning to demand that the discipline attend not just to the historical contours of religions ("the history of religions" or "comparative religions") but to their formal metaphysical articulations as well (hence engaging such subdisciplines as "history of doctrine," "systematic theology," and "historical theology").

Rue's direction in his concluding chapter is hardly uninvolved and free of values. Instead he shares with us some of his own hard-won views and beliefs. The reader can choose to follow Rue here or not. The university does *not*, certainly, assume the role of a religious body approving such a position—or disapproving it. Indeed, it is clearly remaining responsible to one assignment of a contemporary university, which is to assure that carefully reasoned arguments such as Rue's receive a forum for wide discussion. The tone of the last chapter—especially its use of the pronoun "you"—is not something to which we are accustomed in works of scholarship, but I suggest it may well be time for such books to resume their role as arbitrators between the meaningless and the meaningful.

There will be many responses to the problem Rue identifies with his analytical sections, but the logic of our situation is that precisely the amythic response is pluralistic and multiple. Rue's own analytics as well as his conclusions are uncomfortable for most of us—he does not shirk the problems of "extreme pluralism," namely its being "inimical to the integration of our culture" and therefore being "maladaptive," and he can be vituperative about the "health care" industry's cadging bucks from us all when health care should be part of the elementary rights of our contemporary humankind—but what he has to say ought to be heard in many venues of contemporay society.

If there are more postmodern ways of admitting the ways in which we need to reshuffle and reshape our mythic past, I have yet to hear of them. Rue goes beyond such voices as that of Lyotard, who speaks of the death of master narratives. We ought to be grateful that there are such prophetic voices as Rue's to begin the questioning and revisioning that can be the only sort of "salvation" in a radically contemporary world.

Department of Religious Studies   William G. Doty
University of Alabama

Acknowledgments

I once described the contents of this book to a colleague, who immediately attempted to dissuade me from its completion because "those who don't ignore it will condemn it." Perhaps, finally, he will be right. But I persisted nevertheless—partly, no doubt, because there was some therapeutic return in bringing the argument to closure, but not least because others who were patient enough to listen to my thesis responded with varying degress of enthusiasm.

The bulk of the manuscript was written during a visiting fellowship at St. Aidan's College, University of Durham. To colleagues and friends there I owe a debt of gratitude—to some for academic stimulation and criticism and to others for creating an atmosphere of conviviality. Special thanks go to Bishop David Jenkins, Dean Peter Baelz, Irene Hindmarsh, Geoffrey Thrush, Richard Roberts, James D. G. Dunn, Stephen W. Sykes, John McHugh, Deborah Lavin, and Kevin and Becky Lewis.

It is a pleasure also to express my thanks to colleagues at Luther College, several of whom read portions of the manuscript and made valuable contributions to its development. I am especially grateful to Phillip Reitan, John Whelan, Werner Nitschke, Conrad Røyksund, and James C. Hippen.

To H. George Anderson, president, and to the Board of Regents of Luther College, I am grateful for the opportunity of a leave to work on this project. And to the American Lutheran Church I am grateful for a Faculty Growth Award.

ACKNOWLEDGMENTS

Most of all, I am indebted to my wife, Marilyn, for her encouragement and support and for occasionally reminding me that scholarship takes second place to family.

Luther College   Loyal D. Rue
Decorah, Iowa

AMYTHIA

Introduction

It was the best of times, it was the worst of times, it was the age of wisdom, it was the age of foolishness, it was the epoch of belief, it was the epoch of incredulity, it was the season of Light, it was the season of Darkness, it was the spring of hope, it was the winter of despair, we had everything before us, we had nothing before us, we were all going direct to Heaven, we were all going direct the other way.

—Dickens, *A Tale of Two Cities*

The most unsettling irony of contemporary experience is that the finest hour in the realization of creative potential in Western civilization is also a moment in which its self-destructive tendencies have become most evident. Never before in the history of humankind has civilization achieved such powers of self-determination and control over its environment as those achieved by Western civilization in the twentieth century. And yet it is doubtful that any civilization has heretofore experienced such a marked lack of confidence and clarity of purpose.

No single artificial wonder of the world provides as dramatic a testimony to superior technological achievement as the image of a human being standing on the surface of the moon. And no civilization has achieved anything close to the unique perspective on the human condition that is represented by the "blue marble" photographs of the planet earth. The wonders of space flight are rivaled only by the major accomplishments of Western civilization in areas such as agriculture and medical science. Never before in human history has a civilization so enjoyed the luxury of unconcern about its food supply, and never before have humans felt less threatened by disease. The

1

advances in transportation and communications characteristic of the late twentieth century have brought Western culture closer to realizing Alexander's ideal of "one world" than anyone would have dreamed only a few generations ago. Virtually no place on earth has remained unaffected by Western culture, and even those third world leaders to whom Western ideals are anathema are not above consuming the fruits of its creative genius.

And yet, at the precise moment of its greatest manifestations of vitality and creativity, there arise serious questions about the ability of Western culture to survive. The fault lines of degeneration are undeniable, and we are now at a point where the rapid and irreversible collapse of our way of life could begin to take place. Every major city in Western civilization is targeted for destruction by nuclear weapons; violent crime has become a routine feature of life in our great cities; terrorist attacks on Western culture throughout the world are now not only feared but expected. The malaise of the West is profound, penetrating deep into the tissues of social institutions and individual lives. No period in the history of Western civilization has been more extensively shaped by the politics of expediency and self-aggrandizement. Political leaders are not loath to sacrifice the future as they pander to the immediate concerns of voters. The family is becoming dysfunctional as a unit of care and moral instruction. School officials complain that they are not prepared to deal with the severity of the emotional disorders becoming common among our youth. The children of Western culture are unable to imagine a meaningful future, partly because of the bomb, but also because they are conditioned to see the future in selfish terms. The future, for too many of us now, is regarded as something to grab a *share of* and not something to take a *part in*.

Western culture, as this essay will claim, is in a state of crisis because it has lost something fundamental to the achievement of collective coherence and individual wholeness: it has lost a shared orientation in nature and in history. Intellectual pluralism in Western society has finally given way to moral relativism, and under the conditions of moral relativity, individuals identify no necessary connection between rights and responsibilities. Ultimately we lack a cultural mythology that might function as a matrix of shared meanings. Without such a mythology we lack the resources to achieve collective coherence and personal wholeness. And under these conditions, that is, the conditions of *amythia*, there is little chance that Western culture will survive very far into the twenty-first century.

This view is shared by many observers of contemporary culture, but there seems to be little agreement about how we came to this point and what might be done about it. This failure of agreement (which is itself symptomatic of the problem) becomes most clear when we look at contemporary attitudes toward the religious traditions of our culture. Religious conservatives and their cultured despisers may agree rather quickly that Western culture is suffering from an intellectual and moral crisis, and they might even agree that the situation results from a loss of shared meanings, but beyond this point there is very little intelligible discourse. The religious conservative will argue that we must restore the authority of the biblical tradition, for after all, this tradition has shaped the distinctive character of Western culture. The cultured despisers of religion will argue that the Bible has no legitimate claim to authority, since it is the record of an ancient mentality and as such is a source of error and moral confusion when introduced to the modern mind. Anachronistic myths, they would assert, are implausible because they give us fantasies where we need hope. Only a rigorously contemporary myth can place our hopes where our energies can make a difference.

I have tried to be sensitive to the arguments from both sides of this perennial dilemma. There is no question that the distinctive identity of Western culture largely reflects the Judaeo-Christian religious orientation, and to deny the claims that have been placed upon us by three thousand years of history would be foolhardy indeed. Any approach to contemporary problems that involves a wholesale rejection of our tradition would be a recipe for extinction. Such impetuous experiments, where we find them, have never been successful. So we must take great care to preserve a bond of essential continuity with our past. But the importance of the past for preserving identity should not lead us to discredit the demands of the present for intellectual plausibility. Plausibility is no less essential to the achievement of collective coherence and personal wholeness than is continuity of a distinctive identity. No culture has managed to survive solely on the strength of its fidelity to a former way of life and thought. The demands of the present will not be denied, nor will they be well served by efforts to apply to them the solutions of the past.

Every period in history is faced with this problem of resolving tensions between distinctiveness and plausibility, and ours is no exception. But we must not minimize the dimensions of our contemporary crisis with the facile assumption that "this too will pass." There are no guarantees that our form of culture will exist forever. And by all appearances, the alarmists among us are the better judges of historical realities. Ours is *not* like every other moment in history. It is like only a few others; it is like perhaps three or four moments in the three thousand years of Judaeo-Christian tradition.

It is a curious phenomenon of social and cultural evolution that the beliefs, values, and character types producing a new way of life or a new era of history are often the ones least suited to survive under the new conditions. Consider the restless and fiercely autonomous figures who first charted pathways into the American West to make conditions safe for farmers and townspeople. These pioneers were strangely out of place in the settled patterns of life they made possible, and soon they became an extinct breed of men. This phenomenon provides a fitting analogue to the present intellectual and moral crisis. I shall, in fact, be arguing that the mythology we have inherited from our religious past is no longer appropriate to the intellectual milieu it brought forth. The values, habits, beliefs, hopes, and expectations which ordered life for centuries of intellectual history seem to be of little worth to a civilization which has achieved our level of mastery over its environment. They may even, to be honest, prove to be damaging.

The perennial dialectic between distinctiveness and plausibility has, in our time, gone well beyond the point of creative tension to become a source of cultural malaise. The myth we have inherited from our religious past now appears so implausible in the contemporary setting that it has lost its power to captivate the modern imagination and thereby to provide the cognitive resources for collective coherence and personal

4

wholeness. The source of irony in contemporary experience is that the myth which has ultimately generated a scientifically and technologically superior culture is unable to sustain the conditions under which that culture can hope to survive. The irony highlights the paradox of contemporary Western culture: we are now at one of those rare and paradoxical moments in our intellectual history when, for the sake of continuity, we are called to make a radical departure from the conventions of the past.

It is difficult to assess just when the malaise of amythia began to be felt. Certainly Nietzsche was aware of the problems looming ahead for Western culture. But not until Nietzsche's penetrating insight had been distilled by contemporary forms of art and literature did the loss of personal wholeness and social coherence begin to take on the dimensions of amythia.

Underlying the argument of this book is a fundamental conviction that our religious institutions can play a significant role in the revitalization of Western culture. I may be wrong in this judgment; the church may be, as many have argued, too hidebound and too complex to respond adequately to the contemporary challenge. But I see nothing to be gained by giving up on the church; it will not go away. And if the church itself is not brought to make a radical departure from the past, then it will remain a formidable obstacle to any revitalization attempts centered outside the church. The task of averting amythia is to be accomplished not by leaving the church, but by changing it radically.

The paradox of Western culture therefore defines the challenge facing the contemporary church. If the church fails to meet the contemporary demands for plausibility in its expression of faith, then Western culture will continue on its course of self-destruction. But if, on the other hand, the church's expression of faith does not preserve an essential continuity with tradition, there will result an equally fatal loss of identity.

The solution to amythia proposed in these chapters calls for nothing less than the generation of a new venture into mythopoesis. The myth of the Judaeo-Christian tradition fails in its appeal to the modern mind because it employs metaphors powerless to excite the imagination. Nothing short of a radically new constellation of meanings can change that. What is important to the church's identity is that the essence of the tradition does not become lost in the transposition of faith to a new key. This challenge can be met only if we are clear about what the essence of Judaeo-Christian piety has been throughout the tradition. It will be argued here that the truly distinctive element in the tradition has been the idea of Covenant. The challenge of modern culture is, therefore, to transpose the Covenant tradition to new and plausible conventions of meaning.

A transposition of the Covenant tradition calls for an aesthetic reawakening. It belongs to the provinces of art to bring new conventions of meaning into the popular imagination; it will therefore be up to the poets, painters, sculptors, novelists, songwriters, filmmakers, and the like to revitalize Western culture. What I have in mind in this book is not to actually begin the new venture into mythopoesis but rather to legitimate it—or, better, to *commission* the work. This commission asks contemporary artists to reissue the tradition in terms of a new perspective on nature and history. When the early Hebrews finally rejected the nature myths of the ancient Near East, they generated a tradition in which history transcends nature. Nature, in the biblical tradition, became an instrument for God's purposes in history. Our commission calls the contemporary artist to see beyond this perspective to achieve a fundamental reorientation of the tradition. It will not suffice any longer to regard Covenant history as a supernatural process. Nor do we look for a return to the primitive naturalism of the ancient mind with its closed view of history. We must now generate the elements of a myth which regards culture as a natural phenomenon and nature as a historical phenomenon. We commission the arts, therefore, to generate conventions which are consistent with a natural history of the Covenant tradition.

Under conventional categories this book belongs to the discipline of philosophical theology, but I prefer to use the term "natural history of culture" to describe what I do. The title of the book reinforces this view by asserting that amythia is a critical condition within the natural history of Western culture. I will need to explain what I mean by the discipline "natural history of culture." Indeed, I shall have to make the case that there *can be* a natural history of culture, since we are accustomed to regard nature and culture as phenomena sufficiently independent to require their own disciplines for study. This task will occupy our attention for the next two chapters. The focus of these chapters will take us well beyond the boundaries of philosophy and theology, but in the process it is hoped that a fresh and gainful perspective on culture and the religious life will emerge.

The argument of this book begins with a theoretical perspective on the place of human culture within the scope of natural history (chapter 1). It then proceeds to establish the conceptual foundations for a natural history of culture (chapter 2). Chapter 3 takes an overview of the natural history of Western culture to expose the origins and depth of the contemporary intellectual and moral crisis. Chapters 4 and 5 attempt to specify and justify the limits of distinctiveness and plausibility appropriate for the task of transposing the Covenant tradition. The final chapter, which is in some ways out of character with the rest of the book, appeals to the mythmakers of contemporary culture to take up the challenge of amythia.

1

Nature and Culture

Richard Dawkins, a behavioral ecologist at Oxford University, opens an early chapter in *The Selfish Gene* with the line, "In the beginning was simplicity."[1] This obvious allusion to Genesis is followed by an account of how the origins of life emerged as large, stable molecules replaced simpler, unstable ones. While I have not checked with Dawkins personally on this point, it does seem clear enough that he is making a claim for the "scriptural" authority of scientific, especially biological, theory. And why not? It will be one of the fundamental assumptions of this book that no aspect of human life (not even the religious) can be adequately understood in isolation from its biological context. Yet this book is not about biology in any technical sense. It discusses the Judaeo-Christian theological tradition and asserts at the outset that what we do theologically is not biologically unimportant. So committed am I to this assertion that I begin with a summary of an evolutionary perspective which I believe is a prerequisite to any responsible attempt at understanding the past or present theological scene or to any credible urge to chart its future. It may be argued that an introductory chapter of this sort is out of order here because it has nothing to do with theology. I happen to think that evolution has everything to do with theology, and my only hesitation about including this chapter is that some readers might find it an acceptable substitute for more extensive and serious reading on the subject. It is now unpardonable for theological reflection to proceed without grounding itself in a biological self-understanding. It is therefore time we accepted contemporary biology as a *normative* resource for the theological enterprise. This is to suggest not that biology is in any way equipped to determine a theological perspective but that it is in a position to judge the intellectual plausibility of theology.

Natural History

The universe came in, as it were, with a bang. The "big bang," as we now refer to our ultimate origins, happened about 15 billion years ago. At this moment, as Dawkins says, was simplicity. Scientists now believe that the various complicated realities of the universe originated in an unbelievably dense "hot spot" billions of times smaller than a single proton. Such simplicity is not simple to imagine. Within a millionth of a millionth of a microsecond after the big bang, complexity began to set in. First came a separation of the once-unified fundamental forces of nature (gravity, electromagnetism, the strong atomic force, and the weak atomic force). As the universe expanded and cooled, particles of matter (first hydrogen and helium) were formed and transformed by the four forces until they began to achieve stability. In this process stars were born and then died, thereby creating more complex forms of matter which, in turn, stabilized. Simplicity . . . bang . . . diversity . . . complexity . . . stability . . . then more complexity and more stability. And all the while there occurred expansion, cooling condensation, attraction, and organization.

According to the most recent estimates, our solar system was born in this process about 4.6 billion years ago. The diversification, complexification, and stabilization of matter continued after the formation of the earth. In the absence of a protective ozone layer, the earth was bombarded with ultraviolet radiation, precipitating photochemical reactions in the "probiotic soup." The first organic compounds to appear were amino acids which were capable of combining into larger molecules. These were followed by proteins and a host of increasingly complex carbon compounds, the most efficient of which would have the gift of transforming other substances into their own by the process known as autocatalysm. These complex and efficient organisms included some which had nuclei and the capacity to replicate themselves. Life!

The etiquette of growth and reproduction of organisms is the province of the DNA molecule found within the nuclei of cells.

DNA molecules have a most amazing structure; each consists of a double spiral (helix) chain with links composed of the four kinds of nucleotides common to all life forms. Nucleotides are responsible for directing the replication of cells in an organism. The order in which these nucleotides are strung out along the double chains (chromosomes) is informative in the sense that it determines the architecture of an organism: the location, sequence, and quantity of cell production throughout a body. Segments of the chromosomes which contain information governing the manifestation of specific structural and behavioral traits are called genes.

In bisexual reproduction, information contained in the genetic material from one parent recombines with genetic material from the other parent to form the DNA molecule that will be present in every cell of the offspring. There results a reshuffling of the order of genetic material with each generation, so that offspring emerge with unique combinations of characteristics. It is the "job" of individual genes to remain intact during the reproductive process. When we reshuffle a deck of cards, the units remain the same (in a reshuffled deck the queen of hearts remains the queen of hearts). But sometimes copy errors (mutations) occur in the replication of genetic material, and when these random errors occur in reproductive cells (gametes), they result in genetic novelty which then has a chance of being transmitted to the next generation. In the card game of biological reproduction, the queen of hearts may well turn up as the "buffoon of stars" in the next generation.

Genetic mutations are relatively rare and in most cases are harmful. Occasionally, however, errors in replicating the DNA code will bring about new traits which are beneficial. "Beneficial" and "harmful" have meaning relative to the process of natural selection. A beneficial trait is one that enhances the probability of reproductive success for the organism bearing the trait. A trait is harmful if it reduces the probability of reproductive success. This process is the fuel of evolution. Organisms which inherit beneficial mutations will leave more progeny than those which inherit harmful mutations. Beneficial traits will therefore "radiate" throughout a population group, while harmful traits will be selected out. Both in the prebiotic evolution of chemicals and in the evolution of living organisms, there were selective advantages for those organisms which developed greater complexity and efficiency.

The process of natural selection would tend to favor those organisms which inherited mechanisms for the efficient acquisition and storage of energy. Any development which enhanced this ability would have been adaptive (beneficial) vis-à-vis the environment of the organism. Likewise, any mechanism enabling an organism to acquire and store information about the circumstances of its environment would also be adaptive. These two complex functions (energy transfer and information processing) together describe the general characteristics that would bring advantage to individuals, as they are the functions that would most effectively resist the selective pressures operating in the biotic environment:

> A closer approximation to what really happens in organic nature would be to describe it as follows: life is an eminently active enterprise aimed at acquiring both a fund of energy and a stock of knowledge, the possession of one being instrumental to the acquisition of the other. The immense effectiveness of these two feedback cycles, coupled in multiplying interaction, is the precondition, indeed the explanation, for the fact that life has the power to assert itself against the superior strength of the pitiless inorganic world.[2]

Konrad Lorenz has proposed that this dual feedback cycle is the most important feature in any attempt to account both for the direction of evolution from simple organisms toward complex ones and for the acceleration of evolution among more complex life forms.

If there is a Rubicon in evolutionary history, it must surely be the appearance of an organism which possessed the capacity to store more information in its brain than in its genes. This achievement occurred something like a billion years ago among reptiles and started a long and eventful odyssey toward conscious and self-conscious behavior. These primitive reptilian brains were capable of processing information in a rather direct and mechanical fashion, without involving the construction of anything similar to the perceptual world typical of mammalian intelligence. Instead, we can assume that their intellectual life

11

was no more complicated or interesting than a limited repertoire of specific and invariable reflexes to stimuli. It is even
likely that the eyes of these early reptiles were capable of as
much discrimination as their brains were. The ratio of information output (response) to information input (stimulus) was
probably no greater than one to one. And if the character of
stimuli changed appreciably as a result of environmental
changes, there was simply nothing to be done about it. These
brains were hard-wired for very specific transactions.

The next significant spurt in the evolution of intelligence
came roughly 200 million years ago with the arrival of primitive
mammals. As nocturnal creatures these mammals needed an
auditory mechanism that would make them aware of nearby
predators. They also retained (dimly) the visual powers of their
reptilian ancestors. But there was a major difference. In reptiles,
visual stimuli were preencoded in the eye before transmission
to the brain. In contrast, the paleomammalian brain was
equipped to perform an additional encoding function—to integrate the recording of visual stimuli together with auditory
stimuli. The difference meant that mammals were to enjoy an
enhanced experience of reality. With the ability to coordinate
spatial (visual) and temporal (auditory) stimuli, mammals had
acquired a sense that reality had duration as well as location.
An advantageous adaptation of this sort would have radiated
quickly throughout small mammalian populations, with the
result that mammalian brains would be significantly larger
(relative to body size), more structurally complex, and more
plastic than reptilian brains.

And then, about 60 million years ago, vast climatic changes
in many parts of the world altered the supply of food for large
reptiles. Without the flexibility to adjust to new environmental
conditions, they did the only thing they could do—they became
extinct. Now it was safe for mammals to invade the ecological
niches left vacant by the reptiles. This event was followed by
another quantum leap in evolutionary history, the proliferation
of mammalian orders. For those mammals that ventured into
the daylight, vision became an important sense, as it had been
for reptiles. By now, though, there were organisms better
equipped to encode larger quantities of visual information, including refined color discrimination, and to coordinate them

with new sounds. Such development made the information load on the nervous system almost burdensome. Sounds, shapes, colors, and motion all had to be integrated into a consistent spatial and temporal field. The brains that would be able to achieve this function most efficiently would benefit from a distinct selective advantage. By sheer chance of random mutation, some mammalian brains happened to be sufficiently large and complex to be able to perform an operation that was quite radically new: a summation of the flow of information into clusters (subroutines, for the computer enthusiast) representing "objects" in a perceptual world.

The ability to construct a perceptual world of discrete objects turned out to be an enormous advantage which started a new phase of evolution in brain size. For the next several million years (until about 3 million years ago) we find a sustained elaboration of this cognitive function to include the integration of tactile, visual, and auditory sensations. Eventually, too, there was added the ability to recognize recurrent sequences of events, which amounted to a rudimentary apprehension of process. The age of the mammals was a period of gradual encephalization (enlargement of brain mass relative to body mass) with accompanying improvemets in perceptual abilities. At the same time, there was a development toward greater plasticity of the brain, together with more flexibility in behavior. The brain was developing a greater capacity to achieve economy in its encoding, which resulted in greater variability of behavioral responses. As the mammals evolved, they became more perceptive and more creative.

Essential to these developments is the process of speciation. When organisms reproduce in isolated niches, morphological changes resulting from mutations will eventually produce unique traits that are not shared by remote descendants of once common genetic stock. And when the isolated populations are small enough, any adaptations will spread rapidly, so that new species appear. This process exploded in the Cenozoic era. Of course these developments all took place according to the painstaking logic of natural selection. Within some mammalian species the conspiracy of mutation and selective pressures produced dramatic encephalization. With each successive generation, chance mutations furnished a few individuals with larger brains, capable of constructing even more replete and refined perceptual worlds. These individuals would have left more off-spring (with greater genetic endowment), as those who were not proficient at constructing accurate perceptions were at a competitive disadvantage. In short, competition among mammalian species for food and for mates favored the most perceptive individuals which were, of necessity, the ones with the most talented brains.

The truth of the matter is that the evolutionary process I have been describing had many more dimensions to it than I have let on. A great many developments produced important gross anatomical adaptations which any thorough account would not overlook. I have focused on the capacity to construct a *perceptual world* of objects and processes because I take these to be the most decisive operations in the evolution of intelligence. But we are stll a long way off from the emergence of what we normally regard as intelligent behavior, that is, the behavior of human beings. This glorious chapter in the narrative of evolution describes developments taking place over the past 3 million years. As some primates descended from the trees to see what the ecology of the savannahs offered, they developed, more or less simultaneously, a constellation of new traits, each of which was beneficial to the others.

Carnivorous diet. The first meat-eating primates were probably scavengers who tried eating the abandoned carrion of larger predators for want of anything better. For those who were able to make the transition to meat, there were clear benefits. Meat was relatively plentiful, and it represented an efficient source of important nutrients. Eventually primates began to stalk their own prey.

Erect posture. Those primates who hunted in the tall grasses of the savannahs would have been well served by the ability to stand up, which would enable them to command a larger vista. This ability would have given bipedal primates an advantage in spotting potential prey and threatening predators. Bipedal locomotion also had the advantage of freeing the hands for manipulating tools and for carrying food home to the family.

Pelvic restructure. Efficient bipedal locomotion requires a different pelvic structure from that needed for moving or standing on four legs. In order to accommodate bipedalism, the primate pelvis had to be tilted, shortened, broadened, and constricted. The gradually modified pelvis also made possible the successful delivery of babies with larger and, presumably, brainier heads.

Tool use. With the use of improvised and manufactured tools, our hominid ancestors acquired enormous competitive advantages, both in defense and in the acquisition of food. Tool use was followed by the discovery of fire and the construction of simple dwellings. These made it possible to survive extreme climatic and seasonal changes. In addition, the discovery of fire made possible stone splitting, new techniques of animal trapping, and mastication of tough vegetable fibers.

Cooperative predation and defense. Early hominids discovered the principle of security in numbers. The capacity to form and sustain cooperative bonds for hunting and fighting had several advantages. Hunting groups were capable of tackling large game, thereby increasing the variety of food supply. Successful fighting bands could protect groups against dangerous predators and might even reduce competition for resources by taking the offensive against their neighbors. Group cooperation also increased the efficiency of learning and made possible the genius of committees.

Language. Cooperative hunting and fighting could not become well developed without the use of language, however rudimentary. Language would also become an efficient instrument for the transmission of hunting and tool-making skills. Those bands of individuals possessing the ability to communicate effectively would be able to plan their excursions beforehand to great advantage.

Encephalization. Each of the above-mentioned traits affects and is affected by the enlargement and specialization of the brain. Large hominid brains are associated with a greater number of nerve cells in the cerebral cortex and a greater concentration of neural transmitters. Advances in these structural and chemical properties won fitness awards for meeting the challenges of the African savannah environment.

The Emergence of Culture

Far and away the most profound biological adaptation of all time was the inadvertent invention of human culture, which took place over an extended period of time as the above prerequisite characteristics became stabilized. It is doubtful that the emergence of culture was recognized as an achievement in the way that material inventions (the wheel, for example) normally are. A more likely account is that many cultural experiments flourished and withered fairly sporadically over several thousand generations before anything resembling a stable culture developed. In other words, the origin of culture can be viewed as analogous to the genetic origins of traits, that is, by the repetition of trial and success (mutations, selection) until a stable pattern became fixed.

But once human culture did take hold as a stable adaptation to environmental conditions, it advanced rapidly, far more rapidly than would have been possible had it been controlled exclusively by the mechanisms of genetic transmission. This observation is critical to any adequate understanding of the relationship between *homo sapiens* as a biological species and "humanity" as a cultural being. Human culture originated as a specific mode of biological adaptation to environmental conditions; that is to say, it had "survival value." We should never allow ourselves to lose sight of this fundamental insight, so that we come to regard human culture as somehow extrabiological. It is false, misleading, and perhaps even dangerous to slip into this train of thought. The dynamics of culture are continuous with the dynamics of biology. This principle is worthy of our most dogmatic defenses.

We are easily drawn into thinking that culture is discontinuous with nature by the fact that the invention of human culture introduced a radically new dimension into the process of evolution: the extrasomatic formulation of information. But "extrasomatic" should not be construed to mean "extrabiological" or "supernatural." It is about time (and has been for generations) that we put aside the notion that supernatural realities of any kind are operative in human life. In fact, it is about time we began to realize that such notions are potentially threatening to our continued survival. And furthermore, it must be recognized that we are not prevented by anything essential in our cultural tradition from adopting this antisupernatural point of view. Indeed, as I will try to show later, there are strong *traditional* reasons for banishing the supernatural from the tradition. But these arguments will have to wait; for the moment we are concerned with the unique contribution of human culture to evolution.

The capacity for extragenetic information processing among early mammals brought with it the construction of a perceptual world by which organisms could recognize discrete objects and recurrent sequences of events. This perceptual world was not, however, transmittable to other organisms. The *ability* to construct a perceptual world was obviously transmitted by genetic means, but the actual information acquired by individual organisms could not be "objectified" beyond the individual. This situation changed with the arrival of human culture. (There is scant evidence that some animals are able to transmit limited amounts of extragenetic information, but the differences between human and subhuman cultures are so vast that we can ignore the latter for our purposes.)[3] The novelty of human culture was that individuals had acquired the ability to externalize and share the knowledge they possessed. To be precise, human culture was brought into being by the mechanisms for constructing and transmitting a *conceptual* world.

The ability to conceive of objects in their spatial and temporal absence represents a quantum leap in intelligence of great magnitude. Konrad Lorenz has proposed an account of this phenomenon which is both plausible and well supported by the available evidence.[4] Conceptual thought, he suggests, represents a higher system of cognitive organization which bears a gestaltlike relation to a series of lesser preexisting and independent systems. In this view the integration of various individual component functions produced an organizational whole that was qualitatively more than the sum of its parts. The ability to construct and maintain a conceptual world (including the use of language and abstract thought and the capacity to foresee the consequences of one's own behavior) emerged as an adaptive bonus for those higher primates in which the litany of mutation and selection had produced an elaboration of faculties for constructing a perceptual world. There is a well-known story about the invention of a calculating machine which was designed to figure compound interest but which, to the inventor's surprise, turned out to be capable of handling integral calculus as well. In like manner, the complex of mechanisms which evolved to render precise perceptions and efficient motor responses brought with it the serendipitous ability to integrate these functions. And this integration results in conceptual thinking.

Lorenz's account of the emergence of a conceptual world among humans is remarkably similar to the foregoing explanation of the appearance of a perceptual world among lower mammals. In this account the ability to construct a perceptual world came as a result of integrating and summarizing the encoding of visual and auditory sensations. In Lorenz's account of conceptual thought, we find a similar recognition of the importance of cognitive integration. Conceptual thought arrived when humans were able to integrate and summarize information from subsidiary systems of behavior (including complex perceptions, imitative skills, exploratory behavior, subtlety of voluntary movement, memory, and so forth). We might liken these integrative functions to complex networks between individual computers. At both of these dramatic stages in evolution—corresponding to the construction of perceptual worlds and conceptual worlds—we would expect to find a concomitant enrichment of subjective experience.

The neurophysiological mechanisms capable of producing conceptual thought had to be exceedingly complex. Carl Sagan has estimated, for example, that the average human brain is capable of more than 2×10^{13} different brain states (a number greatly exceeding the total number of elementary particles in the entire universe).[5] This figure represents only one measure of the enormous potential for diversity in human experience and behavior. Human beings are capable of so much diversity in their cognitive behavior that the real marvel is that we could ever manage to entertain an idea in common with another individual. On further consideration, however, it becomes clear enough that by its very nature conceptual thought is shared. Ideas are public (cultural) products. And yet it should also be clear that ideas can never be entirely independent of human brains, which are capable of complex integrative functions. This dilemma is resolved by the assertion that conceptual thought (and culture itself) is an *intersubjective* enterprise. Ideas simply do not and cannot exist apart from a medium of information exchange between brains. It is therefore not going too far to declare that human culture exists only to the extent that shared symbols exist. Human culture is, essentially, the sharing of a conceptual world by means of symbols.

The invention of human culture contributes to the process of evolution by adding a Lamarckian element. Lamarck was a French naturalist who believed that traits acquired during an individual's lifetime could be biologically inherited by its off-spring. The usual illustration of Lamarckian evolution is the development of the giraffe's long neck. According to Lamarckian theory, giraffes originally had short necks, but after generations of neck-stretching to reach leaves, the neck gradually lengthened. The increment of elongation achieved by each generation was passed on to the next, and so forth, until giraffe necks were long enough. Lamarckian theory has been thoroughly disconfirmed as an adequate account of how evolution operates. But while the transmission of acquired traits does not clarify the elongation of giraffe necks and such, it does appear to describe developments in human culture. Cultural traditions are cumulative. They make it unnecessary for many important environmental adaptations (the wheel, irrigation techniques, the making of iron, and so forth) to be discovered afresh with each generation. Cultural artifacts are already in place for the next generation, to be "inherited" by the mechanisms of tradition and to be improved upon by successive generations. If we understand evolution as describing a succession of adaptations to environmental challenges controlled by the transmission of relevant information, then we can hardly deny that the advent of human culture was an important evolutionary event which greatly accelerated the rate and efficiency of evolution. There is an essential link between evolution by genetic transmission and evolution by extragenetic (cultural) transmission.

And yet the belief is widespread that differences between biological and cultural mechanisms for transmission are so vast as to be impossible to accomodate within a unified framework of theory and method. This belief prevails even among those who recognize the biological roots of human culture. Evolutionary theory may be thought sufficient to describe life among the animals, but it has nothing to contribute toward an understanding of the life of the mind. Once the evolution of the brain has been accounted for, there is no further hope of insight from the natural sciences. Mind and culture, so the argument goes, transcend brain and biology; humanity transcends *Homo sapiens*. It is appropriate, therefore, for the study of human culture to be conducted independently of the sciences.

This bifurcation of the Western intellectual tradition into two cultures (roughly corresponding to the distinction between the sciences and the humanities) has a complex history, the effects of which will not be overcome easily.[6] It will persist as long as scientists, on the one hand, continue to make excessive reductionistic claims, and as long as humanists, on the other hand, continue to ignore the implications of the sciences for an adequate understanding of human nature.

The Natural History of Culture

The only real hope of overcoming the gap between the two cultures is to develop a consistent theoretical framework together with epistemological principles adequate to the purposes and interests of both sides. One of the best efforts so far to articulate a unifying epistemology appears in the work of Michael Polanyi.[7] Polanyi envisions the edifice of human knowledge as a hierarchy of interpretive frameworks starting with physics and chemistry at the base and working upward to include biology, the social sciences, and finally the humanities. Each successive framework takes as its subject matter a larger range of human experience on the side of the knower and more complex organizations of matter on the side of the known. At the boundaries of contiguous interpretive frameworks, two important conditions prevail. First, an interpretive framework of a higher order (which we may call a "supradiscipline") can never be completely reduced to the particulars of its "infradiscipline" (these are not Polanyi's terms, but they express his meaning). The second, related, principle is that a supradiscipline must be careful not to make assertions that are inconsistent with those of its neighboring infradiscipline. For example, biological theory may never be completely reducible to the particulars of chemistry, but at the same time biologists are admonished to say nothing that would violate the principles of chemistry. In terms of logic we might say that

20

the particulars of an infradiscipline represent necessary but not sufficient conditions for each of its supradisciplines. Another way to say the same thing is to suggest that infradisciplines define the limits of plausibility for supradisciplines.

This way of seeing the matter allows us to make ultimately binding claims for the authority of infradisciplines over supradisciplines without suggesting that infradisciplines say everything that can be said intelligibly. Infradisciplines limit but do not exhaust the intelligible discourse of their supradisciplines. With each particular stratum in the organization of matter, there arise new complexities and new principles of explanation which are accountable to but not deducible from the previous stratum.

Implicit in this viewpoint is the principle that any attempt at a genuine unification of subject matter in our intellectual tradition would have to begin with the lowest (least localized) stratum and work slowly upward. Attempts to reduce supradisciplines to their neighboring infradisciplines should be universally encouraged, even where they appear to have limited chances for success. Reductionism should never elicit objections on principle; it is, after all, the essence of explanation that one phenomenon be described in terms of another. We should predispose ourselves to oppose a particular reduction only when we can demonstrate failure to explain all that must be explained. We might expect that attempts at reduction will at least produce theoretical overlaps between disciplines. Wherever these boundary overlaps have been created (for example physics/chemistry, chemistry/biology, biology/psychology), there have been enormous benefits of insight.

Finally, though, theoretical overlap is perhaps all we can hope for in lieu of a completely continuous unification of knowledge. But areas of theoretical overlap should be enough. They at least represent seams, and not gaps, in the fabric of knowledge. As our curiosity approaches ever more complex strata in the organization of matter, we encounter new problems of interpretation which resist thorough reduction and call into play new principles and methods of understanding which, in a manner of speaking, transcend neighboring disciplines. In one sense biology can never be "more" than chemistry, but in another sense it will always transcend chemistry precisely because some chemicals have achieved levels of complex organization requiring principles of explanation which cannot be deduced from the principles of chemistry. In order to emphasize the importance of infradisciplines to neighboring supradisciplines we might express ourselves in this way: chemistry is a specialized division of physics, biology is a specialized division of chemistry, psychology is a specialized division of biology, and so forth. Here we are presented with a modified vision of theoretical unity within the sciences, a vision which is, in important respects, already accomplished.

But we are still left with a well-guarded theoretical gap between the more-or-less unified scientific disciplines and the human disciplines. This bifurcation of the intellect into two cultures remains an obstacle both to self-understanding and to the achievement of cultural coherence because it allows us to think that we can conduct human affairs adequately without being mindful of our biological nature and limitations. And while the history of this bifurcation may be understandable, we must now learn to regard it as a source of intellectual confusion in Western culture.

The nascent discipline of sociobiology provides us with a good example of an attempt to bridge the disciplinary gap between the study of nature and the study of culture. The aim of sociobiology is to extend the principles of evolutionary biology into the domain of social behavior among animals, including humans. There is no presumption among sociobiologists that all aspects of human behavior can be accounted for in biological terms, but there is an insistence that some of them can be. There is also the implication that those whose business it is to explore and direct human affairs will operate in the dark to the extent that they ignore the importance of biological influences, in the same way that biology can be confounded by an ignorance of physics and chemistry. In spite of its speculative and controversial methods, sociobiology is an especially welcome newcomer on the intellectual scene because it demonstrates very effectively the inadequacies of the doctrine that culture can be clearly distinguished from nature.[8] It is now possible to speak confidently about the interaction between DNA and cultural traditions, a process which has been labeled "gene-culture coevolution." While there is yet no consensus among sociobiologists about theoretical details, we cannot deny the operation of "a complicated, fascinating interaction in which culture is generated and shaped by biological imperatives while biological traits are simultaneously altered by genetic evolution in response to cultural evolution."[9]

Natural history of culture shares an interest with sociobiology in closing the gap between nature and culture, and in a sense they might be said to share the territory between the two, but each with its characteristic emphases. Whereas sociobiology has been primarily fixed upon the biological determinants of culture, the natural history of culture attempts to focus upon the evolutionary implications of cultural history. In the interface of biological imperatives with cultural evolution, the natural history of culture is primarily concerned with the latter.

The task of a natural history of culture can be simply put: it is to narrate the evolution of a particular species of human culture. But to say this is merely to introduce a whole range of subsidiary questions. We need to ask, for example, how "culture" is understood here, we should be prepared to specify what is meant by "evolution," and we must show in what sense cultures may be said to speciate.

Culture. By "culture" I mean a shared corpus of meanings that are viable for transmission among human beings by extragenetic means. Human beings have what can be called a dual system of inheritance. We receive some of our predispositions for behavior from the near and distant past by the process of sexual reproduction, that is, by the transmission of genetic material. For most life forms this process is the only system of transmission. The genetic material of a lion can be passed on to the lion's progeny by sexual reproduction, but what the lion has *learned* in a lifetime cannot be transmitted either genetically or extragenetically. The lion does not have the means for transmitting learned behavior. But eventually, as we have seen, there appeared some animals that had the ability to enlarge the range of their behavior by objectivizing their comprehension of the world around them and communicating symbolically with other animals about the features of the environment. At this point culture becomes an element in natural history. In the term "culture," then, I include both the process and the

23

content of this secondary system for transmitting predispositions for behavior. Human beings therefore have a dual system of inheritance; we can inherit information from the past by the genetic means of sexual reproduction and also by the extragenetic means of a cultural tradition. Both of these systems are rooted in the processes of evolution, and both of them, I suggest, can be analyzed and clarified within the same general evolutionary framework.

Evolution. When I say that the task of a natural history of culture is to narrate the evolution of culture, how do I mean the term "evolution"? Students of human culture have used the metaphor of evolution to describe development in culture for many generations. But what they have meant by the term is hardly familiar to biologists. Or rather, what cultural evolutionists have meant by "evolution" is recognized by biologists as the process of "ontogeny," that is, the growth and development of a single organism throughout its lifetime. Cultural evolution has been compared with the growth and development, say, of an acorn from its germination to its final maturation as an adult oak tree, as if there were in a culture some internal *genius* or *telos* to be worked out in the course of its history. But I wish to avoid this ontogenic fallacy and speak of evolution in a more conventional way. Most biologists would agree that evolution is a process of development that takes place according to the differential survival of replicating entities.[10] A natural history of culture uses the term in this sense. Biological evolution takes place according to the differential survival of *units* of replication, by the differential survival of genes (some survive, others do not). So if we are going to use the term "evolution of culture," we must then be prepared to show how a culture develops according to the differential survival of extragenetic units of replication.

We understand quite well the genetic system of inheritance as a result of theoretical links forged between classical genetics and biochemistry. That is, we understand the genetic process because of our discovery and analysis of the unit of genetic transmission, that is, the gene. It seems reasonable to suppose that an understanding of the process of cultural evolution will depend upon parallel terms—the discovery and analysis of the unit of cultural transmission. A natural history of culture can proceed on this supposition.

I have borrowed a concept from Richard Dawkins and have modified it somewhat for the purpose of discussing the process of cultural evolution. I shall use Dawkins's term "meme" to describe the unit of cultural transmission. Dawkin's gives several examples of memes: tunes, ideas, catchphrases, fashions in clothing, pottery techniques, and so on. "Just as genes propagate themselves in the gene pool by leaping from body to body via sperms or eggs, so memes propagate themselves in the meme pool by leaping from brain to brain via a process which, in the broad sense, can be called imitation."[11] A meme can be regarded as a unit of meaning whch can be replicated in another brain by the apprehension of symbols in the complex processes of social interaction. And once a meme has been encoded in the brain, it becomes an influential factor in an individual's behavior.

To say that memes exist as units of meaning has a certain intuitive appeal, but the concept requires a great deal of clarification before it has significant content. In particular, the neurological and biochemical status of memes will have to be clarified so that the natural history of culture can be shown to be consistent with its infradisciplines. I will address these difficulties in the next chapter, but for the moment let us proceed on the basis of intuitive appeal.

Speciation. An organism can obviously have only a finite number of genes, and organisms that share a sufficient number of genes can be said to belong to a common species. Species are defined in just this way. But it is just as obvious that an individual brain can manage only a finite number of memes, and organisms that share a sufficient number of memes can be said to participate in a common culture. What mechanisms are at work here? At this point we can apply the doctrine that evolution takes place according to the differential survival of units of transmission. The key is to specify how the units are limited. A biological species becomes defined in the process of *selecting out* certain genes. This is the process of natural selection. When left to its own devices of mutation and recombination, nature will propose an unlimited variation of genes. Genes will be proffered for all manner of characteristics: webbed feet, corrugated skin, multiheadedness, and so on. But not all of them can survive. Some of the genes proposed by nature, the least adaptive ones, will be eliminated by the process of natural selection. The selective factors in the environment will edit out lots of bizarre experiments of nature, and what remains after the editorial process will define the gene pool of a species.

Cultures may be said to evolve according to the same principle of differential survival of units of transmission. New experiences and discoveries, combinations of existing ideas, mistakes, misunderstandings, and creativity of every sort will result in the appearance of new meanings, only a limited number of which will be preserved and transmitted in the cultural tradition. Consider, for example, that there are far more paintings and sculptures executed than could ever be preserved in our museums, more songs composed than recorded, more laws proposed than passed, more books written than published, and so on. Some of them are edited out. In general, any culture will generate far more memes than a cultural tradition can ever manage. As a result, memes compete with each other, and the selective agents in the social environment will edit out certain meanings as unacceptable. The meanings that remain after the editorial process will constitute the meme pool, or distinctive identity of the culture. I will consider the details of this process in the next chapter. For the moment it is sufficient to say that natural historians of culture will take as their subject matter the standards and the processes by which a culture generates and regulates its memes.

I should stress here that a natural history of culture is not legitimated by analogy, however sound or dubious, to biological principles. If the evolutionary principle of differential survival of transmittable units applies to both biological and cultural species, then it is by coincidence and not by contrivance. For this reason we must take pains in the next chapter to give intelligible content to the concept of memes and to show how the differential survival of these units can result in the speciation of a cultural tradition.

The perspective I will be taking in this book should now be clear enough. Human culture is a highly organized form of life which under no circumstances should be viewed in isolation from its biological context. In this way of thinking, the study of human culture is a specialized discipline within biology, a discipline which recognizes that human beings have two principal inheritance systems which operate in a complex inter-active mode. This is not to say that the meaning of cultural products is limited to their adaptive significance; it would be misleading to suggest that one cannot appreciate the Italian sonnet form until one grasps its survival value. Yet we cannot deny that cultural products, including the sonnet form, are essentially refinements of a biological adaptation, each of which may or may not have a bearing on the adaptivity of a particular cultural tradition. It is conceivable, for example, that under certain circumstances a literary movement of unusual rhetorical power might be successful in propagating a culture-wide abstention from sexual reproduction. Were such a move-ment to persist for a generation, it would be difficult to deny the maladaptive ramifications for the culture which spawned it. This type of example may sound extreme (the Shakers not-withstanding), but we should nevertheless not underestimate the intimacy of biological aspects of our being with every expression of culture, however remote they may appear. The interaction is so intricate that we are more than justified in bringing biological principles to bear upon our investigations of culture—modified, of course, to reflect the Lamarckian char-acter of cultural evolution. If, in fact, culture is an extension of our biological nature, then something more than mere ana-logical thinking is involved in applying the paradigm of natural selection to the evolution of human culture.

It is appropriate to ask about the bearing of a natural history of culture upon our responsibility as carriers of an intellectual and moral tradition. *Homo sapiens* is a highly successful spe-cies. Its success results directly from the ability of human genes to construct a brain which, in turn, is able to construct a world of memes, and the memes, to continue, have the power to enact patterns of behavior that may ultimately enhance or subvert the survival of brain-making genes. The destiny of the species is entrusted to the constructions of the brain. This point may seem too obvious to dwell upon, but it does highlight the fun-damental *biological* significance of the intellectual life. When it is put forth in these terms, we can hardly overestimate the responsibility we have to husband our intellectual resources and to scrutinize the memes of our culture for their ultimate adaptive value. Nothing could be more difficult or more speculative. Ideas that appear maladaptive at first might turn out ultimately to be decisive for human survival. And it might be argued that some of our fondest truths have been the most threatening to us. Yet despite the uncertainty and the diffi-culty, the adaptive value of our memes must now be accepted as the measure of truth for our time. We must be mindful of the conditions of our survival, and we must construct the cog-nitive conditions which will enable us to obey them. Truth is precisely that which has adaptive significance; and the central responsibility of the intellectual life is to seek the truth.

I might venture to add that the truth is never fully known. Life in a cultural tradition is not unlike the process by which a picture is painted. The painter works with just a few basic colors, and from these he concocts more colors and then applies them to the canvas to create meaningful patterns. In the act of composition there is a constant process of feedback from the canvas to the palette. In the same way, the human nervous system works with a few basic modes of meaning, related di-rectly to the senses. Our sense experiences are integrated to construct the concrete elements of a perceptual world. And these constructions are associated further to construct the ab-stract elements of a conceptual world of memes. The difference of course is that the canvas of human intellectual life is never finished. The feedback continues indefinitely. There is an end-less and irrepressible supply of fresh perceptions to disclose possibilities for new and more satisfying meanings.

It sounds awesome to suggest that the primary responsibility of the intellectual life is to measure all elements of meaning against the canon of adaptivity. The meme pool is too large and too complex for that. And the exercise might quickly de-generate into foolishness. Who would not roll his eyes at an attempt to demonstrate the adaptive significance of the Italian sonnet? But at many levels of intellectual discourse, the canon of adaptivity is apt and should be applied without fear of ridi-cule. We would not wince, for example, at an argument for the survival value of literacy. Nor would we be astonished to hear someone argue the case for the maladaptivity of anarchy. And not least of all the canon of adaptivity has its place in discus-sions of the religious orientation of a culture. Religion is of particular importance here because the religion of a culture expresses the ultimate values by which a sea of memes are judged and are thereby selected either for or against preservation in the tradition. The memes of a religion are therefore crucial for the adaptation of *Homo sapiens* to its environment.

The purpose of this book is not to develop a systematic natural history of the Judaeo-Christian tradition, although I will touch upon some elements of such an enterprise. I am more interested in expressing a certain disposition toward the tradition, insinuated by the evolutionary perspective I have summarized in this chapter. The attitudes with which we regard our tradition are extremely important because they will function as learned biases in the process of cultural selection. My motive in writing this book is to influence the biases that readers will apply in their role as carriers and transmitters of the tradition. To the extent that this effort is successful, certain maladaptive aspects of the tradition will be selected out and new elements will be called forth. Some readers may share the evolutionary perspective that influences my remarks but may disagree about the adaptive significance of particular cultural elements, finding others to select out or to preserve. I am prepared to be encouraged by such a response because it will indicate that the focus of debate about continuity and change in our religious tradition has shifted to a new and promising level of discourse.

2

Myth and Culture

In the previous chapter I argued for the essential continuity of nature and culture. Human culture, properly understood, must always be regarded as an adaptive response to environmental challenges. As such, the capacity for culture evolved by the same logic (mutation, recombination, and natural selection), and by serving the same objectives (survival and reproduction), as did other biological adaptations. To view culture as somehow independent of its biological underpinnings is to risk losing sight of the infradisciplines which define limits of plausibility for the study of culture. It is not overstating the case to assert that any adequate approach to human culture must now find its bearings in the context of natural history. And thus we find value in the prospect of a natural history of culture.

As we renounce the distinction between nature and culture, we are invited to explore the variations in cultural phenomena using models that have been developed for understanding the rest of the biological world. Just as the biosphere has produced thousands upon thousands of species of birds, fish, insects, and mammals (not to mention plant life), so it has allowed the speciation of human culture into various distinctive expressions. Anthropologists have estimated that more than three thousand distinct species of human culture have flourished since the appearance of *Homo sapiens*.

In this chapter I will develop the view that a culture is distinctive as it exemplifies a distinctive religious orientation, that the religious orientation of a culture derives its uniqueness from its myth, and that the myth of a culture is generated by its peculiar constellation of metaphors. I will also argue that metaphors constitute the cognitive substance by which brains construct a conceptual world. To caricature my own argument: a culture *is* its religion; a religion *is* its myth; a myth *is* its root metaphors; and metaphor *is* the way the brain functions. The next assertion, perhaps too obvious a point to belabor, would be that the functioning of the brain *is* the human way of adapting to its environment. This manner of arranging the material serves, once again, to emphasize the continuity of nature and culture, but it will also enable us to make some important observations concerning the principles of a natural history of culture. In particular, we shall be interested in bringing substance to the concept of memes and also to the assertion that cultures evolve according to the differential survival of memes.[1]

Brain, Meaning, and Metaphor

The argument before us will have more precision if we reverse ourselves and begin with the manner in which the brain constructs a conceptual world. We are just beginning to understand the complexities of the brain. For centuries the intricate relations between the mind of conscious experience and the workings of the brain have teased the curiosity of philosophers. Elaborate systems have been devised to explain how the mind and the body can affect one another and yet remain distinct entities. In the past few decades enormous strides in neuroscience have made it increasingly difficult to believe that mind and brain *are* distinct entities. They appear more to be two sides of the same coin. It is now unproductive to maintain that anything occurs in the mind without concomitant brain activity. But acknowledgement of this fact fails to explain *how* the life of the mind is a function of brain states. We may have to wait quite a long time for detailed models of the brain's functioning, but enough can be said now to advance the objectives of this chapter.

The human brain is an action-devising organ made up of approximately 10 billion nerve cells (neurons). These nerve cells bathe in a sea of glial cells which support and nourish the neurons. The brain devises its action patterns by orchestrating a blizzard of electrical and chemical impulses transmitted to it from various parts of the body and from other parts of the brain itself. These impulses pass along the circuitry of the central nervous system, moving from neuron to neuron across narrow gaps between the cells. The point at which information is transmitted from one neuron to another is called a synapse. Each neuron has a central cell body from which extend a number of receptor fibers (dendrites) and a single transmitting fiber (axon). Impulses are received by dendrites and transmitted to other dendrites by branches at the end of the axon. What happens in the synapses between neurons is decisive for the formation of an individual's action patterns. A synapse may be excitatory or inhibitory. In an excitatory synapse the message-bearing axon will release a certain kind of chemical (neurotransmitter), making the membranes of the receiving dendrites more receptive to its impulses. This action accelerates the rate at which the receiving neuron will generate impulses to neighboring cells. In an inhibitory synapse a different kind of chemical transmitter is released, which reduces the potential of receiving dendrites to transmit impulses.

The business of transmitting impulses from the axon of one neuron to the dendrites of neighboring neurons is made infinitely more complex by the fact that most neurons receive input from hundreds and often thousands of neighbors, some of them excitatory and some of them inhibitory. Whether a given cell will signal a "green light" or a "red light" depends upon some form of assessment that takes place within the cell body. At any given moment a neuron may receive many hundreds of excitatory and inhibitory messages which must be evaluated before the neuron itself will send along a message to its neighbors. Whether, and at what rate, a neuron transmits excitatory messages to its neighbors depends upon a variety of factors, including the quantity of red and green lights and the somatic origin of the input signals. In any event, the result of the assessment process is expressed in the rate at which a cell passes impulses along its axon.

Excitatory and inhibitory synapses are equally important to the successful functioning of an organism. If excitation did not occur at the appropriate times and places and rates, then the organism would not be able to devise appropriate action patterns in response to stimuli from the environment. And if inhibition did not occur properly, the organism would remain in a continuous state of uncontrolled convulsions. Our ability to execute finely tuned motor control of every sort (walking, speaking, operating computers, playing the oboe, and so forth) depends upon billions of intricately organized impulses. Everything we do (or do not do) as human beings is partly a function of the way in which this blizzard of neural activity is ordered.

The architecture of the nervous system is equally complex. The impulses we have been discussing originate as input in various sensory processes throughout the body. Their messages are relative to conditions in the environment and also to the internal state of the organism. The impulses terminate at glands and muscles, whose secretions and contractions must be carefully coordinated, again, by a delicate orchestration of synapses. These origination and termination processes are fairly well understood by neuroscientists. But what is not well enough understood is everything that happens in between. The architecture and the functioning of the 10 billion brain cells provide neuroscientists with their most interesting and challenging problems. How are nerve cells lined up throughout the brain, and why are they the way they are? Where are different systems of activity located in the brain? How are the systems interconnected? How (and why) do different neural functions develop at different stages? How is information stored in the brain? How is it retrieved? Why is there so much redundancy in information storage? Why are some impulses carried over long distances (some nerve cells are more than a meter long) and others over short distances? How much information is preencoded in the brain by inheritence, and how much is learned? By what mechanisms does the brain integrate various interdependent systems? Theories abound only to be confounded by new observations. Knowledge advances only to teach us how little we know.

Another avenue of intense interest concerns the evolution of the brain. One thing we do know is that the brain evolved over millions of years of natural selection and that its most important functions bear upon behavioral strategies and tactics for survival and reproduction. The evolutionary approach to the brain has produced some interesting ways of viewing its structure and functions. Indeed, many students of the brain have argued that its structure only begins to make sense in the light of its evolutionary development. Paul MacLean has proposed a theory of the brain which identifies three major structural components corresponding to the reptilian, mammalian, and hominid stages in evolution that I discussed in the previous chapter.[2] MacLean says that the human brain is, in reality, *three* brains interconnected by an ingenious network of neural pathways, each with its own distinctive mentality. The triune brain sits atop the neural chassis, a term by which MacLean designates the spinal cord together with two very primitive formations called the pons and the medulla. These structures regulate the routine bodily functions of the circulatory, respiratory, digestive, and reproductive systems. The three parts of the triune brain are supported by the neural chassis. The arrangement somewhat resembles three scoops of ice cream on a cone, the top two of which have melted to surround the one at the base.

The most primitive component of the triune brain is called the protoreptilian brain, or the R-complex, which can be compared to the kind of brain found in some reptiles. MacLean has associated the R-complex with various action patterns including aggressiveness, ritual behavior, "ancestral" learning, breeding strategies, foraging, and territoriality. Many of the action patterns typical of the reptilian brain are genetic in origin.

Surrounding the protoreptilian brain is the paleomammalian brain, or the limbic system. This portion of the brain has been associated with several complex behavioral patterns, such as classical conditioning, the regulation of the endocrine system, and gross motor control, including sleep and arousal. The limbic system seems to be particularly influential in the stimulation of emotional states. Fear, rage, and sentimentality arise from activity in this area of the brain.

The most advanced component of the triune brain is called the *neomammalian* brain, or the neocortex. This part of the brain is the most complex of all. It appears to be responsible for much of our ability to make detailed perceptions and fine-grained motor responses. The neocortex also houses the language centers, anticipates the future, and recalls the distant past. All of the higher intellectual powers associated with human behavior appear to depend heavily upon the neocortex.

34

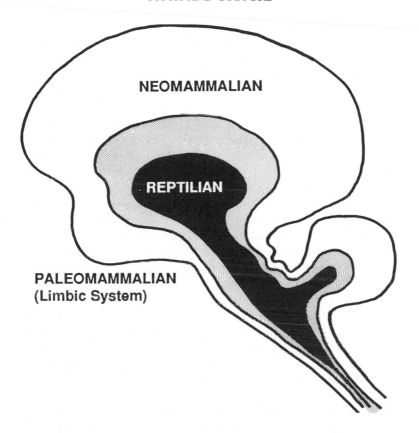

MacLean's theory of the triune brain must continue to be regarded as highly speculative. The human brain does not present itself in clearly distinguished and brightly colored components, as this theory might suggest. Even if the theory is accurate in its assessment of evolutionary stages, it would be difficult to confirm because with each surge in brain evolution intricate structural connections developed between parts of the brain, so that anatomical distinctions became extremely difficult to make. Still, the theory is provocative and may turn out to be a very useful heuristic device.

MacLean's theory has stimulated others to speculate upon the functional integration of the reptilian, mammalian, and neomammalian brains. If we grant the plausibility of his thesis that the human brain amounts to "three interconnected biological computers," what can be said about the organism's obvious capacity for integrating their functions in an orderly and consistent manner? If there are three distinct "drivers" of the neural chassis, by what logic does the brain decide how the vehicle is to be driven?

Robert Isaacson has proposed that the outer layers of the triune brain, the limbic system and the neocortex, function to inhibit action patterns that might otherwise issue from the reptilian brain. In his words, "Basically, I consider the limbic system as regulating the protoreptilian brain, primarily in an inhibitory fashion."[3] And later he adds, "My suggestion is that the neocortical systems use the paleomammalian brain mechanisms to accomplish this suppression."[4] According to this theory, the reptilian brain is merely capable of initiating action patterns that are inherited from the distant past and bring immediate benefits to the organism. The limbic system is capable of initiating action patterns on the basis of temporary associations drawn from the environment. In order to achieve these "conditioned responses," the limbic system would have to inhibit the more archaic "reflexes" of the reptilian brain. And finally, the neocortex ("the brain of anticipation") is capable of devising action patterns based on long-term abstract objectives. To accomplish this purpose the neocortex must selectively inhibit conditioned learning and must further direct the mechanisms of the limbic system to inhibit reptilian reflexes.

Leslie Hart has taken a somewhat different (though no less interesting) approach to the problem of coordinating the functions of the triune brain. Hart suggests that the inhibition of action patterns comes from the opposite direction and is determined less by anticipation of the future than by the perception of *threat*. The old reptilian brain, Hart observes, is relatively small and capable of crude decisions only, but these it can make very quickly and without deliberation. Such a brain can execute action patterns of fight or flight with blazing speed. The mammalian brain, on the other hand, is larger and slower and able to interpret a greater variety of stimuli and to execute a much larger repertoire of responses. But the price of this greater variability is paid in terms of response time. The large neocortex is even more discriminating and versatile than the mammalian brain but, once again, only at the expense of immediacy in response. Hart says the neocortex is much too large and intricate to make appropriate decisions when conditions call for immediate action patterns. Thus when threatening situations arise, the brain "downshifts" to a more primitive apparatus, which is likelier to give an appropriate response. "When the individual detects *threat* in an immediate situation, full use of the great new cerebral brain is suspended, and faster acting, simpler brain resources take larger roles."[5] And again, "In extreme situations, the reptilian brain takes over, as in great rage, abject fear, or panic flight."[6]

Isaacson appears to be suggesting that the distinct functions of the brain are coordinated in the neocortex for the purpose of controlling activities in the deeper structures of the brain. Hart, on the other hand, is saying that the deeper structures "take over" in situations where the organism is threatened. There is a clear difference in the location of "executive" control.

The reality of brain integration is probably more complex than either of these views suggests. It appears that decisive excitatory and inhibitory functions can originate in many parts of the brain, and so it is perhaps misleading to identify an executive region. Humans are capable of withstanding the most acute threats imaginable in defense of abstract (neocortical) goals. At the same time, we have been observed to abandon our fondest ideals in the presence of threat. The correct assumption appears to be that the neocortex and subcortical structures are extensively interdependent and that the integrative function is diffused throughout the brain. While this may be a gross oversimplification, it may nevertheless be useful to regard the brain as a structural unit which acts by consensus rather than by executive control over individual systems.

Still, there must be some regular *process* by which integration is achieved. There is good reason to suppose that the central nervous system operates under the influence of a structural hierarchy for behavior selection. According to this view, the organism would first select a *general* state of arousal (deep sleep, light sleep, wakefulness, or full alertness). The selection of a general state of arousal limits the range of potential action patterns, which must be further selected and refined by the programs of the brain that are relevant to the situation at hand.

This first step in the process of orchestrating neural activity in the organism appears to depend upon the reticular formation. The reticular formation is a complex netlike arrangement of nerve cells at the core of the brain which has ascending and descending neural pathways throughout the brain, from the cortex to the spinal cord. This network receives messages from all the sensory modes of the body and somehow "screens" their impulses for especially noteworthy information to be sent along to the cortex. If the reticular formation has become habituated to a particular smell or sound, it will not send excitatory messages to the cortex. But if there is something novel or potentially exciting in the sensory input, the reticular formation will transmit what amounts to a nota bene message to the cortex which arrives in association with the sensory information. If the evaluation of the cortex is one of alarm, then excitatory impulses will travel back to the reticular formation, which in turn radiates impulses that produce the appropriate level of arousal. But if the cortex decides that the sensory input is not bothersome, it will inhibit impulses to the reticular formation.

To illustrate, I will propose an imaginary experimental situation. Suppose we take two subjects and expose them suddenly to a loud and potentially alarming noise (gunshots, a lion's roar, or whatever), but before we create the noise we tell one of the subjects that the noise is impending and inform him or her of its nature. The other subject remains ignorant. When the noise actually occurs, we can expect the two subjects to exhibit vastly different states of arousal. What happens is that knowledge of the experimental conditions functions as a cortical factor intervening to inhibit the transmission of excitatory impulses back to the reticular formation.

To return to the contrasting models of Isaacson and Hart for a moment, we can perhaps propose a third hypothesis. The situation appears to be the following: the neocortex can inhibit the action patterns of more primitive parts of the brain (as Isaacson suggests) but *only* if it has the necessary memory data to do so. If it does not have the necessary information, then the inhibition will not occur. It is not that the primitive brain *takes* control (à la Hart) but rather that it is *left* in control by a lack of information in the cortex. This model neurologically legitimatizes the Socratic doctrine that what we *know* is decisive for what we *do*, but in this view knowledge of the good leads us to do the good by first preventing its baser alternatives. It also explains why, in the absence of culture, we are condemned to act primarily on the basis of genetically induced impulses.

The importance of language in this process is noteworthy. If any single aspect of intelligent behavior can be associated with the integration of brain functions, it must certainly be language. Elements of our verbal system are localized in particular regions of the neocortex, but the language centers are multiply accessed by a complex neural network so that specific items of verbal information can be drawn upon to influence an enormous array of action patterns. It is not too much to say that the integration of discrete neural systems in humans is orchestrated by the features of a verbal system. Of course no one fully understands how disturbances of the air and ink blots on paper are translated into electrochemical events and then stored in the brain as information to be retrieved when it is needed. But we do know that in human beings the information stored in the brain is heavily influenced by language. In fact, the available evidence suggests that our verbal system is decisively involved at all stages of information processing, including acquisition, storage, association, and retrieval. No one seriously disputes that language finally comes to dominate much of human behavior. The debates begin as we ask when and how the tyranny of language is established.

A competent verbal system cannot be said to be fully in place until early adult life. As it matures, the developing organism acquires operational prerequisites for the verbal life, enabling it to introduce more complexity into its behavior. Infants are born without the powers of speech, and their action patterns are therefore more closely limited to reflexes rigidly established by heredity. During the sensorimotor period the developing child is left to the guidance of the limbic system and learns to associate perceived patterns with its internal states, creating the necessary mechanisms for the types of operant conditioning and observational learning that are typical of many animals.

As this process continues, the organism acquires the motivational elements necessary for further development of information-processing expertise. As language abilities develop, the elements of a verbal system become extensively involved in the encoding of nonverbal memory data. When perceptual information, regardless of the mode of sensory input, is encoded by a language-proficient subject, the information is encoded *verbally as well as nonverbally*, and the associations formed (perhaps in sleep) permit verbal access to information that is essentially nonverbal.[7] In other words, as soon as *some* verbal ability arrives on the scene, it becomes an ingredient in the processing of *all* information, verbal or nonverbal.

I believe that the neural capacity for this dual encoding system is decisive for the development of language, and it may also be the source of what we experience as consciousness. The neural capacity for language and consciousness came about as the editorial pen of nature favored those individuals possessing the greatest redundancy of brain matter. Genes for redundancy of brain matter would be beneficial at any stage of evolution, but their advantage for hominids would have been exaggerated once the rudiments of language emerged. Consider how this situation might have occurred. Symbolic communication among our hominid ancestors probably started out with spontaneous combinations of onomatopoetic utterances and pantomime, one imitating the sounds of nature and the other its shapes and motions. Every successful attempt at being understood would make it possible to abbreviate the sounds and gestures on subsequent occasions and still be understood, at least by those who were on hand to catch each increment of phonemic change. Sounds thus became less and less accurate imitations as they gradually conformed to the vocal apparatus of the imitators. At this point neurological redundancy would reveal a capacity for the dual encoding of information. By the time some primitive antecedent of "lion" came to replace "arrr" (plus gestures) as the symbol for a lion, it would be impossible for ensuing generations to grasp the significance unless the brain was able to use redundant matter to equate dissimilar elements. "Lion" is then encoded in the brain and associated with the encoded memory image of a lion. The language-proficient brain constructs neural equations involving the encoding of symbol as one term and image as the other. Thus we are able to access nonverbal images by encountering an associated symbol, or we can access symbols through perceptual images. See a lion, and you will recall the word "lion"; hear "lion," and you will recall the image.

Once the operation of constructing iconic-semantic equations had started, it would expand at a dramatic rate. When a brain gets the "knack" of naming, it explodes with meaning. Consider the famous episode in which Helen Keller discovered naming. It started with a single iconic-semantic equation:

> Someone was drawing water and my teacher placed my hand under the spout. As the cool stream gushed over my hand she spelled into the other the word *water*, first slowly, then rapidly. I stood still, my whole attention fixed upon the motion of her fingers. Suddenly I felt a misty consciousness as of something forgotten—a thrill of returning thought; and somehow the mystery of language was revealed to me. I knew then that W–A–T–E–R meant that wonderful cool something that was flowing over my hand. That living word awakened my soul, gave it light, hope, joy, set it free! There were barriers still, it is true, but barriers that in time could be swept away. I left the well-house eager to learn. Everything had a name, and each name gave birth to a new thought.[8]

The invention of naming as Miss Keller describes it occurs in each of us, though less noticeably. When toddlers get the knack of naming, they importune their parents with "Wha'dat?" for several months. During this period the primordia of consciousness emerge, and a conceptual world begins to take shape. Once the mystery of language had been revealed to early hominids, they began to name entities that defied imitation: how would one imitate a sunset or the idea of tomorrow?

Iconic-semantic equations established by naming represent the creation of metaphor in its most fundamental form: *this* is *that*. Metaphors are, finally, neurochemical; they amount to the fixation of meaning through the associations of neural matter. And once metaphors have been fixed, they allow the subject to behold objects and their various features in their absence, and this provision makes it possible to carry out cognitive operations limited to the symbolic side of iconic-semantic equations. This is how abstractions are constructed; they are associations between symbols which are, in turn, equated with images. Abstractions are semantic-semantic equations. They, too, are metaphors of a more complex form. Language, once started, feeds on its own creations to discover new realities and new meanings. As it does so, it enriches the texture of conscious experience. Metaphors create more metaphors; the concrete creates the abstract. Lexicographers know this better than anyone. Dictionaries are full of abstract words that transcend their concrete roots. Consider the words we have just used: *metaphor* (carryover), *concrete* (grow together), *abstract* (draw away). These terms are as far from their roots as "lion" is from "arrr."

Cognitive psychologists are divided on the matter of what is actually encoded in the memory systems.[9] Proponents of the "dual code theory" hold that information is stored in long-term memory in terms of sensory images and associated verbal symbols. The "propositional code theory," on the other hand, holds that sensory images fade away, leaving a residue of abstract meanings which are then encoded independently in long-term memory. There are presently no compelling reasons to reject either of these theories. The vivid imagery of dreams seems to indicate that sensory images are retained for a long time. And reports that hypnosis subjects are able to reproduce verbatim conversations from the distant past would tend to confirm that verbal information is stored precisely. These observations support the dual code theory. On the other hand, ample experimental evidence shows that individuals are capable of recalling the "drift" (meaning) of a text or conversation, while the precise wording escapes them entirely. I am inclined to think that something like the dual code phenomenon takes place at the level where semantic primes are built up, but once these have been established, the construction of abstractions could just as well proceed by the encoding of meanings which depend less on sensory images. In any event, neurochemical mechanisms appear to be involved which almost certainly include the production of peptide molecules and the alteration of neural pathways, both of which take place as the brain acquires language.

Until these mechanisms are more thoroughly understood, our notions about language, learning, and memory will remain highly speculative.

Whatever actually takes place in the brain's memory systems, we can hardly fail to recognize that language provides us with the closest thing there is to a common element in all information processing. This common element becomes a powerful and efficient tool by which we draw upon stored information to devise action patterns. And as we continue to develop, we come to rely more heavily upon the verbal system both to interpret the events of the world around us and to coordinate our behavioral responses to them. As subjects become more adept at manipulating verbal symbols syntactically, we observe the development of a coherent symbolic world. And to the extent that a schematic of the world is securely in place, the individual has the ability to orchestrate the entire information system.

This entire discussion has been intended to substantiate the claim that metaphor provides the cognitive material by which the brain is able to construct a conceptual world. If the discussion has become too involved, the reason is that I have been concerned to avoid basing the argument itself on biologically dubious metaphors.

We are now in a position to give greater clarity and precision to the concept of meme that was introduced in the last chapter. A meme is a unit of meaning, and it is also the unit of cultural transmission. A meme is any unit of meaning that can be transmitted from brain to brain without the benefit of genetic means. We might use the term interchangeably with "metaphor," since, as we have seen, the brain can be viewed as constructing its meanings from metaphorical primes. I will prefer the term "meme" here because of the association with genetic units of transmission but also because it avoids confusion with the technical usage of "metaphor" to denote a literary convention. In their simplest form, memes are the expressions of iconic-semantic equations. But like their genetic counterparts, memes may be complex—that is, they may be associated with other memes to form abstractions. "Fido" is a simple meme, while "dog" and "pet shop" are complex. As we go about constructing a conceptual world, we erect a many-layered "house of memes" which is every bit as jerry-built and precarious as a house of cards.

I have promised to construct a series of steps in my argument from the assertion that metaphors (now memes) constitute the cognitive substance of our conceptual world to the assertion that a cultural tradition can be identified with its religious orientation. Before moving ahead with the argument, however, I want to digress for the purpose of illustrating the mechanics of the influence that memes exert on our behavior.

The memes of a culture are constantly engaged in interacting with the gene pool of the culture. They work together on occasion, and sometmes they work against each other. But their purpose is ultimately the same: to devise behaviors that will enhance survival and replication. Let us first take an example of gene-meme opposition. Picture a young couple who are engaged to be married in a few weeks. During one of the couple's late-night planning sessions the young man begins to make sexual advances toward his bride. The impulses to do so originate deep in his reptilian brain, setting in motion a series of genetically induced synapses which are about to express themselves in a particular action pattern, the likes of which got him where he is in the first place. But lodged elsewhere, in his neocortex, there is a countervailing meme (a fairly complex one) which has been transmitted symbolically to his brain and fixed there chemically. In this case the meme is a social rule prohibiting premarital sex, first communicated to him by his parents and then reinforced by various means in the larger context of his culture. He knows that his bride shares this meme. He begins to weigh the benefits of his intentions against the costs. The prospect of social scorn and the possibility of a quarrel that may jeopardize the impending marriage are discouraging. He decides to delay. In doing so, his "no premarital sex" meme initiates a series of synapses which eventually inhibits the genetically induced alternative behavior.

A second example will illustrate how memes and genes can work together. An abundance of evidence supports the view that avoidance of incest describes a behavior pattern that is genetically conditioned. Birds as well as humans and other mammals have evolved complicated mechanisms to ensure that closely related genes rarely mix. When males and females have been raised in proximity from childhood, they are highly unlikely to be sexually attracted to each other. In a massive study of nearly three thousand Israeli marriages, only six marriages were found to have occurred within a single communal care center (kibbutz), in spite of encouraged marriages between unrelated individuals. There appears to be a biological incest-avoidance mechanism operative here, suggesting a form of sexual "anti-imprinting."[10] The universally expressed social value condemning incest probably arises to cover those cases in which siblings are raised separately. Here is clearly a case in which a meme has emerged in culture to objectify and legitimate a program for behavior that is genetic in origin.

Memes function in various complicated ways to both reinforce and combat heredity, and as they participate in the maelstrom of synaptic activity, to exert influence they must contend with thousands of alternative programs for behavior, some of which have been established by heredity and others of which have been established by previous experience. When considered discretely, the programs of the brain amount to internal analogues of special features of the social/physical environment. They contain information about specific environmental features together with instructions for appropriate behavioral responses. But the programs of the brain are necessarily more than discrete units. They are intricately structured in their interrelationships by "master programs" which make it possible for the individual to select among alternative action patterns and thereby to act in a consistent and orderly manner. Coherence in human behavior must therefore rely on the construction of a comprehensive model of the social/physical environment, a model which functions to coordinate the entire system of alternative action patterns. There is no suggestion here that our model of reality must be an explicit theory on which we consciously reflect as we select among behavioral options. To the contrary, it seems to be the nature of these structures that they can provide coherence in our *unreflective* behavior. Such a model of reality, which each of us possesses in varying degrees of complexity and coherence and explicitness, is what I have been calling a symbolic or conceptual world of memes. I will now introduce the term "myth" to describe this phenomenon.

45

Since the nature of myth is germane to the argument of this book, it will be useful at this point to comment on some of its salient features.[11]

Myth, Cosmology, and Morality

If I were to limit the definition of myth to a single characteristic feature, it would be that in myth we encounter the integration of cosmology and morality. In myth we are presented with a unity of the "true" and the "good." This feature of myth violates the modern view that facts are value-free and that it is therefore fallacious to confuse "is" with "ought." But myth does not apologize for confusing cosmology with morality, nor should it. In fact, when we consider the evolutionary value of cosmologies (what is true about the world), we cannot avoid recognizing that they were selected to *serve* morality (how we ought to act in the world). The brain, once again, has evolved as an action-devising organ. The behaviors devised in an individual's brain are executed in the context of a cosmos. They assume the presence of a particular cosmology, that is, the one that is encoded in the brain itself. An intact cosmology is therefore a necessary condition for our normal behavior. In addition, ideas about how the world is would be of no use to an organism except as resources for appropriate behavior. This is not to suggest that a morality can be logically deduced from a cosmology; to argue this point would be to commit the naturalistic fallacy. I am asserting, however, that the integration of cosmology and morality is a *practical* necessity. We simply would not be here if we did not regularly perform this integrative function. Neither morality nor cosmology makes any sense in isolation from the other. Behavior that does not assume a particular world order would be arbitrary, and ideas about the world that are not relevant to behavior would be superfluous. Cosmology without morality is empty; morality without cosmology is blind. I define myth as the *achievement* of an integration of cosmos and ethos, an achievement without which there would be no possibility of achieving personal integrity or social coherence.

The myth of the Judaeo-Christian tradition nicely illustrates the integration of cosmology and morality. In the biblical story we are told that the world was formed out of chaos by a creator God and that this world is structured in a certain way (firmament above, waters of the deep below, and so forth). These are cosmological features. At the same time, we are told that the creator God expects humans to obey his will (as expressed in the law). This is the moral dimension. The uniqueness of myth is that these elements are undifferentiated; they are interdependent features of a unified story. The appropriate behavior for humans is embedded in the features of the cosmos, so that if human behavior displeases God, the social and cosmic order will be jeopardized. The integration in this myth is achieved by fundamental memes which express both the moral preconditions of cosmic order and the cosmic preconditions of moral order.

Myth and the Arts

The achievement of a mythic integration of cosmos and ethos is far more complicated than might be supposed from what I have said here. It is not enough simply to combine cosmology and ethics; the challenge is to combine them in such a way that the result can be ingested by an entire culture. By its nature a cultural myth represents a *shared* vision of cosmic realities and human ideals. The memes of a cultural myth must be available to all members of a culture; to both the young and the old, simple and sophisticated alike. An effective myth is first assimilated in childhood and functions to shape the developing consciousness. We ingest myth early in life and continue to grow in our apprehension of its depths as we periodically reappropriate it throughout life. Myth must therefore be effective at various levels of meaning, and it must be resilient enough to endure the tests of time. The effective myth will be sufficiently simple and entertaining to appeal to the imagination of children, and it will be sufficiently complex and insightful to continue to enrich the imagination of adults. Without universal appeal to the imagination of a culture, a myth will fail to transmit itself and will eventually wither away to become, at most, a historical curiosity.

The achievement of myth is fundamentally aesthetic, and while it would be a mistake to exclude the contribution of any

47

art form, there is nevertheless a need to emphasize the importance of the literary arts. This is appropriate because of the narrative structure of myth. The importance of the aesthetic dimension of myth cannot be minimized; it would be far better to exaggerate this dimension than to obscure it. We are thus justified in the assertion that the arts themselves are properly judged for their contributions to myth. Such a claim may appear excessive, but it is no more outrageous than our previous claim that cosmology and morality have meaning only in relation to one another in the context of their mythic integration. Here we are simply adding an essential third element to the fabric of myth. If cosmology is defined as a configuration of memes supposed to be true statements about our physical and social environment, and if morality is defined as a configuration of memes that specify behaviors appropriate to this environment, then we might well define the arts as the mechanics of expressing and transmitting their integration. Under this definition, the role of the artist is to craft the conventions of meaning by which ideals of human life in the world are narrated for popular consumption.

At this point our definition of myth is complete. Myth is now defined as an *effective* integration of cosmology and morality, or, to put it differently, myth is the undifferentiated presence of cosmos, ethos, and pathos. In myth we encounter a symbolic world in which the full range of human experience (intellectual, moral, and aesthetic) is synthesized and interpreted.

It is difficult to overstress the importance of effectiveness when speaking of myth. It is not enough, I repeat, simply to combine cosmology and morality; the trick is to integrate them in a compelling and imaginative way. Somehow the memes of a myth must find their way into the chemistry of the brain. But this penetration does not just happen. The elements of a myth are established in the brain by an elusive process—so elusive, in fact, that cultural traditions often represent the process as the work of supernatural agents. Christianity, for example, has traditionally held that apprehension of the Gospel comes as a gift of the Holy Spirit. But while the process of ingesting a mythic vision may be somewhat perplexing, there is no virtue in making it completely obscure. It is possible to communicate myth from brain to brain without the intervention of supernatural agents, but little is known about the science of this process. In fact, to call it a science is misleading; we are more on the mark if we speak of the art of transmitting myth. Indeed, the process of transmitting myth *is art itself.*

The role of the artist is to *con-fuse* cosmology with morality and to give this insight public form. The artist sees into the world in such a way that possibilities and imperatives for human action are disclosed. The artist perceives an overlay of human ideals on nature. It is then necessary to express this overlay in symbols, that is, by creating memes. Such memes, if they are effective, will be replicated in other brains. This manner of regarding the vocation of the artist might prompt the objection that it excludes much of what is normally called art and includes much that is normally not called art. Much of what passes as art is simply craftsmanship. A craftsman is one who explores a form or technical medium for its own sake, and many craftsmen have exploited forms and techniques to the point of mastery without achieving art. A craftsman is an artist only when he or she formulates and transmits meanings which inform, however indirectly, the execution of behavior in the world.

At the same time, our definition of art will exclude those propagandists and advertisers who attempt to manipulate the specific actions of individuals without achieving any significant impact on their perception of the world. There is a fine distinction between propaganda and advertising, on the one hand, and art on the other. The definitive criterion is whether or not the individual's apprehension of the interdependence of nature and human behavior is clarified.

But if our definition of the artist's vocation excludes craftsmen and propagandists, it will also include some surprising characters. We might include, for example, prophets, priests, parents, journalists, teachers, clinical psychologists, and politicians. The decisive factor is whether these professions are engaged in the formation and transmission of memes that integrate intellectual, moral, and aesthetic experience.

I have been discussing art and the role of the artist in a way that threatens conventional understandings of the vocation. "Artist" now appears to describe a class of individuals as large and amorphous as that described by "friendly." Anyone can be friendly, and everyone is friendly at one time or another. In the same way, anyone can be occupied with the transmission of mythic memes, and everyone does so to a certain extent. Yet I do not want to go this far. The emphasis, again, is on the invention and successful transmission of memes which integrate experience, and the effectiveness of this work is not unrelated to the mastery of form and technique. I would like to be understood as arguing for the retroactive designation of the artist. An individual is not an artist by self-declaration or by training. The artist is an individual who is especially resourceful at generating mythic memes and/or is especially effective in transmitting these memes to other individuals. It so happens that the most resourceful generators and the most effective transmitters have been those who have special technical skills and the mastery of forms.

No particular artistic medium has a monopoly on the generation and transmission of memes in a culture. Cultural traditions are normally transmitted by a synergy of art forms; song, verse, narrative, drama, dance, painting, sculpture, and so forth work together to convey a pattern of meanings—a story(mythos)—which discloses a reality imbued with human ideals. The artists at work in any culture will generate more possibilities for a cultural myth than can ever be preserved, which inevitably produces a climate of competition among memes for acceptance into the popular imagination. The resulting editorial process of preserving some memes and discarding others eventually leaves a culture with a constellation of memes to define its distinctive mythological tradition. The character of a culture is thus shaped by what it allows to be preserved as art. This, in fact, is the selective process by which distinctive cultures are speciated. In civilized societies this editorial process becomes institutionalized, and this institution I call religion.

Myth and Root Metaphors

All human cultures develop by the selection and accretion of memes, and a natural history of myth discloses no exception to this rule. At the center of every mythic tradition there is a nucleus of meaning which exerts both generative and regulative influence on the development of the myth. I will follow Stephen Pepper in calling this nucleus of meaning the "root metaphor" of a myth.

> The method in principle seems to be this: a man desiring to understand the world looks about for a clue to its comprehension. He pitches upon some area of common sense fact and tries if he cannot understand other areas in terms of this one. The original area becomes then his basic analogy or root metaphor. He describes as best he can the characteristics of this area, or, if you will, discriminates its structure. A list of its structural characteristics becomes his basic concepts of explanation and description. We call them a set of categories. In terms of these categories he proceeds to study all other areas of fact whether uncriticized or previously criticized. He undertakes to interpret all facts in terms of these categories[12]

The corpus of a mythic tradition is complex, including a rich variety of stories, sayings, legends, folk tales, legal codes, and so on. Tracing the sources of these elements is an enormously complicated process, but generally the elements of myth can be said to reflect two things: first, the heuristic power of the root metaphor to generate new meanings, and second, the historical experience of the culture. These elements come into focus in the imagination of artists to produce a constant supply of fresh interpretations of collective experience.

The root metaphor of a myth will suggest new meanings and will also both limit and legitimatize meanings which arise from novel experiences. The root metaphor can be viewed as the foundation of a culture because it is the primary cultural expression of the integration of cosmology and morality. To this primary expression there will accrete a constellation of qualifying and clarifying memes. The root metaphor defines, in the most fundamental way, the nature of the cosmos, and together with its qualifying memes, it establishes the coordinates by which individuals will understand and conduct themselves in relation to their environment. A similar situation exists in the sciences, where the direction of research is conditioned by paradigms which, like a root metaphor, exert both generative and regulative influence.[13]

The root metaphor of the Judaeo-Christian tradition is, without doubt, the most ancient and common root metaphor in the history of human culture. It is, quite simply, the metaphor of *human personality*. This root metaphor is held in common by most cultures, from those of primitive animists to those of modern day monotheists. It asserts that the characteristics of the cosmos conform to those we recognize in ourselves and in other persons—that personality (including the motives and emotions we experience in ourselves) is the ultimate source of explanation for all that happens in the world. It is not difficult to understand why the root metaphor of personality has been so prevalent in human culture. Human beings are inveterate social animals, and our most significant experiences come to us through interaction with other persons. Indeed, most of the mass of the human brain is given over to functions that facilitate human interaction. The human brain is an instrument specialized for the process of communication with other persons. It makes good sense, then, that when this brain set about understanding its environment it naturally fixed upon the metaphor which was most available and provided the richest associations.

The essential differences between the Judaeo-Christian myth and other anthropocentric myths are to be found not in the root metaphor itself but in the accretions which have developed to qualify it. The Judaeo-Christian myth is distinguished from others by virtue of the memes it has constructed to limit and amplify possibilities inherent in the metaphor of personality. According to the experience of a culture, the root metaphor will be limited in terms of one or many, male or female, forgiving or demanding, intimate or remote, and so on. Various options for qualifying the root metaphor of a myth can be expected to emerge in the course of a culture's history, and the distinctive character, or essence, of a mythic tradition can be seen as the result of decisions which are made concerning the omission or transmission of these alternative memes. As a culture encounters new experiences, it is faced with the challenge of preserving its identity against the inevitable onslaught of new alternative memes which emerge to compete with established memes. It is important, therefore, for a culture to achieve a vision of its distinctive identity together with the procedures by which memes essential to this identity can be reinforced and also by which memes contrary to this identity can be expunged. As I shall argue later, the Covenant has functioned as the distinctive element of identity in the Judaeo-Christian tradition.

Myth, Social Coherence, and Personal Wholeness

There is a fundamental ambiguity in the structure of human existence, stemming from the fact that evolution has selected for behavioral predispositions which oppose one another. The ambiguity is experienced in the ever-present dilemma between selfish and sacrificial behavior. Human beings are predisposed by natural selection to behave selfishly and in so doing to achieve a state of biological equilibrium, or homeostasis. We get hungry; we eat. We get cold; we clothe and house ourselves. We get scared; we defend or run. We become curious; we inquire. We anticipate deficiencies; we acquire and hoard resources. And so on. The relentless challenges of the social and physical environment present us with a stream of major and minor disturbances which drive us toward restabilizing solutions. Natural selection has long since eliminated those individuals who were not predisposed to behave in this selfish mode. But at the same time, there are adaptive limits to selfishness. Evolution has also selected against those individuals who were incapable of compromising their own immediate needs for the purpose of advancing the cooperative goals of a social group. It can be argued (and has been) that this sacrificial behavior is in reality a veiled form of selfishness, that is, that short-term sacrifice is but an investment toward long-term gain. This statement may be true enough, but it does not alter the fact that sacrificial behavior is costly to the individual and very often beneficial to others.

The ambiguity of human existence is that human beings everywhere have both collective and individual needs for order. Collectively, we share a need for coherent systems of cooperation in order to achieve common goals—for example, food production and distribution, exchange of labor, defense, and so on. Individually, we have a biological need to achieve homeostasis and, as an extension, we need to achieve a sense of direction and meaning in our personal lives—that is, the sense that our mundane activities have value relative to the near or distant future. It takes little reflection to discover that the needs for social coherence and personal wholeness are intimately related. Individuals cannot be expected to achieve homeostasis when the social context of their lives is in a state of disarray. At the same time, we cannot expect a society to function harmoniously when its individual members are disoriented and beset by anxiety.

I have already said that it is in the *nature* of myth to represent an overlay of cosmology and morality. I now assert that the principal *function* of myth is to provide the cognitive conditions under which collective and individual needs can be met within the context of a unified ideology. A shared myth is the source of both social coherence and personal integrity. The myth of a culture functions to establish a social contract in which collective and individual "orders" coincide. Myth, in other words, creates a synergy of individual rights and social responsibilities.[14] Human existence manifests the dual principle that survival of the individual and the satisfaction of individual needs ultimately depend upon the stability of the group and that survival of the group ultimately depends upon individual possibilities to achieve homeostasis.

For social order to emerge, it is essential that individuals make occasional sacrifices. One method for achieving the orderly sacrifices of individuals is to force them to behave in certain ways—that is, to formulate a set of rules and to impose them by establishing an enforcement agency. The extreme example of this approach is the totalitarian police state. But the use of naked power is finally an inefficient strategy and one which encourages deception and brutality. A far more effective method of persuading individuals to make the sacrifices necessary for social coherence is to get them to ingest willfully a set of memes which can elicit the necessary sacrificial behavior. This is the function of myth; the result of ingesting a myth is to achieve an interface of individual and collective orders.

And when this process is complete, there is seldom a need to enforce the ideals of a group from without.

Much of the world's significant literature and drama centers upon the great difficulty and yet the great urgency of the willful sacrifice of self-interest. The perennial dilemma between self-fulfillment and self-sacrifice is often resolved by the paradox that the individual is ultimately fulfilled by a sacrifice made in the interest of others. Central to every cultural myth is the imperative that individual sacrifices must be made for the welfare of the group. Myth is the ultimate legitimator of sacrificial behavior. In some cultures sacrifice is elicited by the promise of an eventual reward. In some, individual sacrifices are made because the myth issues commands from a transcendent source of authority. And in totalitarian societies the sacrifices necessary for social coherence are produced by open threat. Every cultural myth is potentially capable of supporting totalitarian rule. If the myth of a culture loses its appeal to the imagination, its memes will not be internalized, and then the myth may well be used to legitimate the use of force. It goes without saying that cultural degeneration is in clear evidence whenever we observe a discrepancy between the imperatives of a cultural myth and the voluntary behavior of a significant number of individuals. As the synergy of individual rights and social responsibilities breaks down, there begins a slide in culture toward amythia.

The classic example of a culture failing to achieve an interface of collective and individual order is ancient Rome. The Roman Empire was capable of providing for the collective needs of its citizens but was not successful in satisfying their personal needs for wholeness. Pax Romana provided for the administration of orderly systems of food production, division of labor, defense, and so on, but the official myth of emperor worship did not appeal to the imagination of the local populations that were being newly admitted to the empire. Individuals who were unable to find meaning in the official myth were left to their own devices to achieve a sense of personal integrity. There emerged an ideological void which was filled by all manner of religions and practical philosophies competing at the local level to relieve the anxiety of individuals. The result was a perilous

55

ideological pluralism throughout the empire. And under the conditions of ideological pluralism, there was an erosion of both social coherence and individual wholeness.

Myth and Religion

A considerable amount of time and energy has been spent in disputing the proper definition of religion. Some observers of the religious life insist that religion is entirely a matter of the heart and cannot be defined obectively. For our purposes religion will be given a straightforward and empirical definition. Religion is the institutionalization of the myth of a culture. The religion of a culture can be identified with the institutional structures which have been created to regulate the myth of a culture. The literal meaning of "religion" ("binds together") derives from this function. To be more precise, religion is associated with those centers of power and authority in which decisions are made concerning the memes that will be preserved or expunged. Religion is, therefore, the principal agency of meme selection in a culture. Religious institutions render an official interpretation of the myth and establish the structures for its perpetuation and application. The chief instrument of religion in the West has been the worship service, the ceremonial means by which the myth is transmitted and reinforced. In the worship service we encounter the memes which religious authorities consider to be central to the myth; the purpose of worship, therefore, is to present the myth in its purest and most effective form.

The worship service is essentially an aesthetic event. In the worship service the arts are concentrated; they saturate the individual to create an artificial occasion in which life's varied experiences are absorbed and unified into the coherent perspective of the myth. But the worship service is also essentially a public event. If it is effective, the worship service will induce an overlay of individual and collective experience as well as an overlay of cosmology and morality. The many become one and the cosmos becomes imbued with meaning as the experiences of individuals are clarified and oriented by the drama of the worship service. There is a sense in which the worship experience bears a functional similarity to dreaming. As the individual dreams, the brain organizes various experiences of the day and gives them coherent meaning. The worship service, too, contributes coherence to discrete experiences. We might say that the worship life of a community is its collective dream life.[15]

The worship service is the principal instrument by which the biochemical conditions for social coherence and individual wholeness are established. Here the memes which order individual and collective life become fixed in the brains of initiates and reinforced in the brains of the already faithful. But while the worship service may be the most important setting for transmitting a myth, it is not the only one. It must be followed by all manner of supplemental reinforcement in homes, schools, and other venues of social interaction. Religious authority will therefore assert itself in every dimension of social life to make certain that memes incompatible with the "official" myth will not take hold, for if they do, the plausibility of the myth will begin to break down and the conditions for order, both individual and social, will be threatened by amythia. Here we note the fascinating and ambiguous relation between the arts and the religion of a culture. Religion absolutely depends upon the arts, for without the forms of art the myth cannot be expressed. But at the same time, the arts represent the greatest threat imaginable to religion, for in the arts new meanings will emerge, some of which may threaten to displace the fundamental memes of the myth.

Our definition of religion as the agent of meme selection in a tradition appears rather unwieldy in the context of a pluralistic culture. Under the conditions of pluralism, the agents of meme selection are highly diffused. In fact, this diffusion serves as an appropriate definition of pluralism. A culture is pluralistic to the extent that authority affecting its meme selection is decentralized. In contemporary culture decisions about which ideas and values will be preserved and transmitted are as likely to be made by television producers, book publishers, journalists, educators, legislators, and disc jockeys as they are by religious figures. Religious institutions now appear to play a rather minor role in a clamor of authorities, each attempting to fix memes in the brains of individuals. In the medieval period, when the church exercised monolithic authority, there was a centralization of power over the management of myth. In such times the most powerful figures in society were artists, who crafted memes, and bishops, who regulated the transmission of memes. The origins and implications of pluralism in Western culture will be explored in the next chapter. For the moment I simply observe that, as pluralism advances in a culture, there results a crisis of authority which decentralizes and, as in the case of Western culture, secularizes the institution of religion.

Summary

Our primary concern is with the vitality of contemporary Western civilization. I began with the observation that just as Western culture is reaching the heights of its creative potential it is beginning to manifest disturbing signs of degeneration. It is now pertinent to question whether this culture will continue to survive beyond the present century. Any hope of restoring the conditions of vitality to Western culture must begin with an understanding of what sort of reality a culture is. Only then can we appreciate the source of our malaise and begin to take appropriate measures to assure our survival.

I have taken the view that human culture cannot be understood apart from its natural history. A natural history of culture shows that the capacity for culture is itself a product of biological evolution, emerging as part of an extremely long and fortuitous series of adaptations of life forms to the environmental conditions of this planet. The capacity for culture is a major factor in the successful adaptation of human beings. The capacity for culture is a property of the human brain, but the *achievement* of culture is a function of a community of human brains. The process by which a community of human brains creates a stable culture begins with the establishment of metaphors which objectify information about the environment and make it possible to share and transmit a large corpus of meanings (memes). The acquisition of memes expands the behavioral repertory of the human brain by introducing abstractions and, with them, the formation of cooperative goals, purposes, and commitments. The invention of memes brings order to a community of individuals by regulating behavior through the orchestration of impulses in the nervous systems of individuals. But this achievement of order does not just happen. Information stored in the brain—if it is to be information and not mere data—must be organized into a coherent system or framework, a universe of meaning in which discrete predispositions for behavior are integrated, thereby making it possible for the individual to choose among various alternatives. Only under these conditions can we expect human behavior to be orderly and meaningful.

I have used the concept of myth to describe this phenomenon of building up a coherent symbolic world to integrate information about the environment with appropriate patterns of behavior. And we have seen how this world is constructed on the basis of a constellation of metaphors, which functions to generate and regulate the systematic accretion of a vast number of qualifying memes. We have further observed that cultures differentiate themselves on the basis of the distinctiveness of their myths. By perpetuating a myth shared commitments are formed, and a system of shared commitments guarantees the conditions for personal wholeness and social coherence. In civilized societies the transmission of a myth will be institutionalized as the religion of a culture.

What I have been attempting here is the construction of a theoretical view linking the viability and adaptivity of a culture to the viability of its myth, and, ultimately, to the viability of its root metaphors. And I have tried to do this in a way that clarifies the biological dimensions of these elements. If a culture manifests signs of degeneration—that is, the loss of shared commitments and the resulting breakdown of social coherence and personal wholeness—then we are justified in laying the blame on a failure of the tradition to transmit its distinctive myth successfully, a failure which results in the condition of amythia. The causes of this phenomenon promise to be extremely complex, and we must now turn to an exploration of these.

3

The Crisis in
Contemporary Culture

The Origins of Crisis

*Then the Lord came down to see the city and the tower which
those men had built, and he said, "Now then, these are all
one people and they speak one language; this is just the beginning of what they are going to do. Soon they will be able
to do anything they want! Let us go down and mix up their
language so that they will not understand one another."*
—Genesis 11:5–7

It has become somewhat conventional in the contemporary
period to describe the problems of human existence as resulting
from alienation. Everything from sexual inadequacy and labor
disputes to the doctrine of sin has been reduced to the dynamics
of alienation. In fact the idea of alienation, however imprecisely
defined, does seem to strike a responsive nerve for us. Experiences of estrangement, separation, homelessness, ambivalence, suspicion, and isolation, along with the anxiety typical
of each, have become all too familiar to us. Our difficulties in
maintaining equilibrium in our personal lives and in keeping
our institutions functional give us a sense that there is something fundamentally disjunctive in our present circumstances.
Crime rates increase, mental illness strikes with greater frequency in every socioeconomic class, families disintegrate as
often as not, alcoholism reaches epidemic proportions, and
stress seems to be a problem for everyone.

No doubt, a certain amount of disjunctive experience is present in every culture at any given time and much of it is not

situation-based at all. Nor is it entirely negative. To some extent alienation may even be regarded as a necessary source of vitality and social change and should not always be seen as a sign of cultural maladaptation. But when disjunctive experiences reach excessive levels of frequency, intensity, and ubiquity, and when there are insufficient means at our disposal for coping with them effectively, then alarm is justified. When alienation becomes the *substance* of a social ecology (as seems to have happened in Western culture), then we might conclude that the cognitive conditions for personal wholeness and social coherence have become attenuated.

The disjunctive character of modern civilization has been recognized for generations by the social sciences, each of which has constructed its own theoretical and experimental apparatus for defining and measuring it. I would probably embarrass myself beyond repair if I suggested that anything approximating a consensus exists in the social sciences regarding the nature and extent of psychological and social problems. And yet when one reads the literature, it is easy enough to conclude that much of what we perceive to be obstructive to personal wholeness and social coherence arises from the sheer complexity of our civilization. The number of physical and emotional ailments, for example, that have been linked to stress tempts one to believe that the many role demands imposed by a complex society have actually threatened our capacity to achieve good health. The sociological literature generated by the concept of anomie (literally, "normlessness") and its role in the etiologies of delinquency, deviancy, mental illness, and alcohol and drug addiction suggests that these problems are somehow directly related to the intellectual and moral pluralism of the modern age. The psychological literature directed toward evaluating the situational aspects of anxiety suggests that psychological homeostasis is less attainable in a complex intellectual and moral environment. And the failure of our political institutions to define and execute social goals and programs amid the increased clamor of competing special interests might also, it would appear, be assigned to the pluralism of values in modern society.

Alienation may well be the peculiar phenomenon of our contemporary social ecology, but its sources must ultimately be traced to the inescapability of conflict—psychological, social, and political—between norms, values, expectations, ideas, and the like. In other words, the immediate crisis in contemporary culture is one characterized by our inability to cope effectively with conflicting memes. We are a culture overwhelmed with meanings.

A natural history of culture is inclined to regard extreme complexity in a culture as maladaptive. When a culture becomes so complicated that its members no longer feel secure and its institutions begin to work at cross-purposes in their pursuit of collective goals, we might then expect the culture either to simplify itself by some radical transformation or else to collapse. In either case the immediate crisis promises an interesting future. The purpose of the present chapter is to trace the historical antecedents of the contemporary crisis and to speculate about where it might end.

The Emergence of Christian Culture

To assert that the crisis of contemporary culture is a function of disjunctive complexity implies that there was a time when it was not so, a time of pristine cultural unity. Of course there never was such an age of absolute integrity, especially in the political sense. The ideal of cultural unity has been present in the tradition from antiquity and was most forcefully expressed in Augustine's *City of God*. Augustine's vision was that the church was eternal, and thus the temporal state must be seen in a subordinate position, serving the spiritual ends of the church. The authority of the church was none other than God's own authority on earth and was therefore absolute. The entire medieval period can be seen as a sustained effort by the church to realize this theocratic vision of culture. But politically speaking, the unity of the West under medieval ecclesiastical dominion was not entirely forthcoming. Throughout the medieval period the ideal of Christian unity was frustrated by an abundance of fiefdoms, duchies, baronies, kingdoms, city-states, urban leagues, prince-bishoprics, and independent religious and military orders, each making their own noises about authority. But politics alone doth not a culture make, and even Augustine did not see the church as something to replace the secular domain; the state was to be encouraged as long as it did not interfere with the church's mission. The Christian ideal was rather one of spiritual communion, a unity of souls that transcends temporal powers. And in this sense we cannot deny that by the eleventh century Christianity was eventually able to achieve, to an impressive degree, a monolithic culture.

Christian unity, however, was not fashioned overnight. It took centuries of dedicated work under the most difficult of circumstances. The Christian era began in an environment much like our own, characterized by international strife, social upheaval, and personal anxiety. And even as the church spread throughout the Roman world, it gathered up a constituency that would eventually threaten to destroy it with theological diversity. The first step toward a unified Christian culture was therefore to establish theological orthodoxy within the church. And no sooner was this accomplished, in the mid-fifth century, than the social order of the empire dissolved into the agrarian dark ages as classical culture gave way to local pagan traditions. Much of the credit for cultivating Christian unity at the grass roots must go to Pope Gregory the Great (A.D. 540–604), who inspired monastic communities to carry the church's mission into the heathen countryside of the early Middle Ages. Only after centuries of grafting the Christian myth to the folkways of the *pagani* were the foundations of Western culture finally secure.

In the tenth century, monasticism again served as the principal agency of the papacy in its efforts toward ecclesiastical reform and the political restoration of European society. Not until the eleventh century, however, can one truly speak of a unified Christian culture. It is then that the efforts of monastics paid off and everything began to slip into place in what Christopher Dawson called a "centripetal movement" toward Christian unity.[1] In the eleventh century the papacy was finally able to rescind a centuries-old tradition of lay investiture of clergy, thereby making good its claim to be the supreme spiritual monarch of Christendom. The following period of prolonged papal supremacy, 1075–1250, we can designate as the golden age of Christian unity. This age saw the virtual fulfillment of the medieval ideal of a common culture unified under the spiritual leadership of the church.

63

Our interest is drawn toward the mechanics of achieving and maintaining this common culture. As the discussion of the previous chapter showed, the character of a cultural tradition is determined by the process of selecting which memes will be transmitted in a society and which ones will not. What we observe in the medieval period is a high degree of centralization of selective authority over the meme pool. Christendom as a cultural unity was able to emerge largely because the church was successful at monopolizing the means of cultural transmission and limiting the range of meanings that would be fixed in the biochemistry of medieval European brains. The first five centuries of the faith were preoccupied with defining what the limits of orthodoxy would be. And once theological controversy had calmed down, official doctrine was wired into the educational experiences of the monasteries. Literacy during the Middle Ages was virtually restricted to the clergy, and the education of the clergy was almost singularly defined by a program of classical and religious training cast in the sixth century by Cassiodorus and augmented a century later by Isidore of Seville. These were two of the most influential figures in all of Christian history, not because they were original thinkers, but because their work determined which memes would be transmitted throughout the formative period of Christian culture.[2]

Scholarship in the Middle Ages was placed unconditionally in service to the Christian proclamation. There was no scholarship for its own sake but only for the sake of advancing the Christian faith. Much of monastic education included the study of classical pagan texts, but these were generally held in suspicion, as a necessary evil; their merit was limited to their usefulness in promoting the Christian myth. Typical of the age were the views of Pope Gregory the Great, who held classical studies in complete contempt but who, oddly enough, was indirectly responsible for the preservation of much classical material. Gregory claimed, "The same mouth cannot sing the praises of Jupiter and the praises of Christ."[3]

Much the same attitude prevailed in the church's regard for the arts. Sculpture and monumental architecture were scarce in the early Middle Ages, and the only significant figure art was confined to the illustration of manuscripts. Here, too, there was no art for art's sake but only for the sake of the proclamation. Medieval figure art is highly symbolic, often to the degree of pantomime. Human figures were represented not for their intrinsic beauty but solely for their religious significance. There may have been attempts to stray from the straight and narrow religious subjects, but we do not know of them. The church was single-minded about what it allowed to be preserved as art and would have selected out any aberrations of the fanciful artist. Musical traditions were rich during the Middle Ages, and much musical material was transmitted because it was well suited as an accessory to prayer and worship. But very likely much of the popular music of the day—that is, music composed to accompany song and dance—succumbed to the obscurity of the past because it had no useful spiritual applications.

Matters were no different when it came to science and nature. Interest in natural science was limited to its function as a source of Christian allegory. Consider the following passage from the *Physiologus*, a popular type of natural history book in the early Middle Ages:

The lion has three characteristics; as he walks or runs he brushes his foot-prints with his tail, so that hunters may not track him. This signifies the secrecy of the incarnation of the Lion of the tribe of Judah. Secondly, the lion sleeps with his eyes open; so slept the body of Christ upon the Cross, while his Godhead watched at the right hand of the Father. Thirdly, the Lioness brings forth her cub dead; on the third day the father comes and roars in its face, and wakes it to life. This signifies the Lord's resurrection on the third day. . . . The pelican is distinguished by its love for its young, as these begin to grow they strike at their parents' faces, and the parents strike back and kill them. Then the parents take pity, and on the third day the mother comes and opens her side and lets the blood flow on the dead young ones, and they become alive again. Thus God cast off mankind after the Fall, and delivered them over to death; but he took pity on us, as a mother, for by the Crucifixion He awoke us with his Blood to eternal life. . . . The Unicorn cannot be taken by hunters, because of his great strength, but lets himself be captured by a pure virgin. So Christ, mightier than the heavenly powers, took on humanity in a virgin's womb.[4]

This passage illustrates the medieval subordination of scientific knowledge to theological ends. Most things were passively accepted on the basis of authority, even (or perhaps especially) those which were fantastic, magical, or miraculous. There was no attempt to scrutinize accounts of nature by observation or experiment; the point was to apply them. Any interest in nature that did not contribute to a clarification of the myth was considered an idle waste of time and was summarily dismissed. Witness St. Ambrose: "To discuss the nature and position of the earth does not help us in our hope of the life to come. It is enough to know what the Scripture states. . . . Why then argue and raise a controversy?"[5]

The general point is to show that the character of a cultural tradition takes shape by selectively removing from circulation those memes which are not seen to clarify and reinforce the myth. The process is plain enough: if a meme does not fit, it is pronounced unfit. By this process a common Christian culture came to flourish in the high Middle Ages. But it was not to last. As we shall presently see, the unity of Christian culture was progressively dismantled as the church lost its monopoly of authority over the selection of memes.

Renaissance Humanism

The Renaissance was a many-sided and many-layered phenomenon, and my point here is not to comment on all of its dimensions but only to stress that its effect was to legitimate new independent sources of authority over the selection of memes in Western culture. These were, to anticipate the argument, the authority of the classical tradition and the authority of human resourcefulness.

By the mid-thirteenth century, the great flower of medieval Christendom had begun to wither. A conflux of problems sent the church into a prolonged tailspin from which it would never fully recover its power. The last Christian outpost in Palestine fell to the Turks in 1291, opening the door for their entry into Europe. Europe itself was entering into a period of economic decline which was to affect the church's financial position greatly and bring it increasingly into conflict with emerging nations. Monasticism was weakened by financial drainage to the papacy, by the ravages of the Black Death, and by invasions of mercenary soldiers. The intellectual and moral fiber of the clergy was eroded by illiteracy, simony, debauchery, and other abuses. The papacy was weakened by ineptitude, by the removal to Avignon and the subsequent papal schism, and also by intense criticism and the growing popularity of conciliarism. And in addition, theological controversies were flaring up again. Such developments, and more, had a cumulative negative effect on the morale of the church and of society in general.[6] The church was progressively unable to perform its functions and ceased to be an effective custodian of culture. Those who might have looked to the church's authority for help found only disappointment. Under these conditions, mysticism began to appear as a form of anecclesiastical religious life. But these were also the conditions for ripening a new form of *secular* life.

The Renaissance started in Italy, if indeed we can say that anything so complex could have started in one place. But it started in Italy nevertheless. And it did so because in Italy, though not in the rest of Europe, the city had never quite disappeared into the agrarian patterns of the Middle Ages, and the Renaissance was primarily an urban affair. Italian cities like Venice, Florence, and Rome offered financial opportunities for the emergence of a new class of educated laymen. And these cities attracted Byzantine refugees as the Turks advanced westward, thereby providing the scholarly resources to further stimulate the growing interest in classical Greek culture. Opportunity, resources, and the decomposition of the church conspired to produce a new aesthetic sensibility and a new way of life for an educated elite class.

The aesthetic character of the medieval period had been exclusively religious. That is to say, nothing was considered beautiful or worthy of preservation unless it could be shown to glorify God and to extend his kingdom. But in the Renaissance a new aesthetic principle arose. This is to say not that the Renaissance was antireligious but merely that there emerged a new willingness to regard nature and the human figure on their own terms rather than exclusively as symbols for a higher truth. What contributed to this new willingness more than anything else was the renewed influence of classical culture. Gradually, as a result of the revival of scholarship in the twelfth century, suspicion of pagan literature subsided. Already in the fourteenth century, Dante was highly conversant with the secular literature of the ancient world, and just a generation later Petrarch was amassing a huge library of classical authors and extolling the value of these texts on their own merits and not simply for their contributions to Christian piety. Soon enough, all over Italy, we find artists and scholars infatuated with the prospect of recovering classical ideals. Among other things this infatuation brought with it a new appreciation for Plato.

The environment of the early Renaissance released readers of Plato from their Augustinian blinders, enabling them to see his doctrine of humanity in a new light. The Platonic concept of *areté*, excellence, was now understood to be the realization or fulfillment of one's essential human nature through the process of *paideía*, education. The classical concept of *areté* therefore became for Renaissance scholars and artists the basis for a new aesthetic and a new vision of humanity. Classical culture charmed the artists and thinkers of the early Renaissance and sent them in search of their own expressions of essential humanity. The emerging aesthetic principle regarded something as beautiful or worthy of preservation if it could be shown to glorify humanity and clarify the human condition—that is, if it expressed what is essentially human. The painting, sculpture, literature, drama, and music of the Renaissance are completely miscomprehended if we fail to see in them a passion for exploiting the limits of creative human resources.

The concept of *areté* finds its peculiar Renaissance rendition in *virtù*, the watchword of Renaissance humanism. *Virtù* can be variously translated as "valor," "ability," "courage," "resourcefulness," "genius," "vigor," "prudence," "ambition," "skill," and the like. In nearly all cases it is associated with the heroic. The heroic ideal of Renaissance humanists was the radically free and self-sufficient individual who had the courage to take on difficult tasks and who had the intellectual and physical resources to succeed. Renaissance humanists strove both to achieve and to display virtù. Knowledge of the classics was generally thought to confer the intellectual ingredients of virtù. And thus the new class of artists and scholars did their best to imitate the classics in their speech and in their exploits. The athletic traits of virtù could be cultivated only by rigorous physical discipline. The humanists were not afraid of hard work, and they applied themselves diligently to a regimen of scholarship and physical activity. Such a paideía was expected to produce specimens of virtù: individuals who were clever, defiant, well mannered, physically well conditioned, and able to paint, make music, and quote Cicero and Homer to boot. But eventually the penchant for imitating classical ideals led to pretentious excesses. And thus there arose, for example, the practice of classicizing names: Johann Müller became Regio-montanus, and Hiero Fabrizio became Hieronymus Fabricus da Aquapendente. The excesses of humanism tended to degenerate into a shallow, self-indulgent, and sometimes trivial way of life.

As imitation of the classical world became more extreme, the importance of Christianity began to fade. The doctrine of divine Providence was for some humanists replaced by the classical notion of *Fortuna* (fate). Fortuna served as a recognition that there are some limits on the ability of human beings to shape their own destiny, but in most matters human life depended on the ability of an individual to seize the day, that is, to recognize an opportunity and to use one's resources to turn it to one's own advantage.

One should not, however, take the impression that the Renaissance was widely regarded as an overt revival of paganism and therefore a rival to the Christian myth. Indeed, there were significant attempts to justify the ideals of the new learning on theological grounds. We need only consider the likes of Giovanni Pico della Mirandola, who aspired to synthesize Judaism and Hellenism in a Christian theological system and whose "Oration on the Dignity of Man" put the new humanism in theological terms, or Egidio da Viterbo, who considered Plato a pre-Christian Christian, or Leonardo Bruni, who said that classical literature bore the mark of divinity, or humanist educators like Vergerio and Sadoleto who embraced the intellectual and aesthetic ideals of Hellenism without feeling that they were compromising Christian theology and morality.

The excesses of Renaissance humanism and its tendency to displace Christian ideals in some quarters were eventually moderated by the influence of a more substantive Christian humanism from the North—where literacy remained in the province of the clergy—and by the Reformation and religious wars which were to follow. But there was no undoing the major innovations of Renaissance humanism. The humanists brought forth into Western culture many new ideas; however, the contribution of most lasting significance was that humanism introduced new authorities alongside the church. Scholarship, philosophy, and art were freed from their exclusive role as handmaidens of theology to become "pure scholarship" and "pure art." The authority of pre-Christian traditions would henceforth rival that of the church, and so too would the authority of the creative human spirit.

Reformation

The Protestant Reformation ignited when two rather independent and powerful dynamics converged. They were a growing nationalistic resentment of Rome and the wave of theological controversy that was unleashed by biblical and patristic scholarship. These movements came to a crisis in Germany, where the sparks were fanned by the powerful influence of the new press. The result of the Reformation was devastating for anyone who longed for a restoration of a unified Christian culture. The authority of scripture was established decisively, and the wars which followed the Reformation created a situation wherein theological divisions and national boundaries reinforced one another.

After its resettlement in Rome, the papacy became embroiled in Italian power politics and lavish ventures of artistic patronage, both of which were enormously expensive. The mounting financial pressure produced measures for increasing taxation on church lands as well as elaborate schemes for extracting money from ecclesiastical positions. When a post became vacant, its income was typically called to Rome, and when posts were not vacant there was always an opportunity to create new ones for sale to the highest bidder. Nowhere were there fewer financial resources and less political organization for resisting papal enormities than in Germany, which was a patchwork of civil and ecclesiastical jurisdictions. And nowhere, therefore, did the resentment of Rome reach such extremes. The situation came to its flashpoint in 1517 when Pope Leo X authorized a campaign for the sale of indulgences in Germany. Frederick the Wise, elector of Saxony, was particularly put off because the sale of indulgences threatened to interfere with his own schemes to raise money. At this point Martin Luther entered the scene, and as he did, economic and political issues joined forces with theology to create a climate of crisis.

The theological dynamic for the Reformation really began when there existed both the inclination and the means for holding church doctrine and polity in judgment. The prolonged abuses of the fourteenth and fifteenth centuries left no want of inclination, and the means were refined by the scholarship of the Renaissance. Knowledge of Greek was one of the fruits of the Renaissance, and if humanist scholars stressed anything, it was the importance of returning to original sources for original meanings. Thus the scriptures and the writings of the church fathers became more important than ever to the reformers. It was now possible for biblical and patristic scholars to sort through the original sources and to find important discrepancies between current practices and original teachings. This enterprise became something of a passion among learned men who sought reform in the church. Not only did the reformers believe the church should be held accountable to its origins, but they began to see that the laity also had rights of access to these original sources. Erasmus and Luther both agreed with the earlier teachings of Wycliffe, Hus, and the fourteenth-century mystics that nothing, not even the ministrations and interpretations of the church, should be allowed to interfere with the impact of scripture on individual souls.

The church had customarily insisted upon custodial rights when it came to the scriptures and had on several occasions since the ninth century explicitly forbidden not only vernacular translations but the very reading of the Bible by laymen. But by the end of the fourteenth century, vernacular translations were proliferating rapidly. By 1522, when Luther produced his own German translation of the New Testament, there were already fourteen others in German and four in Dutch. Access to scripture became a central issue between the church and its critics precisely because the Bible was increasingly cited as a legitimate source of criticism. But the church was not successful in suppressing the lay readership of the Bible, so scripturally inspired criticism continued to mount. And the criticism was not limited to the cloistered disputations of scholars. Once printing presses got into the act, the issue of church reform became a movement of the masses.

No one was more instrumental in bringing about this movement than Martin Luther. Luther's prodigious biblical scholarship and his irascible disposition led him to judge the church at the bar of scripture on many critical points of doctrine. He was especially agitated by abuses of the sacramental system, which he thought had finally reduced God's salvation to a mere commodity mongered by the church for its own profit and at the expense of poor Christian peasants. The sale of indulgences became Luther's pretext for a general assault on the abuses of the mechanical church. His allegations won both the grateful admiration of the German people and the unmitigated scorn of the pope. The situation came into focus at Leipzig in 1519 when Luther explicitly denounced the authority of the pope and ecclesiastical councils when they were not supported by scripture. This pointed assertion that scripture was the ultimate authority led to Luther's excommunication and the division of Christendom into armed camps.

Luther's altercation with the church was followed by a century of religious wars which had theological dimensions as well as political ones. In fact, once the Reformation was under way, it became increasingly difficult to tell where theology left off and politics began. In some cases (for example, England and Germany) religious issues gave secular rulers an opportunity to strengthen their hand. In other cases (for example, Spain and Italy) secular powers were used to purify the religious environment. In general it can be said that the Reformation strengthened the powers of secular monarchs considerably and helped to reify nationalistic sentiments which had been so influential in starting reform movements at the onset. It can also be said that post-Reformation Christendom tended to realign itself to conform with national boundaries. The result was to have far-reaching consequences for the future of Christian culture. Theological diversity continued to increase as denominations defined themselves against one another. When theological differences become reinforced by national and linguistic identity, the conditions are set for a divergence of intellectual, moral, and aesthetic experience. The psychological and social implications of the Reformation were far more lasting than the theological and political issues which produced them. As Dawson puts it: "The Baroque culture integrated asceticism with mysticism, and humanism with popular culture, through the common media of art and liturgy; but in the Protestant world, the religious culture of the masses, which was derived from the Bible and the sermon, had no access to the imaginative world of the humanist poet and artist. Thus it is on the popular level that the differencs between the two cultures are most obvious and their separation most complete."[7]

The Reformation then, like the Renaissance, produced not only a wave of new meanings in Western culture but also new authority structures for the generation and regulation of meanings. The consequences of the Reformation in terms of stimulating complexity and the subspeciation of Western culture are still being realized.

The State

In 1648 the Peace of Westphalia marked the end of a century of religious wars. The treaties centered upon the nation-states of Europe and asserted their sovereignty in settling their own affairs without interference from either the emperor or the pope. The Holy Roman Empire was finally reduced to a mere formality, and it was virtually the same with the papacy. Pope Innocent X condemned the final treaty as "null, void, invalid, iniquitous, unjust, damnable, reprobate, inane, empty of all meaning and effect for all time."[8] But the papal condemnation was barely noticed and universally disregarded; it became crystal clear that the church would no longer be a serious participant in matters relating to political settlements. Thus since the mid-seventeenth century, the legitimate independent authority of the Western nation-state has been assumed. The Peace of Westphalia, however, stands as a mere exclamation at the far end of four centuries of development. The emergence of the nation-state is closely linked to the beginnings of a money economy. Feudalism and its various localized institutions were well enough suited to the decentralized agrarian economy of the Middle Ages, but as towns flourished and trade expanded, there came a need to expand bureaucracies and to centralize political and military power. The pressure for this development came primarily from the new capitalists and burghers who preferred the strong hand of a king to the provincial rule of a landed nobility.

In general we can say that the process of nationalizing Europe, starting with the emergence of a new economy, was greatly accelerated by the Renaissance and the Reformation; the former provided theoretical legitimation and the latter generated the social and political upheaval which could be settled only by powerful secular rulers. The result was to bring Europe away from the Augustinian model of church-state relations into the Erastian dawn of the modern era.

The theocratic vision of Augustine clearly saw the state as subordinate in authority to the church. Indeed, civil authority was derived from ecclesiastical authority. The value of the state was entirely instrumental; like philosophy and the arts, the state was legitimated by its service to the Christian myth. This view came under attack from political thinkers of the early Renaissance, whose views were provoked both by the writings of antiquity and by observations of centrifugal forces which were rapidly eroding feudalism. Admiration of the civic virtues of ancient Greece and Rome led some Renaissance scholars to new insights about the nature of collective life. And eventually it came to be seen that civil law, and not faith, was the true ground of social coherence and that the state was not merely an instrument but an entity with intrinsic value.

One of the earliest proponents of these Erastian views was Marsiglio of Padua, who lived in the first half of the fourteenth century but whose works were widely circulated in the fifteenth century when the monarchs of Europe were beginning to display absolutist tendencies. Marsiglio was infatuated with the ideal of an autonomous lay state, and he was irritated by the church's interference in secular matters. His political theory idealized the northern Italian city-state in the same way that Platonic and Aristotelian theory idealized Athens. Marsiglio makes frequent references to Aristotle in arguing for the autonomy of the state, just as he makes frequent references to the Bible in his argument that the papal claims to independent ecclesiastical jurisdiction were bogus. Marsiglio in fact reverses the medieval doctrine of church and state by advancing the theory that the church is a part of the state. The church is merely an association of Christians whose primary identity is found in the state, and the church's only legitimate role is to encourage the moral and spiritual conditions most conducive to the achievement of civil ends. Even legislation concerning crimes of heresy, if such be necessary to preserve order, is properly the function of the state, not the church. To the extent that the church opposes the authority of the state, it becomes a source of social strife and should be held accountable to civil law.

From the views of Marsiglio it is but a quick step to the Machiavellian divorce of politics from morality. Marsiglio was sufficiently wary of absolutism to declare that legislation is the province of the citizenry and that laws should therefore substantially represent public opinion. But Machiavelli had less respect for the wisdom of the masses. He believed that a strong and unified society could be held together only by an absolute ruler, one who embodied the ambition and resourcefulness typical of virtù. Machiavelli had a sincere admiration for the civic virtues of the ancient world and was heavily influenced by the political dysfunctions created by divisions among Italian city-states. He was motivated by a desire to articulate the foundations of a unified state. The true state is built upon civil virtues which are codified in civil law. But law requires legislation, and here Machiavelli could see no way around the need for an absolute ruler who had the ability to consolidate and maintain power and who had the strength of character to use this power for the security and preservation of the state. Whatever means were necessary to achieve and maintain a unified state were justified, even though they might transgress the conventions of morality, whether Christian or pagan. To Machiavelli, the state is an end in itself, and the wise prince should elevate the preservation of the state above morality: "When it is absolutely a question of the safety of one's country, there must be no consideration of just or unjust, of merciful or cruel, of praiseworthy or disgraceful; instead, setting aside every scruple, one must follow to the utmost any plan that will save her life and keep her liberty."[9] For Machiavelli morality and law serve the state, and the state shall be the judge of virtue.

Such absolutist theories of the state were subsequently ratified by the experience of the Reformation, which relied for its success upon the predisposition of secular rulers to use their power to establish social order. Where social order was disrupted by religious controversy, secular rulers claimed the authority to intervene. Indeed, on many occasions they were urged to do so by religious leaders, with the result that the autonomy of the state became a fixture of doctrine within Protestant theology as well as a fixture of civil law. The leaders of the Reformation had no qualms about the effects of an autonomous state upon the integrity of the Christian myth. Luther's doctrine of the two kingdoms can be seen as a form of theological apology for the independent state. God had created two kingdoms, and both stand under his rulership. The state bears the same relation to the church that the Law does to the Gospel. While the state is considered to be independent of the church, there is no suggestion that it would in any way be inimical to the Christian myth.

The extent to which the authority of the sovereign state was recognized by the end of the Reformation period can be seen in the principle *cuis regio, eius religio* (whoever controls the region controls the religion). This principle was affirmed in the Peace of Augsburg in 1555 and was later reaffirmed in the Peace of Westphalia. It assigns to secular rulers the power to determine the religion practiced by their subjects. Thus the state claimed the authority to determine which memes would and would not be allowed to transmit themselves throughout culture.

The point of this entire discussion bears upon the proliferation of authorities in Western culture. We have already seen that alongside the authority of the church there stood the authority of the classical traditions and the authority of human resourcefulness. And then we observed that the Reformation asserted the authority of scripture. And in the immediate discussion we have seen the extent to which the independent authority of the state was established. Within a mere four centuries the integrity of Christian culture was to give way to an emergent pluralism, the extent of which had not been seen since the demise of the Roman Empire. But it was not to end here, for the authority of the scientific method was also asserting itself.

Science

It is not possible to speak of the recognition of the scientific method as an independent authority until the beginning of the seventeenth century because not until then was the scientific method explicitly formulated by Sir Francis Bacon. And we cannot really speak of the institutional aspects of the scientific community before the formation of scientific societies in the mid-seventeenth century. But here again, these events are end points which were preceded by a conflux of discrete developments. One of the most interesting questions in Western intellectual history asks why, when the early Greek philosophers came so close, the methods and fruits of science did not appear much earlier. But it is difficult enough to discern why science appeared when it did, in the sixteenth and seventeenth centuries, without speculating on the reasons for its not appearing when it did not.

Several prerequisite conditions emerged during the Middle Ages, both material and intellectual, without which modern science would have been inconceivable. Discovery of the New World was important for the rise of science because it stimulated a spurt of commercial activity in far-off places and brought forth new scientific instruments that were needed to improve methods of navigation. The discovery of gunpowder prompted a flurry of investigation to discover new means of defensive and offensive warfare. The artistic realism of the Renaissance gave rise to new methods of calculating visual perspective which were eventually useful to astronomers. The recovery of classical learning brought the speculations of ancient philosophers, many of whom anticipated modern theories, to the attention of European scholars. The introduction of Arabic numerals to the West was an event of obvious importance to modern science. The Renaissance rejection of scholasticism eventually brought the authority of Aristotelian cosmology under scrutiny. And as the cities of the Renaissance flourished, there were new opportunities for interaction between the practical mentality of the craft tradition and the theoretical mentality of the scholarly tradition. These developments and others helped to create the conditions under which scientific inquiry could evolve as an independent enterprise. And as it did so science plainly showed itself to be a new worldview with structural, functional, and methodological aspects.

When considering the rise of the modern scientific worldview, one is likely to think of the Copernican revolution and its new conception of the structure of the universe. It is difficult to measure the impact of the new heliocentric theory on the consciousness of the fifteenth century, but if the discomfort of the church is any indication, we must conclude that this impact was considerable. The Copernican revolution, in fact, did nothing less than present to the Western mind a totally new map of the universe with profound implications regarding the place of humanity in nature. Furthermore, and more important, it was to dislodge the authority of Aristotelian cosmology completely, clearing the way for new speculations about the functioning of nature.

Medieval science was characterized by its emphasis on teleological explanations. Under the influence of Aristotelian physics, no phenomenon in nature—not even a simple event like the falling of a rock—was thought to be sufficiently explained until it was shown to have an end or purpose. A rock falls. Why? Because it is the *telos* of such bodies to be at rest. Ultimately, of course, all events could be explained by reference to a system of nature which was controlled by Providence, that is, by a purposeful God. This understanding of the teleological function of nature was gradually replaced by descriptive accounts of natural phenomena. Descriptive accounts skirt the question of *why* an event occurs and merely show *how* it occurs. Little by little the final (teleological) causes of Aristotelian science were regarded as less satisfying than efficient (descriptive) causes. Efficient causes were infinitely more satisfying because they tended to enhance the ability to predict and control natural events. The ultimate explanation for practitioners of modern science, therefore, was to be set out not in terms of Providence but rather in terms of natural laws which described the regularity of mass and force within dimensions of space and time. The events of nature came to be seen less as products of God's will than as functions of natural laws.

The passionate search for regularity in nature eventually produced a more far-reaching innovation: the invention of a fairly well defined method for generating new knowledge about nature. Medieval science depended heavily upon the deductive method of inquiry. The accepted procedure was to pursue conclusions by applying the rules of logic to a body of general principles. The major limitation on this method was that the Middle Ages had no systematic and reliable method for discovering the truth of general principles to begin with. General truths were either assumed by common sense or accepted on the strength of authority. But as the interaction of practical craftsmen and theoretical scholars began to bear fruit, it became more evident that firsthand critical observation and the meticulous recording of data were of central importance for the falsification as well as for the construction of general assertions. Renaissance scientists such as Leonardo and Vesalius followed the new practice of repeating experiments and recording their observations, and they had good reasons for being less impressed with what Aristotle or Galen had to say than with their own experience. As pioneering scientists began to exchange and reflect on their work, a systematic method gradually materialized and received its most explicit formulation from Bacon.

It seems that once scientists had become more self-conscious about their methods, they achieved a sense of common identity and began to realize that science was itself an independent entity. Shortly after Bacon's death in 1626, scientific societies began to appear in Europe, the most notable being the Academy of Experiments in Florence, the Royal Society of England, and the French Academy of Sciences. The influence of these groups on the progress and prestige of science was dramatic. Prior to the formation of these societies, scientific investigators carried on their work in relative isolation from their colleagues, and there were no standard organs for the dissemination of scientific knowledge. Nor was early modern science welcomed into the universities. But the societies provided for significant (and often international) contact between individuals and soon began to publish their own journals for the circulation of ideas. The activities of scientific societies meant that science would become a cooperative and authoritative enterprise. By the end of the seventeenth century, the century of Descartes, Leibniz, Harvey, Hooke, Newton, and Boyle, there could be no doubting the authority of the scientific method and, indeed, of the scientific community itself.

It would be misleading to create the impression that the new science was seen by all as a threat to Christianity. To the contrary, despite the scoffs of Luther and Melanchthon at the Copernican theory, and the church's treatment of Galileo, the new science was seen by many as fully consistent with the Christian myth. In fact, as the fruits of science became more abundant, the widespread belief emerged that scientific inquiry advanced the discovery and admiration of God's handiwork. Galileo's remark that mathematics was the language of God's creation and Kepler's remark that scientists were merely thinking God's thoughts after him are adequate expressions of the climate of opinion by the mid-seventeenth century. These observations lead us to emphasize the general point that, while the emergence of new authorities (that is, the classical traditions, individual resourcefulness, the scriptures, the state, and science) may have created problems for particular religious doctrines, there was no appreciation of the possibility that any of these would undermine the root metaphor of the Christian myth (God as person). In fact, as we have seen, this root metaphor functioned in each case to legitimate the new authorities.

Pluralism

It is useful to identify two stages in the development of Western cultural pluralism, the first extending from the mid-thirteenth century to the mid-seventeenth century, and the second from the mid-seventeenth century to the present. Soon after the fall of the Roman Empire and the subsequent ruralization of Western civilization there began a steady movement toward the reunification of culture centered upon the leadership of the Christian church. This centripetal movement culminated in a golden age of Christian culture which flourished from the mid-eleventh to the mid-thirteenth century. And then, in the thirteenth century, there was a reversal of motion and centrifugal forces began to dismantle the unity of culture. Gradually the church lost its monopoly over the instruments of cultural transmission as various other authorities asserted themselves. By the mid-seventeenth century the first stage of disintegration was virtually complete: we find a diffusion of custodial power among a plurality of authorities. After this point all the equations were different, and the church was left to share its influence in Western culture with the secular state, the scriptures, the classical traditions of literature, philosophy and the arts, and, finally, modern science. We have briefly reviewed the legitimation of these determinants of culture.

But the legitimation of these primary authorities was, in a way, only the beginning of pluralism, for a second stage of diffusion was yet to create diversity within each of them. The period since the seventeenth century, while it cannot be said to have uncovered new types of authority (except, perhaps, the authority of the market), had the effect of transforming the dynamics of cultural transmission and accelerating the growth of diversity. The second stage of cultural diffusion, beginning with the Enlightenment, has continued down to the present day.

A natural history of culture must necessarily concern itself with two decisive phenomena which characterize the period since the late thirteenth century. One is the proliferation of selective agencies, and the other is the attenuation of selective activity. These two dynamics correspond to the two stages in the diffusion of meanings. Pluralism emerges in the first stage, and by the end of the seventeenth century, as we have seen, it was *there*—a reality, a fact of life. And pluralism was clearly not going to go away. The only thing that could be done about pluralism was somehow to account for it and justify it. In the first stage, then, we find a gradual pluralization of authorities, and in the second stage we find a further diversification together with a legitimation of pluralism itself. And once plu-

81

ralism gained theoretical justification it became difficult to find good reasons for the exclusion of any meanings whatsoever from the meme pool.

The exploration of nature by modern science presented to the modern period a world of neutral facts and mechanical laws which appeared totally indifferent to the world of human affairs. The challenge for the new philosophy was to find a place for the autonomy of human choice and intellection alongside the morally neutral realm of material nature. It fell to Descartes to orient modern philosophy generally on the basis of a dualistic metaphysic. Descartes reasoned that the reality of the human mind and the reality of the material world were, in fact, separate. They reflect a fundamental metaphysical distinction between spiritual substance and material substance. The implication for the apparent contradictions between science and religion was clear: the world of religious sentiment and moral discourse could not be in conflict with the world of scientific theory because their subject matters were ontologically distinct. Much of subsequent modern philosophy can be seen as a heroic attempt to save this metaphysical dualism from its inherent difficulties. Descartes's solution to the modern challenge, while basically unstable, was convincing enough to make possible for the moment the peaceful coexistence of science and religion.

While philosophers were busy puzzling over the metaphysical and epistemological foundations of pluralism, social changes were brewing that would pluralize the political realm. The alliance of the merchant class with absolutist monarchs, which had brought feudalism to an end and had created the modern nation-state, was beginning to fall apart with the continued expansion of the middle class. Eventually the dynastic monarchies of Europe were seen to be just as repressive as a feudal nobility. When appeals to monarchs met with no success, the middle classes organized their resistance. Political revolutions, first in England and then later in America and on the European continent, brought forth constitutional democracies. Philosophical legitimations of democracy are evident as early as the sixteenth century in the social contract theories of Francois Hotman and the anonymous author of *Vindiciae Contra Tyrannos* and in the early seventeenth century in the social contract theory of Robert Bellarmine. But the classic defenses of the social contract were elaborated by Locke and Rousseau.

The extension of political enfranchisement was consistent with the general tendency of the Enlightenment toward greater toleration in every aspect of human affairs. The principle *cuis regio, eius religio*, which had given the new states power to intervene in religious affairs, was in practice repealed by the Enlightenment mood for absolute toleration in matters of religion. Early figures to anticipate this mood were Michel Montaigne, Jeremy Taylor, John Milton, and Roger Williams, but the most influential voice for religious toleration was that of John Locke. Locke argued the Cartesian line that religious belief was a matter of conscience and occupied a realm that was not to be violated by the authority of the state.

But the legitimation of pluralism was not to stop with mere religious toleration. Cartesian dualism contributed to the notion that we have no access to the beliefs and opinions of other minds, and without such access there are no grounds for judging them to be false. Joseph Glanvill, an early advocate of complete toleration and freedom of thought, argued the virtues of an open mind over the evils of dogmatism. His appeal for tolerance was later reinforced by the likes of Pierre Bayle, Anthony Collins, and Voltaire. Religious toleration was eventually expanded to include Catholics, Jews, Protestants of all stripes, and even agnostics and atheists.

The attack on religious intolerance was generalized to include attacks upon censorship of the press. In the sixteenth century, as soon as civil and ecclesiastical authorities had recognized the power of the press as a transmitter of culture, licensure laws were put into effect. Prohibited books were indexed, and unlicensed printing was made punishable, often by death. The battle against censorship of the press enlisted some of the greatest luminaries of the Enlightenment. John Milton was by far the most eloquent and inspired many subsequent defenders of the free press. Milton's *Aeropagitica* was written in response to the censorship imposed in 1643 by the Long Parliament. Milton argued the standard plea for a free press, that truth can prevail only when falsehood too is allowed expression: "Let the truth and falsehood grapple. Who ever knew truth put to the worse in a free and open encounter? . . . She needs no policies, no strategems, no licensings to make her victorious. These are the shifts and defenses that error uses against her power."[10]

Milton's arguments have been echoed in virtually every test case for free expression since his time. By the end of the seventeenth century there was, if not a free press, at least a much liberated press in Holland, Germany, and England. Others were to follow, so that since the nineteenth century (with obvious setbacks) freedom of the press has been considered throughout the West as an inalienable human right.

Freedom of worship and freedom of the press are among a constellation of civil liberties upon which people in Western nations insisted from the end of the seventeenth century. Civil liberties—including rights of petition, free elections, fair and speedy trial, appropriate fines and punishments, and so forth—were initially demanded by the merchant class to safeguard their persons, property, and commercial activities from the caprices of civil authorities. The merchant classes had the sagacity to insist that civil liberties be written into constitutional law, for they would then be much harder to expunge than ordinary statutes. Eventually, of course, the civil liberties which had been designed for an elite class were demanded by the masses. By the end of the eighteenth century, England, America, and France had all made constitutional provisions for civil liberties, and the remaining Western nations were to follow suit in the nineteenth century.

In the eighteenth century there were several innovations in the area of education. During this century responsibility for education started to devolve upon the state, as Protestants had long believed it should. Protestants also supported education for the masses, though this goal was not to be fully realized until the nineteenth century. As the eighteenth century progressed, the schools became targets for advancing Enlightenment ideals. There were efforts to free curricula from traditional influences and to eradicate religious superstition by introducing liberal doses of natural science. Reasonableness, tolerance, and a critical bearing were the chief virtues of eighteenth-century education. Rousseau and the romantic movement reacted against the artificiality and conventionalism of rationalist education and stressed the importance of adapting the curriculum to the nature of the learner, and they also stressed the importance of cultivating the full and spontaneous expression of the individual. In the nineteenth century, as a result of the Industrial Revolution, education was democratized and further diversified to meet the needs of a more complex economy. Soon the ideals of universal literacy and a freethinking populace were to approach realization, and as they did so the effects of pluralism began to accelerate.

Some readers will object to my concluding this historical survey on the very eve of the Industrial Revolution. Many of the developments that have contributed to the contemporary crisis are arguably more recent. I certainly would not disagree. But it has been my purpose here only to identify the developments which created the cognitive conditions for the contemporary crisis. These took place, I believe, between the thirteenth and the nineteenth centuries. In this period the generation and legitimation of pluralism occurred. And this pluralism is the source of complexity in contemporary culture. Once pluralism had appeared and had been justified, it was inevitable that the diversification of memes would begin to accelerate beyond control, especially after the expansion of literacy. The period from the Renaissance to the Industrial Revolution therefore set in motion the dynamics that would swell in the nineteenth century and would then erupt violently in the twentieth century to produce the frenzied society of rapid change and unprecedented diversity that Alvin Toffler was to describe in *Future Shock*.

Today we are left with a culture having so little integrity of character that it lacks clarity of purpose. We are no longer a coherent culture but a complex assemblage of subcultures. The common meanings that might provide fiber for commitments are lost in the clamor of competing memes. The church, once a tidy hierarchical entity, is now a kaleidoscope of liturgical, theological, moral, institutional, and stylistic differences. Only extreme theological romantics continue to speak of the Universal Church. The truth is that there are now more varieties of religious orientation than we can keep track of. Ever since the Reformation, Christian churches have shown a pronounced tendency to split over trivial issues and thereby to proliferate.

But the Judaeo-Christian tradition is no longer alone in having influence in Western culture. All the major religions of the world and some of the minor ones have a presence too, as do a multiplicity of so-called secular belief systems. There has been a parallel diffusion of the authority of scripture as well. Luther believed that if the Bible were placed in the hands of a literate layperson, the Holy Spirit would make God's word clear. But lay access to the scriptures has produced more variations of interpretation than Luther could have dreamed possible. There is no denying that the Bible is used to support a diversity of opposing views on almost any theological or moral issue. The nation-state is no longer simply identified with monarchs as was the case when its independence was first accomplished. As political participation has broadened and as civil liberties have been achieved, the modern state has become something of a free-for-all of civil and military bureaucracies, political parties, and special interest groups representing the views of every ethnic, professional, industrial, and economic group imaginable, each with its own ideology and institutional framework. Diversity within the scientific community has grown exponentially. The division of scientific labor has produced so many disciplines, subdisciplines, and cross-disciplines that universities cannot keep abreast of them. And within each there exists a diversity of theoretical perspectives. We can still identify scientific societies, but they are held together less by common intellectual interests than by concern for the place of science in national budgets and educational curricula. Diversity in literature and the arts is rampant. Whereas the arts once conspired to promote the transmission of the Christian myth, and then later the values of an elite, they have now become completely democratized to serve a bewildering range of interests, including purely aesthetic problems of exploiting artistic forms as well as virtually any subject matter that can manage to identify a market.

Contemporary Western culture is characterized by an anarchy of meanings. We have no effective way to select memes out of circulation because any efforts to do so are prohibited by one form or another of entitlement. There is no heresy, just variations of piety; there is no treason, just nuances of loyalty; there is no pornography, just art. Any meaning, *all* meaning, is legitimate. Every charge of unacceptable meaning is counter-charged as a violation of human rights. We are therefore increasingly a deregulated culture. Deregulation is certainly not the way in which our culture fashioned its existence from the chaos of the Dark Ages, and it is hardly the way we will survive. In simpler times, in the age of coherence, nearly every occasion for social interaction somehow reconfirmed common meanings to provide a fabric for shared commitments. But in contemporary culture each occasion for social interaction is brimming with possibilities for conflict between values, and each moral situation becomes a moment for internal conflict of values. The proliferation of authorities together with the reduction of selective activity has created a situation in which value conflicts, both internal and interpersonal, are unavoidable, and such conflicts tend to undermine the possibilities for personal wholeness and social coherence. Insofar as we have internalized a plurality of authorities, and insofar as we affirm a wide range of meanings legitimated by them—and that is what participating in Western culture has come to mean—we have created the conditions for the further disintegration of our culture. The real question facing us is whether or not we can stand the strain of too many meanings.

What would happen in nature under similar conditions? Wherever we find a reduction in selective pressures in nature, there follows a rapid increase of diversity in gene pools. And this process will continue until environmental limits are reached. We observed this phenomenon at the close of the Mesozoic period. When the great reptiles became extinct, there followed a proliferation of mammalian species. When limits were reached, competition introduced new selective factors to limit diversity. We can expect the same dynamics to affect our cultural life. Conflicts of value are easily tolerated when circumstances allow. But where are the limits? How well equipped is a pluralistic culture to handle an eventual political or economic crisis of any magnitude? Have we gone beyond the psychological and social limits of diversity that are consistent with the survival of our culture?

I shall address these questions presently, but first I must digress slightly on the matter of liberty. The tone of this chapter so far will strike some readers as reactionary. To begin with,

I have described the breakdown of medieval culture as a source of problems in Western culture, but most readers are likely to view it as a solution because it brought freedom of expression, freedom of worship, possibilities for social mobility, the wonders of science, and so on. In short, the breakdown of medieval unity brought forth the conditions for individual liberty and social progress. This is the enthusiastic view of the Enlightenment, and it is a perspective which I wholeheartedly share. I am myself a grateful child of the Enlightenment, and I enjoy my liberties as much as anyone. I dread the prospect of returning to a restrictive cultural environment. But it is precisely because I cherish liberty that I fear its excesses. We now need to worry about the consequences that too little shared meaning will have for the stability of the social order. If our intellectual and moral life degenerates into the discord of private meanings and the unrestrained pursuit of selfish ends, then we will be unable to sustain the kinds of commitments that are necessary to maintain social and political institutions. And if we do not maintain these institutions, we will have played into the hands of totalitarianism.

We must be mindful of the dangers of too little freedom on the one hand and too much on the other. The political expression of too much meme selection is totalitarianism, and the political expression of too little meme selection is anarchy. Neither of these is an acceptable option because neither is consistent with the twofold requirements of social coherence and personal wholeness. But we must not overlook the fact that these extremes tend to produce their opposites. What we need to know is whether we have at the moment drifted too far toward excessive diversity. And in addition we need to consider whether we have the resources at our disposal for regenerating shared meanings without resorting to repressive measures.

The Depth of Crisis

In the previous chapter I made the point that the brain is a vast repository of programs for behavior which are built up by the complex interactions of heredity and environment. I also noted that it is necessary for individuals to have at their disposal the means for selecting appropriate behaviors from the repertory of alternative action patterns. Without such means, individual behavior would appear inconsistent and arbitrary, and the grounds for social cooperation would be lost. The importance of a verbal system was considered in this context, as was the necessity of constructing a comprehensive symbolic model of the social/physical environment to organize the evaluation of experience and the selection of appropriate action patterns. I used the term "myth" to describe the comprehensive symbolic framework in which these operations interface. I made several general observations concerning the nature, structure, and function of myth. The nature of myth, it was maintained, is to integrate cosmology with morality—that is, to construct an overlay which reveals the organic connection between what is true of the world and how we ought to behave in the world. Without this integration, neither cosmology nor morality has any significant bearings. As to the structure of myth, I argued that root metaphors play a role of key importance. A root metaphor is the fundamental equation of cosmos and ethos which provides a nucleus for the further elaboration of meanings to inform the interpretation of experience and the devising of behavior. On another level, I said that the function of myth is to resolve the ambiguity of human existence by providing the means by which individual needs for homeostasis might be satisfied in the context of social cooperation. By this function, a shared myth may be said to create the basis for a synergy of individual rights and social obligations.

On the basis of these observations, we argued that a widely shared myth constitutes the fundamental cognitive conditions for personal wholeness and social coherence, and by extension of these principles, it can be seen that such a myth is decisive for the adaptivity of a culture as well as for its individual members. From the point of view of a natural history of culture, therefore, the question we have put to ourselves regarding the social and psychological limits of pluralism quickly dissolves into a question about the effects of pluralism upon the myth of Western culture. It has been part of the argument of this book that the incidence of maladaptive behavior in Western culture, both individual and collective, is an index of the maladaptivity of its myth. And furthermore, if there are signs of maladaptivity, any hope for the long-term survival of culture must focus upon the need to redress inadequacies in the myth itself. In the remainder of this chapter I intend to show how pluralism has undermined the effectiveness of the Judaeo-Christian myth to foster personal wholeness and social coherence.

The substance of the argument before us will be that the pluralism peculiar to Western culture has strained the root metaphor of the Judaeo-Christian myth to the point where it is no longer seen as a plausible integration of cosmology and morality. When cosmos and ethos disintegrate, human values become relative and subjective. Moral relativism represents a fundamentally unstable situation which encourages selfish behavior to the detriment of personal commitments to collective ideals. As commitments dissolve, social institutions become dysfunctional, incapable of providing for the homeostasis of individuals. And as this happens, even more personal anxiety is injected into the situation so that individuals are even less likely to be able to make the sacrifices necessary to maintain social institutions. And so on. This process of cultural degeneration is already well under way in Western civilization. The ultimate danger is that, when social institutions begin to collapse, individuals will withdraw from participation in public life, leaving the political arena vacant just at the moment when social disorder worsens. And such a situation sets the stage for a minority of zealots to lay hold of the instruments of power for the purpose of engineering a forceful imposition of social order. We must never lose sight of the fact that human beings must have order in their lives, and to the extent that they perceive their circumstances to be disorderly, they will be vulnerable to the attractions of totalitarian rule.

The Impotence of God

The main point of the argument at hand is that extreme pluralism is inimical to the integrity of culture and must therefore be seen as a maladaptive development. But if so, we must wonder how Western culture has managed to survive as long as it has under conditions of pluralism; after all, pluralism began to appear in our midst as early as the thirteenth century. The obvious answer of course, is that the large-scale impact of pluralism was forestalled by the restriction of literacy and education to the elite classes. But it must also be seen that from the beginning there have been sufficiently compelling attempts to demonstrate the consistency of new meanings and new agencies of selection with fundamental meanings in the tradition. I am referring here above all to the theological tradition which has endeavored to enlarge theological principles to accommodate new meanings and, wherever possible, to reduce new meanings so as to preserve traditional ones. Thus the theological tradition has managed, for a very long time, to sustain the effectiveness of the root metaphor of the Judaeo-Christian myth (providence, or the personality of God) as an adequate metaphor for integrating cosmic realities and human ideals. And this impression has softened the impact of pluralism and has to some extent obscured it. As long as God could be shown to be approving of this or that new meme, it was possible to overlook all kinds of inherent difficulties. But this theological tradition was bound to become threadbare. In the first stage of pluralism, it was common to appeal to the root metaphor of the tradition to legitimate nontheological cultural innovations.

We have seen evidence of this practice in theological defenses of the independent state and the authority of science. The plausibility of these new authorities might be said to have been nourished by the metaphor of the divine person. But as pluralism matured, there was a gradual reversal, and it more frequently became necessary to defend the plausibility of the personal metaphor on the strength of nontheological meanings. Those frameworks of meaning which fed initially upon the personal metaphor were eventually called upon to keep it alive. The difference in theological problematics from the seventeenth century to the nineteenth makes this process plain enough. Efforts to maintain the personal metaphor have become more desperate as pluralism has become more evident, but it is now painfully clear that the metaphor of God as person is no longer able to serve the human imagination as a root metaphor must: it cannot integrate cosmos and ethos. God as person has become, if not a dead metaphor, then one that is pathetically dependent on a network of nontheological life-support systems.

One reason for the decimation of the personal metaphor has

been the fact that, as pluralism advanced, there was a reduction in the occasions for reinforcing it. Peter Berger, following Weber's distinction between Church and Sect, has shown how the advent of pluralism introduces new problems of social engineering for assuring the transmission of myth:

> A theoretically important variation is between situations in which an entire society serves as the plausibility structure for a religious world and situations in which only a subsociety serves as such. In other words, the "social engineering" problem differs as between religious monopolies and religious groups seeking to maintain themselves in a situation of pluralistic competition. . . . When an entire society serves as the plausibility structure for a religiously legitimated world, all the important social processes within it serve to confirm and reconfirm the reality of this world.[11]

If the personal metaphor were to remain vital, it would therefore become necessary to construct sociocognitive boundaries between those who resonate to this metaphor and those who do not. In the formative stages of pluralism, these boundaries were easily constructed through the social isolation of agnostics and atheists. But as pluralism advanced and as civil liberties were established, it became impracticable to do this. And as soon as there were enough agnostics and atheists on hand to make a difference, a difference was indeed made, so that eventually any mention of God in the public realm was construed as a violation of civil liberties. This phenomenon is no doubt less evident in nations with an established state church, but even these nations have seen significant changes. In England and Scandinavia, for example the treatment of religion in state schools during the past few generations has generally shifted from indoctrination to academic understanding.

In the previous chapter I noted that the worship service is the principal venue for establishing and reinforcing the central memes of the Judaeo-Christian myth, and I also argued that the worship service is insufficient in itself to assure that their transmission is successful. But now, under the conditions of cultural pluralism, the worship service is almost the only public occasion for social interaction where the reinforcement of

92

God talk is still allowed. God talk is now practically confined to an interlude lasting one hour per week in the stream of human affairs, hardly enough to make any noticeable biochemical difference. The point is that the necessary social-psychological conditions for assuring the viability of the personal metaphor no longer exist for the majority of persons in Western culture. These conditions may exist for members of isolated groups such as the Amish but not so for the rest of us, nor are they likely to be restored, television evangelism and the Moral Majority notwithstanding. But we must not assume that the disappearance of God talk from the fabric of routine social intercourse is the fault of civil liberties movements alone. After all, at one point there were enough agnostics and atheists on hand to ban God from the public realm, and they presumably came from somewhere. Apostasy is never spontaneous.

The topic of theological disillusionment is as ancient as it is complex. It appears in Old Testament texts such as the Book of Job. What has continued to baffle philosophers of religion is why some people give up religious beliefs rather quickly, while others, faced with exactly the same range of evidence, continue to hold to them and, on the other side, why some individuals find arguments in support of religious beliefs compelling, while others do not. These observations have led some people to argue that religious belief does not have a cognitive dimension at all.[12] What clearly emerges from the preceding discussion is that the matter of theological disenchantment can be understood only with reference to the nature of myth.

To return again to the previous chapter, I defined myth as an effective integration of cosmology and morality; similarly, myth was said to express the undifferentiated presence of cosmos, ethos, and pathos. In myth we encounter a symbolic world in which the full range of human experience (intellectual, moral, and aesthetic) is synthesized and interpreted. It must be said that the integrated symbolic world of myth cannot directly be falsified. Truth and falsity, in fact, are not entirely relevant to such complex symbolism. The most important feature of myth is that it is shared, that it is effective in grasping the imagination of an entire culture and thus in shaping the consciousness of its members according to an undifferentiated vision of truth, goodness, and beauty. Yet on some occasions in our experience the elements of myth become momentarily differentiated. Matters of truth do have an indirect and unspecifiable bearing on the effectiveness of myth in the imagination. The cosmological elements integrated into a myth, for example, may be isolated and set forth in propositional form where they can be tested for their truth value. The same possibilities for isolation apply to the moral and aesthetic elements. It may be inappropriate to judge a myth true or false, right or wrong, beautiful or banal, but it is appropriate to raise such questions against the intellectual, moral, and aesthetic particulars of a myth.

The effectiveness of a myth itself, however, transcends these subsidiary critiques. It is conceivable (though unlikely) that each of the cosmological, moral, and aesthetic elements in a myth may be judged independently untenable while the myth as a whole remains effective. In fact, any combination of tenable and untenable constituent elements is compatible with the final effectiveness or ineffectiveness of the myth itself. This is the reason, for example, why the completely falsified cosmology of the biblical narrative has not resulted in a decisive discreditation of the Judaeo-Christian myth as a whole. While the falsification of biblical cosmology has left the myth implausible for many, it has not had the same effect on everyone. For some, the myth is validated by the strength of its moral vision alone or by the charm of its mystery and simplicity. This complex relation between the myth as an integrated whole and its constituent cosmological, moral, and aesthetic particulars has muddled the entire philosophical discussion of religious belief.

Disenchantment with the Judaeo-Christian myth can be associated with any combination of critiques of its components, but it becomes more likely when scrutiny is brought to bear on more than one front. Thus as the cosmological elements of the myth were undermined by the advances of modern science, the moral vision of the myth became more exposed. If the myth is already untenable on cosmological grounds, then any occasion for scrutinizing the moral vision (for example, unusual and undeserved suffering or even the evidence of moral decency among non-Christians and moral indecency among Christians) could easily result in total disenchantment.

The combined attack of cosmological and moral evidence has strained the ability of the metaphor of God as person to interpret human experience and direct human behavior adequately. It has become very difficult for twentieth-century minds to discern a purposeful God standing behind the complexities of chance and necessity in nature. And it is equally difficult for the twentieth century to discern a just and loving God standing behind natural and historic disaster. But that the idea of a personal God can be maintained on both fronts is hardly to be expected. It represents a cognitive feat that can be accomplished only by desperate means, such as denying the validity of science (for example, fundamentalism), or abstracting the personality of God beyond recognition (for example, process theology), or by isolation from contemporary culture (for example, sectarianism), or by living the fragile life of extreme cognitive dissonance. Few are willing or able to pay such prices, and many therefore take the alternative path of tacit or professed apostasy.

Already in the seventeenth century, Spinoza recognized the difficulties inherent in maintaining anthropomorphic categories to speak about God:

> For example, if a stone falls from a roof on to someone's head, and kills him, they will demonstrate by their new method that the stone fell in order to kill the man; for, if it had not by God's will fallen with that object, how could so many circumstances have all happened together by chance? Perhaps you will answer that the event is due to the facts that the wind was blowing, and the man was walking that way. "But why," they will insist, "was the wind blowing, and why was the man at that very time walking that way?" If you again answer, that the wind had then sprung up because the sea had begun to be agitated the day before, the weather being previously calm, and that the man had been invited by a friend, they will again insist: "But why was the sea agitated, and why was the man invited at that time?" So they will pursue their questions from cause to cause, till at last you take refuge in the will of God—in other words, the sanctuary of ignorance.[13]

Spinoza could not manage the exhausting mental gymnastics necessary to maintain the personality of God, and thus he set out to elaborate a nonpersonal metaphor for integrating cosmology and morality. He defined God as a substance containing infinite attributes, each expressing eternal and infinite essence. Basically, of course, Spinoza was only attempting to speak of God using the metaphor of nature, but few others could manage his mental gymnastics. Nor was there any need to do so, for the cosmological and moral inadequacies of the personal metaphor were overwhelmed by the social-psychological mechanisms, still intact in the seventeenth century, for reinforcing the idea that God was a person.

But much has transpired since the seventeenth century, and Spinoza's remark about the sanctuary of ignorance adequately describes the failure of the personal metaphor to bear the weight of explanation for the popular mind of the twentieth century. The metaphor has become impotent even for many who continue to identify with the church. Contemporary Christians and Jews tolerate use of the personal metaphor because there is no adequate substitute for it, but not many find that it clarifies their experience as a root metaphor should. The primary reason is that the metaphor has become transparent. That is, it is seen *as* a metaphor. In MacLeish's terms, the metaphor of God as person is *seen* but no longer *means*:

> A world ends when its metaphor has died.
> An age becomes an age, all else beside,
> When sensuous poets in their pride invent
> Emblems for the soul's content
> That speak the meanings men will never know
> But man-imagined images can show;
> It perishes when those images, though seen,
> No longer mean.[14]

The personal metaphor no longer means because the modern mind has assimilated various memes which obstruct its meaning. Metaphors can work in our thinking only when they clarify the lesser known in terms of the better known. This, in fact, is a useful and common definition of metaphor. Throughout most of the Judaeo-Christian tradition, therefore, the "better-known" idea of personality was used to clarify the "lesser-known" phenomena of nature. The personality of God was a most useful instrument for understanding the reality of the cosmos as well as the reality of human affairs. But in this century a cognitive "gestalt switch" of infinitely profound significance has shifted the idea of personality so that it is no longer the instrument of knowing but is now an object of knowledge. That is to say, natural phenomena are now much better understood by the nonpersonal metaphors of science, and personality has itself become the lesser-known object of scientific study. The metaphor of personality has shifted from the status of the *explanans* (the explainer) to the status of the *explanandum* (the explained).

This shift has enormous implications for theology. We now understand personality to be shaped by, *determined* by, complex hereditary and environmental factors. Even if we cannot demonstrate the causal factors in lavish detail we are dead convinced that they are there. But if a person is for us a product of heredity and environment, then what becomes of the metaphor of God as person? If God is person then he (he!) must have a heritage. What sort of genes did he inherit? Were his parents tall or short? Were they red, yellow, black, brown, or white? Is there a history of schizophrenia in the family? And what about the environmental factors? What sort of relationship did he have with his mother? Was he abused as a child? Was he well educated? What sort of religious upbringing did he have? These questions are of course ridiculous when they are applied to God. It is not my intention here to demonstrate my irreverence or to argue against using the personal metaphor. I merely want to call to the reader's attention the reason why, in fact, the metaphor of God as person has already become impotent as a root metaphor in the minds of twentieth-century men and women. Virtually everyone in Western culture has assimilated enough biology and psychology to know that persons are shaped by hereditary and environmental factors. And for precisely this reason we are increasingly dissatisfied by the use of this metaphor as an explanation for why things happen. Children, certainly, resonate to the personal metaphor but only as long as they remain biologically and psychologically innocent. When they discover genes and operant conditioning in school they are set up for a major disenchantment. It is also clear enough to the modern mind that the personal metaphor cannot be used without engaging the kind of specificity that makes it objectionable to various elements in a pluralistic society. In the Old Testament YHWH is male, in the New Testament Jesus is white, among the Moral Majority God is a defender of capitalism, and so on. To speak of God as a person is to create alienation.

Curiously enough, however, we still hear talk of God as person. In fact, recent religious revival movements (backed by a surge in spiritualist theology) are emphatic about the intimacy of the personal God. But the question remains as to whether this use of the personal metaphor can generate a shared myth. The intimacy of God characteristic of spiritualist religious movements is avowedly a privatization of God. The Holy Spirit speaks to the individual who has bracketed the evening news together with everything learned in school and who manages to crawl into a private sanctuary of meditation where the concerns are likely to be immediate and selfish. This is not the God of socially constructive shared meanings, and it is certainly not the God of the cosmos. But this is not the place for a critique of the new spiritualism. I will merely say at this point that the spiritualist revival is symptomatic of decline in Western culture and not a harbinger of restoration, and the reason is that it pushes pluralism to extremes by completely subjectivizing God.

We return now to the effects of the impotence of God upon the myth of Western culture. The critical observation is that, once the root metaphor of God as person has lost its place in the imagination, there follows a disjunction of cosmology and morality. This disintegration of cosmos and ethos has been recognized for generations now and has been explored fully by philosophical movements as diverse as positivism and existentialism. But the disintegration of cosmology and morality is no longer merely a problem for academic philosophers; it has become part of the popular climate of opinion in contemporary culture. In practical terms the consequence is that human values have lost their organic connection with the cosmos and thereby also their objective status. Nature is now conceded to be "value free," and human values are regarded as mere subjective conventions. The world of human affairs is therefore relative no longer to cosmic realities but only to its own accidents of history. The continuity of cosmology and morality, which we have observed to be the singular achievement of myth, seems nowhere evident in contemporary thought. There are now, in fact, popularly approved sanctions against any attempts to locate objective values in the universe. This disjunction of cosmology and morality is both a result of pluralism and an additional stimulus for its progression. Science (cosmology) and politics (morality) are now, more than ever, ontologically distinct, and they interface only on the level of mutual benefaction, science relying on politics for its funding and political programs relying on science for their technical applications. But it is universally considered a breach of logical necessity to look for memes by which cosmological facts and moral values can be reconciled. Again, if this doctrine were limited to an academic elite, there would be no cause for alarm, but now that it has become a fixture of popular consciousness, we must expect to find its negative consequences for personal wholeness and social coherence.

Amythia

It will come as no surprise to the reader when I now declare that the contemporary crisis in Western culture can be described as amythia, a quite simple notion which follows directly from what I have already said about the nature and function of myth. On the most general level, amythia describes a cultural condition in which the level of shared myth falls below that which is required to provide adequately for personal wholeness and social coherence. On the particular level, it is found when individuals lack the symbolic resources for locating the meaning of their experiences and actions in the context of purposes which transcend their immediate needs. Amythia results when cosmology and morality are not effectively integrated by a root metaphor. It has been our argument that amythia has descended upon Western culture because under the conditions of pluralism the root metaphor of God as person has failed to transmit itself effectively. The metaphor is seen but no longer means.

When a plausible root metaphor is effectively transmitted by a culture, then the members of the culture have the means of

99

orienting their lives. Individuals are presented with a limited range of goals and purposes, legitimated by the root metaphor, to which they commit themselves. And the values embodied in these goals and purposes are perceived to be objective. The perceived objectivity of values actually elicits commitment to them. I become committed to an ideal when I am unable to see it as optional for my life, that is, when I see a particular ideal to be integral to a fundamental order, which includes me, that will be damaged by violating the ideal. I am committed to an ideal when I find myself saying, "relative to me and my concerns this ideal is more important"; "this value has a claim on me"; "this is a value to which I must submit"; "this is a value which it is not my option to ignore." And so on. Facts operate in our cognitive life in precisely this way: if there is a brick wall in my path, it is not my option to ignore it; I must submit.

But where there is no integration of cosmology and morality, human values cease to function in this way. Values then become part of a range of options for orienting one's life. Under the conditions of amythia, it becomes necessary for individuals to search for meaning and values which they find it personally rewarding to serve. This cognitive condition has been variously described in more particular terms as nihilism, alienation, anomie, loss of identity, and existential crisis and by other more or less helpful constructs. Contemporary culture is overwhelmed with these themes in its art, literature, philosophy, and popular social science journals. These expressions all acknowledge the loss of "traditional" objective values and the urgent need that this loss imposes upon the individual to find a "sense of self" amid the range of options available in a pluralistic culture. Until the individual finds a sense of self, he or she will remain in a state of intellectual and moral confusion which can easily develop into nihilism. In an amythic culture it is not unusual for individuals to pass through a nihilistic phase, especially following the point of disillusionment when one discovers that there are "no objective values" and that "everything is relative." Nihilism, the conviction that human life has no enduring purpose or meaning, represents the complete breakdown of personal wholeness. The danger of nihilism is that it generates anxiety which is very often resolved in depression, aggression, or addiction.[15] The probability that these highly maladaptive symptoms will appear is much higher for those individuals who have limited social, intellectual, and even financial resources to conduct a successful search for meaning. It goes without saying that no social order is consistent with widespread nihilism.

But nihilism remains a constant threat to an amythic culture. While most individuals are able to achieve a sense of self by entering into various roles and pastimes offered by the pluralistic society, this achievement is inherently precarious because it is backed not by commitment to objective values but by preference for self-selected values. Robert Bellah and a small group of researchers have explored this important problem in the context of American society:

> Now if selves are defined by their preferences, but those preferences are arbitrary, then each self constitutes its own moral universe and there is finally no way to reconcile conflicting claims about what is good in itself. All we can do is refer to chains of consequences and ask if our actions prove useful or consistent in light of our own "value-systems." All we can appeal to in relationships with others is their self-interest, likewise enlightened, or to their intuitive sympathies. . . . In the absence of any objectifiable criteria of right and wrong, good or evil, the self and its feelings become our only moral guide.[16]

One trouble with this situation is that individual preferences can change with the seasons, and as they change, individuals are thrown once again into another desperate search for a sense of self. Contemporary life therefore begins to resemble a succession of passes over the abyss of nihilism. But this is not the only trouble. When the individual self becomes the sole source of moral guidance and when commitments are reduced to personal preferences, then the value of social institutions becomes privatized. Under the conditions of amythia, our participation in social institutions and social processes is conditioned by self-interest alone. We can see this trend toward selfish participation in contemporary attitudes toward family life, education, work, and political process.

Throughout most of our history, the family has functioned

as the primary unit of care and moral instruction in society. But this is no longer the case for many families. The crisis of the contemporary family has complex origins, but there is little question that the mode of selfish participation is a major factor. The family is increasingly regarded as a convenience; it is becoming a base of operations from which individual family members can pursue their own heroics in the pluralistic society. As long as the family makes no demands that interfere with extrafamilial exploits, then it will continue to be convenient. But when problems arise in the family and when demands are met with resentment and refusal to sacrifice, then the family becomes a battleground of self-interest. Stress builds, tempers flare, unseemly things are said, sometimes violence enters in, and soon enough the family becomes an obstacle to self-fulfillment. As this happens, individuals will take measures to reduce or discontinue their participation. "It's just not worth it anymore" is the familiar complaint. Every reader, I have no doubt, can fill in the details of this formula from personal experience or from the experience of relatives and close friends. The mode of selfish participation in family life is so widespread in contemporary society that it affects each of us.

The mode of selfish participation also affects our educational institutions. Every society constructs institutions for socialization which ensure that individuals will acquire the necessary values, attitudes, and skills that form the fabric of social expectation. In the democratic West our schools have been regarded as a necessary element for the preservation of a free society. We once regarded an education as a training ground not simply for useful technical skills but for the *civil arts*. Young men and women were given the responsibility of becoming educated because a democratic state presupposes an informed and critical electorate. But at the same time, an education was regarded as a great privilege. Education was both a privilege *and* a responsibility. But education seems to be neither of these any longer. Anyone who encounters university students these days cannot escape the impression that education is now regarded among our youth as *currency*, as something that can be mongered for their own advantage, to purchase a better job or a place in graduate school.

Students are now grade conscious in the extreme. They want to know precisely what will be included in their exams so that they will be sure not to learn anything that will not advance their immediate interests. Sometimes they will try to negotiate for a better grade because they "need it"; whether they need it for self-esteem or to impress a graduate school does not matter. The evidence points in the same direction: the educational process is there to serve their private concerns, and they tend to invest themselves in learning only when it is clear that they will enjoy direct benefits. There is no sense at all that sound education advances the ideals of a larger society; they simply do not have the means for operating on that level of valuation. These are not isolated impressions; I hear colleagues from all over Western culture complaining of the same selfish motives. And surveys of American students' reasons for attending a university corroborate these impressions. According to statistics compiled by the American Council on Education, the most common reason for attending a university shifted in the late 1970s from "to develop a meaningful philosophy of life" to "to secure a better job."[17]

The institution of work has also been privatized. I will use a personal example here, although it is, I believe, representative of general circumstances. As part of a college history requirement, my father wrote a brief family history in which he also reflected extensively upon his future career. It is clear that there was a single, unquestioned criterion in his selection of a career: *service*. He was a man fortunate enough to have several options, but his options were limited by considerations of where and how he could be of greatest service to self-transcending values. I have no reason to suspect that my father was unique in this respect; his attitudes toward work reflected those of his generation. But now, in the vast industry of career counseling we seldom encounter the notion of service. A career seeker who has several options is now encouraged to select a career on the basis of self-interest and success potential. Career counselors use "interest inventories" to determine the preferences of their clients. Even those who select service-oriented careers often do so because they profess to "get satisfaction from helping others." The relevant questions for career-seekers are: how much money? how much prestige? how much op-

103

portunity for influence or self-expression? how little grief? and in general, how much personal satisfaction? We must assume that these same standards of self-interest are held by those who have few options and are forced by economic necessity to take the comparatively unattractive jobs. What cognitive means do they have for finding value in their work if it does not measure up to the standards of high salaries, high prestige, and creativity? When the value of one's work is perceived in selfish terms, then we can expect that a substantial percentage of the work force will fail to find meaning in their jobs. Under these conditions it should come as no surprise when productivity drops and unemployment rises.

An amythic culture is inherently threatening to democracy. This point becomes clear when we examine the modes of political participation that will appeal to individuals under the conditions of amythia. Individuals who are inclined to judge everything by standards of self-interest will either be drawn into the political arena at points of entry that are narrowly consistent with their immediate concerns or, if they fail to find such points of entry, will become disinterested in political process altogether. That is, they will become either cause-oriented activists or politically apathetic. Political process then becomes characterized by competing special interest groups, each with a tendency to identify the good of the nation with its own programs. Politicians will sacrifice the common good to win votes in single-issue elections. Political parties will proliferate to meet the needs of diffused political visions that follow the dissolution of objective social values.[18] Sharp ideological differences will tend to weaken more traditional forms of social bonding characteristic of local communities. The fabric of economic life will coarsen as corporations attempt to monopolize industries and as cartels begin to take economic hostages. Special interest groups will become expert in the techniques of power and propaganda. The political arena might then become "a breeding ground of extremist doctrines that expose the nakedness of power, of ruthless creeds and embittered ideologies."[19] The press will tend to become more politicized, and as it does so, the public will encounter wildly exaggerated and divergent reports of the "facts." Masses of people begin to sense an impending crisis. Anxiety and insecurity spread. The military establishment oozes closer to the surface of political activity, where it is courted by political coteries. Under these conditions, routine social and economic problems will appear larger than they really are, and overreactions become common. Local crises (for example, unemployment and shortages of goods) appear with greater frequency to create dislocations of social and economic structures and to disrupt the already precarious life orientations of individuals, bringing them closer to the abyss of nihilism. Survivalist and terrorist groups organize and withdraw. Economic order declines rapidly, the military is forced to choose a partner, and the sun goes down.

Can this scenario really happen? Is it possible that an ancient and venerable culture could be decimated by something as simple as a lost metaphor? Yes, it could happen. It *is* happening. And in one sense we might even argue that it *has* happened. The character of Western culture was shaped by the process of meme selection, as I have repeatedly observed. Memes that were considered detrimental to the shared ideals of the Christian myth were selectively removed from circulation. But now, under the conditions of extreme pluralism, where the only selection that makes sense to us is self-selection, we have lost our character. The dominant character of contemporary Western culture is therefore a character achieved by default; it is the ultimately fatal character of selfishness. And the question that now faces us as a culture is whether or not anything can be done to prevent total collapse. How is amythia to be treated? By what means are the conditions for personal wholeness and social coherence to be restored? It is the argument of this book that these conditions depend ultimately upon a restoration of myth. Before we can address this issue, however, we must consider, briefly, two serious reservations about the very possibility of a mythic restoration in contemporary culture.

The first of these reservations concerns the peculiar form of amythia experienced in contemporary culture. We have defined amythia, basically, as the absence of a shared myth. But the contemporary mentality of the West seems to have added a dimension to its amythia: it rejects the possibility of mythic restoration *in principle*. It is one thing for a root metaphor to lose its grip on the imagination of a culture, but it is quite another for the imagination then to seal itself off with the doctrine that it is fallacious to attempt any sort of integration of cosmology and morality. This is the doctrine of amythia, which, as already mentioned, has behind it the full authority of the philosophical community.

But I am unconvinced by this doctrine. I may agree that the root metaphor of God as person is not plausible enough to engage my imagination and to reveal to me nonoptional ideals, but this statement does not necessarily imply that no metaphor whatsoever could get the job done. And to appeal to the theory of relativity as cosmological proof of the absurdity of beholding objective values is, it seems to me, a way of begging the question. There may be limits on the extent to which individuals can share their perspectives, but these do not preclude the possibility of achieving common moral commitments any more than they have precluded general theoretical agreements in the scientific community. The doctrine of amythia is even less persuasive when we consider that nature and culture are not discontinuous. Culture is a part of nature, as I have insisted throughout this essay. And for this reason I find it difficult to affirm on the one hand that nature and culture are one while on the other hand denying the possibility of achieving a compelling vision of the integration of cosmology and morality.

The second reservation has to do with the resources at our disposal for restoring an effective myth. This is essentially a strategic question. The options appear to limit themselves either to a repristination of the traditional Judaeo-Christian myth or to the generation of an entirely new fabric of symbolic meanings. There is reason to believe, however, that neither of these strategies hold much promise. The first option, attractive as it is to fundamentalists and latter day evangelicals, could be pursued only by the most dogged and mindless rejection of the scientific worldview that has emerged in the past three centuries. But this approach simply will not wash, for while modern science may represent a body of ideas that Judaeo-Christian culture cannot easily live with, these are hardly ideas that we could learn to live without. In an environment of widespread illiteracy, the anti-intellectual strategy of repristination might have some success, but in the contemporary setting, it can only aggravate the condition of amythia. The other strategy, which amounts to ideological revolution, does not appear to have any more potential for success than repristination. Cultural traditions have enormous momentum which is not easily discouraged. It is extreme naivete to believe that a cultural tradition can simply be replaced by an entirely new set of meanings. There is an undeniable urge in human beings to remain true to the past, to remain in a state of essential continuity with one's tradition. A sense of continuity is the stuff of personal and cultural identity. To reject an ancient tradition outright and to install a new one in its place is to underestimate the former and to overestimate the latter. Any attempt to follow this strategy would result in greater intellectual and moral nihilism than presently exists under the conditions of amythia. Moreover, the strategy of ideological revolution would necessarily involve the same ruthless denial of intellectual freedom as the strategy of repristination.

The only reasonable hope for overcoming the condition of amythia in Western culture is to follow a strategy of cultural transposition. That is, we may hope to restore the conditions for personal wholeness and social coherence by transposing the distinctive character of the Judaeo-Christian myth to a new and plausible root metaphor. In this way we may hope to satisfy the perennial demands placed on any cultural tradition: the demand for distinctiveness and the demand for plausibility. If, therefore, we are to meet the challenge of amythia, we must be aware of both the limits of distinctiveness and the limits of plausibility. In essence, the challenge is to achieve a new mode of piety; one that continues to affirm essential continuity with our tradition and that, at the same time, has the power to captivate the imagination of the modern mind in a way that will elicit commitment to ideals that transcend immediate concerns.

4

The Limits of
Distinctiveness

*If a Religion or a Republic is to live long, it must often be
brought back to its beginnings.*
— Machiavelli, *The Discourses*, book 3, chapter 1

The Covenant of Survival

In the introductory chapter of this book, I expressed a concern about the survival of the Western cultural tradition. The second chapter asserted the fundamental biological significance of culture: culture is a specifically human mode of adaptation to the environment. The ensuing argument has been that a cultural tradition can remain adaptive only if it has an effective myth which will function to bind individuals together by virtue of shared commitments to the ideals embodied in the myth. If the effectiveness of the myth is disrupted, the culture will decline into a maladaptive state of amythia. The previous chapter argued that Western culture is now in a critical period of amythic decline because radical cultural pluralism has undermined the plausibility of its root metaphor. The chapter closed with a suggestion that the adaptivity of Western culture can be restored only through a regeneration of myth. I cautioned, however, that there are limits to be observed in this quest. On the one hand, any new expression of myth must take care to preserve the distinctive identity of the Judaeo-Christian tradition, and on the other, it must be plausible enough to elicit commitment.

This chapter will advance the claim that from its beginnings the distinctive feature of the Judaeo-Christian tradition has been the centrality of the Covenant. The primary element of

108

self-identification among the people of Israel and, later, the Christian Church has been the affirmation of continuity with the Covenant community. The Covenant has always been the matrix of personal wholeness and social coherence for this tradition. In each of its periodic moments of reformulation, the distinctive concern of the tradition has been to reformulate the Covenant. Any assertion, therefore, of a claim to essential continuity with this tradition must make good its claim to represent the true Covenant community. And if, as I suggested in the previous chapter, the challenge of amythic culture is to transpose the distinctiveness of the tradition to a new metaphor, then it must clearly be seen that the challenge before us is to transpose the Covenant.

At a slightly more abstract level, this chapter will also be advancing the claim that the Covenant has consistently been regarded by the community as an expression of the *conditions of its existence*. In their efforts to renew the Covenant the people of God have been ultimately concerned to confirm their commitment to observe those conditions without which the Covenant community would cease to exist. In maintaining that the Covenant is the distinctive feature of the Judaeo Christian tradition, I am saying that what has *not* varied in the tradition is the centrality of the Covenant as an expression of the conditions of existence. What *has* varied throughout the tradition is the specific manner in which the conditions of existence have been understood. The variants in the tradition are the cosmological frameworks from which "existence" has taken its meanings and the modes of piety which have been regarded as appropriate thereto.

It should be evident where this approach is leading us. If the adaptivity of Western culture is to be effectively restored, it will be necessary to avert the present condition of amythia by transposing the Covenant tradition to a more plausible root metaphor. That is to say, we must find a way of discerning and expressing the conditions of our existence such that individuals will be drawn into a new mode of piety by committing themselves to the service of these conditions. These are the terms of renewing the Covenant for our generation. Indeed, they have been the terms of Covenant renewal for every generation. It may be objected that this interpretation of the Covenant faith

reduces the character of the entire tradition to that of a survivalist community. In fact, this is precisely the point that I
wish to argue. The distinctive feature of the Judaeo-Christian
tradition has always been its concern for maintaining the Covenant, and the language of the Covenant has always been the
language of survival. Ideas about what surviving actually
means and how it is achieved have varied, but the Covenant
itself, as an expression of faith, has always expressed the logic
of survival. A contemporary claim to be the heirs to the Covenant will therefore attempt to express what survival can mean
in the context of a contemporary cosmology, and it will attempt, furthermore, to devise the means to elicit the commitment of individuals to appropriate behavior.

This may be as good a point as any to answer objections to
what might appear to be an inherent contradiction. On the one
hand we have already argued that the root metaphor of God as
person is implausible and is therefore an unfit vehicle for transmitting myth. But on the other hand we have claimed that the
distinctive feature of the Judaeo-Christian tradition, to be preserved at all costs, is the idea of Covenant. The objection will
be that we cannot have it both ways, that any suggestion of
Covenant necessarily involves the personal metaphor. After all,
Covenant in the Judaeo-Christian tradition has always implied
a personal relationship between God and his people, so to speak
of Covenant apart from this relationship is either to contradict
oneself or to corrupt the meaning of Covenant. This objection
must be brought into the light of the fact that the Judaeo-Christian Covenant has always been unilateral. It is not the type of
juridical covenant that is negotiated between two parties of
equal or even unequal status. It is always one-sided; the terms
of the Covenant are God's terms. The Covenant is every bit
as impersonal as an ultimatum.

A related objection will be that the centrality of the Covenant
in the Judaeo-Christian tradition derives from the distinctiveness of the personal metaphor. If anything is distinctive in this
tradition, it must be the consistency with which God has been
understood in personal terms, or rather the consistency with
which humanity has been understood in theological terms, in
the image of God. The only possible response to this objection
is to beg the reader to view these matters in slightly more

formal terms for the duration of the argument. We shall not violate the biases of even the most dogmatic defenders of the personal metaphor if we say the following: the Covenant faith of the Judaeo-Christian tradition is fulfilled in a relationship between humanity and the source of existence. This formulation deliberately leaves open the question of how "source of existence" is to be understood. I would not argue for a moment against the claim that the tradition has consistently viewed the source of existence in personalist terms. But I would argue that there would be no sacrifice of distinctiveness if it ceased to do so. In fact, I would like to say that to maintain the Covenant within the contemporary limits of plausibility *requires* a discontinuation of the personal metaphor. The contradiction, then, I would insist, is on the backs of those who continue to speak of God as person, for to do so is to prolong a mythia and thus to preclude the restoration of an adaptive myth. In other words, to persist with the personal metaphor is to violate the Covenant of survival.

This line of reasoning assumes the survivalist character of the Covenant, the demonstration of which has been promised in the present chapter. But before we move ahead with a survey of Covenant history, it will be useful to settle upon a method for doing so. There are special problems involved with any attempt to speak of the "essence" of a long tradition. This is especially true when we consider the Judaeo-Christian tradition. If, indeed, a common essence is presented as descriptive of both Judaism and Christianity, then one is hard-pressed to account for Christianity's claim to be independent of Judaism. But on the other hand, if Christianity is described by its own distinctive essence, then one knows not what to make of its insisting to be essentially continuous with the ancient traditions of Israel. The problem is one of sorting out the decisive elements of continuity and discontinuity. I hope to resolve these difficulties by employing the locution "modes of piety" together with the idea of distinctiveness. The argument will be that the entire Judaeo-Christian tradition can be shown to have a continuous and distinctive character, its fidelity to the Covenant. But at the same time, the tradition has manifested different modes of piety, divergent enough to account for major discontinuities.[1] I will use the term "mode of piety" to refer to a distinctive manner of appropriating the covenant tradition. A mode of piety is to be understood from the point of view of a participant in the Covenant; it expresses the participant's own grasp of what the Covenant means and how it functions. It is the participant's comprehension of the manner by which one enters into the Covenant and by which one remains in the Covenant, as well as a vision of what consequences are implied by being in or not being in. A mode of piety is the logic by which an individual and/or group idealizes the relationship between humanity and the source of existence. It is, in brief, an expression of the memes at work in the heads of those who identify themselves as being "in" the Covenant. Sometimes a mode of piety may be quite explicit about speculative matters such as cosmology (the nature of the universe) and soteriology (the logic of salvation), but this specificity is not always evident. When these cognitive elements are not explicit, we may therefore assume not that they are nonexistent but rather that they are only tacitly known to the participant. At points it may be necessary to supply these elements in order to complete our presentation of distinct modes of piety.

Before I embark on a survey of the Covenant tradition, I will repeat myself here by offering a formulaic expression of the Covenant theme. The Judaeo-Christian Covenant tradition can be reduced to three rather simple affirmations:

1. God is the source of existence.[2]

2. The human condition is suspended between life and death (existence and nonexistence).

3. The Covenant is an expression of the conditions of existence.

Variations on this theme define the distinctive modes of piety which constitute the Covenant tradition.

The Emergence of the Covenant Tradition

Just when, where, and how the Covenant tradition first appeared in history is a problem of infinite complexity. It will be necessary for our purposes to reach some conclusions about the origins of the Covenant, for we can hardly speak of modes of Covenant piety that predate the Covenant tradition. One of the difficulties we are up against in formulating a clear picture of Covenantal origins is that the only extant accounts are those of a civilized people recalling, with all their theological biases engaged, their distant precivilized beginnings. The credibility gap produced by this retrospect of several centuries has produced a confusing array of perspectives on the character of life and religion in the precivilized phase of Israel's history.

Of one thing we can be fairly certain, namely that in the tenth century B.C.E. a historian, conventionally called the Yahwist, wrote the first comprehensive narrative of Israel's history. And we know that this work, which is scattered throughout the Pentateuch, was controlled by the Covenant theme. Less clear is the extent to which the Covenant theme was already present in the sources which the Yahwist had to draw upon. By the time of the Yahwist's writing, the available sources for generating a narrative history would have been rich and varied. There were legal traditions and creation myths from Mesopotamia, fertility dramas from Canaanite civilization, epics about various ancestral clans, poetic oracles of various prophets, legends about floods and baby boys in bulrush baskets, accounts of slavery and deliverance, stories to account for features of natural landscape and place names, war stories in vast supply, and tales of many gods. There was such variety because the newly founded kingdom of Israel (the official origins of which the Yahwist was attempting to fix) was assembled from a confederation of tribal units, each of which had been formed by a conflux of elements from different parts of the Fertile Crescent, some from civilized backgrounds and others from nomadic backgrounds. Each of these elements, we may assume, had its own traditions to bear.

The task of the Yahwist was to draw these elements together into a coherent historical narrative. But we may not assume that the Yahwist was the first one to attempt to bring diverse cultural elements into focus. The process of integrating these traditions must have started much earlier, even before the initial formation of the tribal confederacy. The Yahwist, then, represents a layer of tradition which relied upon the efforts of an earlier layer of tradition. But the layer of tradition upon

113

which the Yahwist drew must itself have had sources to draw upon. And so we appear to be left with a stack of traditional layers taking us far back into the period before the monarchy. The question we must ask is this: what is the earliest point in this process at which we can identify the influence of the Covenant theme? In our earlier discussion of the emergence of Christian unity, we spoke of centripetal forces bringing together diverse cultural elements under the control of the Christian myth. A similar process was at work in the emergence of the Covenant tradition. But at what point did the Covenant theme enter the process to control the centripetation?

I will illustrate this process of emergence, as I imagine it, with a homely example. A favorite game I play with my children is "the story game." In this game, the hearer provides elements for the teller, and the teller must weave the elements into a coherent whole. If my role is that of hearer, I might say, "O.K., now *you* tell a story about an elephant, a Halloween mask, two boys, a mountain, and a snowstorm." Then I wait for the teller's imagination to bring these elements into focus by attaching them to a central theme. The freedom granted to the teller in this example is almost without limitation, and so too is the range of stories I might expect to hear. But if I were to provide another element to assist the teller in controlling the various bits, then the outcome would be much different. Suppose I say, "Tell me a story about an elephant, a Halloween mask, two boys, a mountain, a snowstorm, and a little girl who gets lost and then struggles to find her way home." Now the teller has a central theme to control the development of the story. There is still room for considerable variation, but the possibilities have been greatly limited. Now the various elements (mask, mountain, and so forth) will find their place in the story in terms of how they facilitate or frustrate the girl's homecoming.

The Covenant theme functioned as such a controlling device in the development of Israel's cultural tradition. When this device appeared, it provided a nucleus of meaning to which the various discrete elements might cohere. It also provided a basis for the extraction of material by storytellers. The amount of material brought into the cultural milieu of the tribal confederation would have been enormous, and it could have been managed only by the selective agency of a controlling meme. The Covenant was the meme, but just where it came from and just when its influence commenced is frightfully difficult to determine.

The biblical narrative tells us that the Covenant theme was already present in the stories of the patriarchs (Abram, Isaac, and Jacob). This is not very likely, though the patriarchal stories were eventually given a prominent position in the final narrative and must therefore have been well preserved and strongly represented in the conflux of traditions. The major contribution of the patriarchal narratives to the tradition, it seems to me, was their powerful longing for land and lineage. The patriarchs were nomads who roamed about on the fringes of civilization.[3] They had no legal status, and their livelihood was quite precarious, especially when water and grass became scarce. Those who found the opportunity to do so were quick to settle down. The unfortunate ones continued to wander, preoccupied with insecurity and with the hope of growing large enough in numbers to avail themselves of the milk and honey of settled life. In the final analysis, however, there is too little evidence, biblical and/or archaeological, to support the view that the religious life of the patriarchs could have generated the controlling theme of the Covenant.[4] Perhaps all we can say about these stories is that they had a certain affinity with the Covenant theme, and for this reason they were eventually preserved in the biblical narrative.

It is much more plausible to look to the Sinai experience as the primary source of the Covenant tradition. Few episodes in the Judaeo-Christian tradition have generated more speculative commentary than the events surrounding the Exodus and Sinai experience. The commentary is appropriate because of the biblical emphasis on these events as normative for Israel's faith, and the commentary has necessarily been speculative because of the dearth of resources for reconstructing the historic events.[5] Still, a few things can be said with confidence. That the Egyptians took slaves out of Palestine and put them to work on building projects during the early thirteenth century is not seriously doubted by any historians. We also know that Moses is an Egyptian name and, further, that there was a seminomadic group known as "Israel" in Palestine before the end of the thirteenth century. We know that Palestine in the late thirteenth century was rife with turmoil and that the cities of Canaan were vulnerable to conquest by tribes of seminomads. And we know that the destruction of many cities named in the biblical account of conquest has been confirmed by archaeological evidence. In other words, the chronology and general conditions reflected in the biblical narrative of the period from the seventeenth century to the thirteenth century appear to be basically correct. While this is not much to go on, the general accuracy of the biblical record invites us to use it as a basis for further speculation.

It is entirely conceivable that a small band of runaway slaves could have escaped from Egypt in the first quarter of the thirteenth century. It would have taken considerable courage and capable leadership, but when the moment was right, a few hundred men, women, and children might have beat the odds and made their way across the Red Sea to the safety of a mountain hideout on the Sinai peninsula. Within a short while the members of the group would become filled with ambivalence and confusion about their situation. Life in the wilderness for a band of ill-equipped runaways who were unaccustomed to the nomadic life would have proven every bit as harsh and cruel as the oppression of slavery. To turn back now would be suicidal, but to go forward offered less promise still. What would become of them? How were they to manage? The situation called for the most charismatic form of leadership imaginable. Moses, son-in-law of a Kenite priest, found a way to lift their spirits and lead them on. The oppression of slavery, the harrowing experience of escape, and the challenge of the moment were not, he told them, meaningless. They must go on. They would be looked after; they must not lose hope. Yahweh would see to their safety. They must not forget the suffering and indignity of slavery. Consider our good fortune; we escaped with life and limb against all odds. You see? Yahweh has *already* provided for us, and he will go on providing for us if only we will trust and follow him. Moses' vision of a God that had drawn these people up out of oppression and humility and had taken them unto his own provided the runaway slaves with a way to find significance in their suffering. They were not to die in the wilderness; they had been called out of slavery for a purpose—God's purpose—and what God had in store for them would be clear in due course.

With Moses' encouragement the group moved on and settled for a time at Kadesh, a sizable oasis to the south of Palestine. There these people would have encountered several wandering nomadic clans of the sort that dreamed of land and lineage. Here there would have been the opportunity to share stories, the Moses group telling of its miraculous escape from Egypt and the nomadic clans telling of their hopes to acquire land. Stories of this sort would have revealed their natural affinity for one another; memories of a remarkable past and dreams of a promising future were grafted together to produce something of great power. Now we can speak of a community with a fundamental sense of history and mission. Yahweh's purpose was becoming clear.

Any consideration of the call of Moses and the Sinai experience cannot overlook the importance of the divine name. The name "Yahweh" is a curious one in the history of religions. It is likely that the name was known among the Kenites (and hence Moses' familiarity with it), but the meaning it acquired in Israel's history appears to be original and thus, it could be argued, marks the beginning of the distinctive faith of the Judaeo-Christian tradition.[6] The precise meaning of the name is enigmatic. While the linguistic evidence is inconclusive, it appears to be a derivative of the Hebrew verb "to be," though the exact form is disputed.[7] The name has many possible meanings: "I am who I am," "I create what I create," "I am he who calls into being." It is difficult here to avoid the distinction of Yahweh as the "source of existence," but there are additional provocative associations. The traditional rendition, "I am who I am," sounds like an evasive response to the question "who are you?" In the ancient world to possess the name of another was to possess some measure of power over that individual. Yahweh's evasion of full disclosure would therefore suggest that his nature was not at the disposal of human beings; Yahweh was not to be manipulated. This interpretation is consistent with Genesis 32:29, where God refuses self-disclosure after wrestling with Jacob, and also with the prohibition against idols (Exodus 20:4).

We are not mistaken if we conclude that Israel believed from the beginning that God's nature was not to be known. Yahweh is known only by his creative word, which had called Israel itself into existence. Yahweh is not to be manipulated by humans; he calls Israel into relationship with himself on his terms alone. Israel's influence, if it had any, was over its own fate, and this influence was realized by its mindfulness of Yahweh's word and willing compliance with it. Thus the elements of primitive Yahwism begin to cohere in the desert as a result of Moses' role as mediator of divine oracles. Now we have a people with a keen sense of identity, united by a common vision of their past and a common hope for the future. This vision was anchored in the conviction that Yahweh had given them their existence, and he would sustain them in their hopes as long as they observed his word. A group thus constituted would have more going for it than all other bands of nomads it was to encounter as it pressed forward to realize its vision. And as these encounters took place, Israel grew in numbers only to validate its mission further. The conversion of new clans meant the accretion of new stories which were adjusted to the norms of primitive Yahwism.

But the conversion of additional clans also meant that the group would become socially much more complex, so that new forms of organization and identity would need to be invented. These would include a refinement of worship and rules of moral conduct. We might conjecture that the original mode of Covenant piety emerged in the process of these refinements. The idea of Covenant would not have occurred to the Sinai group as a model for understanding their relationship with Yahweh. The language of legal pacts and treaties is not the common parlance of slaves. But suzerainty treaties would have been familiar to seminomads on the fringes of Canaanite civilization in the mid-thirteenth century,[8] and such a model would have been ideal for a community that was growing by the accretion of large units. To frame the Yahwistic faith as a Covenant would have solved a couple of major problems for the Moses group. In the first place, it would provide a useful form for a summary statement of the Yahwistic creed. This would have provided both a core for worship and a tribal pledge of allegiance for new members of the group. And second, a Covenant would have provided a useful framework for articulating rules of moral conduct and the consequences of transgression that would have been necessary for the social regulation of a larger group. We might further suppose that the Ark of Yahweh came into existence in the process of refining worship. The Ark, a symbol of Yahweh's presence, probably originated as a compromise between those who felt an object of worship was necessary and those who objected to graven images. And in addition to these developments, it is likely that the beginnings of a quasiprophetic tradition appeared as the demands of an enlarged group exposed Moses' limitations.

This entire account of the emergence of the Covenant tradition is highly speculative, as any such account will necessarily be. But in any event we must assume something similar to this reconstruction, for it is nearly impossible to believe alternative possibilities on either extreme, that is, an Egyptian or Sinaitic origin, on the one side, or a Canaanite origin, on the other. As to the details of the primitive mode of Covenant piety, we can say very little, so the following must suffice. Members of the earliest Covenant community were aware that Yahweh was the source of their existence. They had a simple, this-worldly, and communal sense of what that meant. They were a preliterate and unsophisticated people and did not possess the resources for cosmological speculation. For them existence meant life; it meant safety, land, food, and children for a community in a hostile and unpredictable environment. They also had a sense that these things would be theirs if they held fast to the words of Yahweh, who had called them up out of obscurity and despair into existence and the promise of existence as a people. Yahweh made a Covenant with these people, and in this Covenant *was* their existence. To enter into the Covenant was to enter into life; apart from the Covenant there was death, literally and inescapably. These were rustic folk who had only a glimmer of the scale of events going on around them. Their cosmos had very narrow horizons, yet their vision was steadily expanding as their numbers increased. Rustic as they were, these people of the Covenant knew the difference between life and death, and the difference lay in their awareness of the conditions of their existence and in their compliance with these conditions. From its very beginnings Covenant piety involved a question of life and death:

See, today I set before you life and prosperity, death and disaster. If you obey the commandments of Yahweh your God that I enjoin on you today, if you love Yahweh your God and follow his ways, if you keep his commandments, his laws, his customs, you will live and increase, and Yahweh your God will bless you in the land which you are entering to make your own. But if your heart strays, if you refuse to listen, if you let yourself be drawn into worshipping other gods and serving them, I tell you today, you will most certainly perish.

[Deuteronomy 30:15–19]

Tribal Mode

The biblical account of the occupation of Canaan is recorded in the books of Joshua and Judges. Here the occupation is represented as a sudden and violent conquest which delivered the land of Canaan thoroughly into the hands of Israel. Thereafter the land was apportioned among the twelve tribes of Israel. As tempting as this narrative is, we now know that the process of occupation was protracted and considerably less violent than the biblical account indicates (though there was undoubtedly some bloodshed). Nor was the occupation thorough in the sense that Canaanite culture was entirely displaced by the immigration of seminomadic Israelites. Archaeological discoveries and biblical scholarship concur to give us a picture of the settlement period as one involving sporadic immigration followed by a long period of social assimilation and cultural syncretism.

At Kadesh we see two important developments taking place simultaneously. First, there was a refinement and normalization of the main features of Yahwism as a Covenant tradition. And second, there was a significant enlargement of the constituency of the community that took its primary identity from this tradition. As the community enlarged it would have divided itself into a spectrum of tribal units loosely united by a common Covenant identity. How many tribal units were involved cannot be known, for the tradition of twelve tribes was not fixed until after the settlement. The enlarged tribal league eventually developed a military dimension and set out sporadically from its seminomadic base at Kadesh to realize its dreams of becoming civilized.

During the period of the late thirteenth century, the land of Canaan was in political shambles and would have been vulnerable to invasions, especially those which were well organized and fueled by a mission. Eventually a few Israelite tribes gained a foothold in Canaan, and from the initial penetration subsequent invaders would have had strong allies to assist them in their own efforts. Nor was the resistance of the Canaanites so very discouraging. Canaanite feudal society was unusually brutal, so that the have-nots of society would have been predisposed to be receptive to the possibility of a new order.[9] There would have been no advantage for the immigrant tribes in mistreating the indigenous population of their new territory. In the first place, the Canaanites were closely related to the immigrants both racially and linguistically. Furthermore, if they were going to enjoy the civilized life, the immigrants would have to learn its arts from someone, and there would be no better resource than the already settled population. The period of the settlement, then, must be viewed as a period during which the Israelites adjusted themselves to their new physical/ social environment.

The difficulties of this adjustment cannot be minimized. The immigrants were a seminomadic pastoral people, and the Canaanites were civilized and agricultural. The difficulties had not least of all to do with religious differences. The agricultural pattern of life in Canaan was based upon a particularly rude form of polytheistic fertility religion, which would have appeared repugnant to Yahwists. The challenge to the Covenant community was precisely how it could manage to become a civilized agricultural society without sacrificing its distinctive identity as the people of Yahweh. Here the tension between plausibility and distinctiveness was heightened. On the one hand, the Israelites were committed to the agricultural life (promised by Yahweh), which necessarily involved the acquisition of agricultural techniques. But in Canaanite civilization, the techniques of agriculture were indistinguishable from the rituals of the fertility cult. How could the Israelites plausibly practice agriculture without involving themselves in the fertility cult? How could they lay hold to Yahweh's promise without becoming Baalists? On the other hand, the Israelites entered into this situation with countervailing commitments to a God who tolerated no rivals and no images, and they understood full well that to abrogate their solemn Covenant with Yahweh was to violate the conditions of their very existence. The contradiction between plausibility and distinctiveness is obvious. The Covenant tradition promised the settled life but then prevented its practical realization. Here was a situation in Israel's history (not the last!) in which continuity of the tradition called for a radical departure from its own conventions.

At this point we need a brief excursus into Canaanite polytheism. The cosmological framework of Canaanite religion is typical of the ancient worldview which radiated throughout Near Eastern civilization from Mesopotamia as early as the third millennium B.C. According to this worldview, the universe was defined by three distinct layers. The upper layer was the abode of the gods. The lower layer was occupied by vast seas and the powers of chaos, death, and destruction. Between these layers was the earth, anchored by mountains and separated from the upper and lower worlds by solid fixtures constructed by the gods to prevent a watery chaos from breaking in upon the earth. The cosmic order expressed in this worldview was understood to result from struggles among the gods. It was a relatively fixed order but was not defenseless against major disruptions. Mesopotamian peoples believed that their activities were crucial in renewing the primordial order of creation. By reenacting a cosmic drama on the day of the New Year, the order of the universe and the fertility of the earth could be restored. This is the general context of Canaanite religion, a worldview with which the seminomadic Israelites could have been only faintly familiar.

The Canaanite pantheon was presided over by El, the "creator and father of gods and men" and the "creator of all creatures."[10] While El is represented as taking a consort (Asherah), he plays an austere role in the fertility drama. The principal deity in both legend and ritual is Baal ("lord," "rain," "husband," "prince of earth"). Baal is represented as a king who earns his kingship by defeating his major opponents, Yam (the powers of the waters) and Mot (the powers of death and drought). The principal goddess is Anat (sister and consort of Baal), who is known for both her sexuality and her prowess in war. There were many other gods, including various astral deities, but these that I have mentioned are the ones featured in most mythic cycles. In one illustrative cycle Baal contends for power with Mot and enters into the underworld domain of the antagonist, whereupon messengers bring to the earth word of Baal's death and the loss of vital rain. Anat languishes in Baal's absence from the earth and seeks to avenge his death by killing Mot and strewing his remains over the earth. Anat intercedes with El on Baal's behalf, after which Baal and Mot both return for a final cosmic battle from which Baal emerges victorious. A sacral cosmic marriage ensues, and life is restored to the earth. It is assumed that such myths were dramatized ritually at various sites and times with the attendance of song, dance, food, drink, sacrifices, and ritual prostitution. And by such ministrations was the fruit of the land assured.

We know that when the Israelites occupied Canaan they appropriated some of the Canaanite worship sites and agricultural festivals.[11] Israel formed a confederation of twelve tribes which served various military, social, and religious purposes. And we know that the functional center of this confederation was a central sanctuary where political and military deliberations were held and where the Covenant with Yahweh was reaffirmed annually in a New Year's festival of agricultural origins. But what is not known with sufficient clarity is the precise extent to which this New Year's festival, as well as other celebrations at other local sites, involved elements taken over from the Canaanite fertility cult. There is among some biblical scholars a residual belief that Yahwism simply transformed Canaanite religion by a cooptive historicizing of the established sites and festivals of the fertility cult. This interpretation represents an oversimplification of the settlement period, as will be appreciated by anyone who grew up around farmers and understands how deeply rooted their notions about the machinations of nature are. Yahwism was without question a formidable religion and ultimately expunged the baser elements of Baalism, but its initial concessions to Canaanite fertility worship were undoubtedly more extensive than a quick transfer of the significance of cultic festivals.

123

We should see the tribal mode of Covenant piety as far more complex than a simple relabeling process. We are better advised to look for traces of a more extensive adjustment of Yahwism to the conditions of agrarian life. If Yahwism had failed to assimilate the basic elements of the Mesopotamian cosmology, it would have become a hopelessly inconsequential religion for the needs of an agricultural society. At the same time, it is an obvious fact that the Covenant theme continued to be transmitted on Canaanite soil. The only reasonable explanation for these circumstances is that there developed a cosmic dimension within the Covenant tradition. During the period of settlement, then, the Mosaic Covenant was complemented by a *cosmic* Covenant. Here we can use the term "controlled syncretism" to describe the appropriation of Canaanite religion by the Covenant tradition. Elements of Canaanite fertility religion entered into the worship of Israel, but their character and influence were conditioned by the Covenant meme. The cosmic events known to the Canaanites were now laid in alongside the historic events of the primitive credo, as Yahweh becomes the king of the universe and assumes (more or less) the roles previously played out by El and Baal.

The full force of the cosmic Covenant celebrations of the tribal period has been mitigated by later revisions of the Pentateuch, but we can still see major themes of the cosmic Covenant well preserved in various other Old Testament texts:[12]

1. Yahweh constructs the cosmos
   [Proverbs 8:22–31; Psalms 104:9]

2. and binds the elements in a cosmic Covenant
   [Jeremiah 5:22; Job 26:12–13; Jeremiah 33:20]

3. by overpowering cosmic monsters.
   [Psalms 74:12–17; Psalms 89:9–10; Isaiah 27:1; Isaiah 51:9]

4. The cosmic Covenant is broken,
   [Isaiah 24:5; Genesis 6]

5. bringing destruction upon the earth.
   [Isaiah 24:18–20; Genesis 6:13–17]

6. The earth is restored by renewal of the cosmic Covenant. [Genesis 9:8–17; Isaiah 54:9–10; Hosea 2:18; Ezekiel 34:25–29]

Admittedly, this is pretty bland stuff when compared with the orgiastic flavors of the Baalist fertility rites, but the essential elements for the guarantee of order in the cosmos and bounty in the fields are well represented. We are justified in conjecturing that the Covenant community celebrated this cosmic Covenant in connection with the New Year (Feast of Booths?), to the accompaniment of song, dance, food, and drink.[13] The precise origins and universality of the ceremony are hopelessly obscure. It is doubtful that the typical conventions of fertility worship were followed, but even if they were practiced initially, they died out rather soon. It may have taken several generations to coordinate a New Year's festival of this sort with the other major festivals of the Israelite calendar, such as the Feast of Weeks, at which the Book of the Covenant (Exodus chaps. 21–23) was read in connection with a Covenant renewal ceremony. But as these festivals became coordinated, the connection between the cosmic Covenant and the Mosaic Covenant became more apparent.

What we observe in the period of the settlement is an adjustment of the Covenant tradition to the new conditions imposed by the cosmology of an agricultural society. The response of the tradition was to *transpose* the Covenant to conform to the new cosmological orientation. The tradition still understood Yahweh to be the source of its existence, and it still understood that to violate the Covenant was to violate the conditions of their existence. But the Covenant itself, as an expression of these conditions, changed to reflect the demands of an agricultural society. The conditions of existence were perceived anew. The Book of the Covenant, for example, includes laws to govern agriculture: to be "in" the Covenant meant to observe these laws. No longer merely concerned with the oppressions of slavery and the desert, on the one hand, and the promise of land and lineage, on the other, the cosmological horizons of the Covenant community broadened to include the mysterious powers of the cosmos and the frail balance of nature. God changes too. Now Yahweh appears also as a nature God, as the king of the universe whose covenantal blessings include cosmic harmony and the return of the seasons as well as safety, land, and lineage. And if the conditions of existence have changed, so too have the consequences of violating them; now the Israelites perceive the terrifying forces of chaos to be just a broken Covenant away. The Covenant is now seen on a cosmic scale—or rather, the cosmos is seen in Covenant terms.

Nationalistic Mode

After two centuries the limitations of the tribal confederation in Israel were beginning to show through. This form of government was no longer adequate to the new challenges of the environment. Problems of both internal and external origins finally led the confederation to recognize that Israel could be saved only by another radical departure from the conventions of its past. The Book of Judges ends with a summary of the internal disorder that had come to characterize the period of the confederacy: "In those days there was no king in Israel, and every man did as he pleased" (Judges 21:25). Here is a poignant expression of amythia following, as it does, an account of gang rape and intertribal warfare. The period of the judges reflects a system of localized and sometimes arbitrary authority, a system which would appear anarchic as social and commercial interaction between tribes increased, a system in which Israel hankered for unity. But disunity among the tribes of Israel only left the confederacy more vulnerable than ever to the aggressions of the Philistines, who were threatening to extinguish Israel in order to safeguard their own interests. At the very moment when crime, injustice, and tribal disputes were increasing within, Israel was also becoming engaged in border incidents with a formidable external threat.

These tense circumstances eventually resolved themselves in the establishment of a monarchical government in Israel. This was a transformation of major proportions for Israel, for the selection of a king and the subsequent flourishing of strange new bureaucracies would have brought about social, political, and religious dislocations all over the region. Here, then, was another set of circumstances which put the Covenant community into a bind between plausibility and distinctiveness. It

126

had become clear that the existing Covenant was no longer an effective basis for order. It had not generated the social institutions (military, economic, and judicial) which were consistent with Israel's survival under new conditions. And to this extent the Covenant had become implausible. With their very existence at stake, the people clamored for a new order: "Give us a king to rule over us, like the other nations" (I Samuel 8:5). But how could Israel choose a king and become "like the other nations" without sacrificing its distinctive identity as the people of Yahweh? After all, *Yahweh* was their king, and he would brook no rivals; to choose another would be to abrogate the Covenant and jeopardize Israel's existence. The kings of Israel's neighbors (Egypt and Mesopotamia) were regarded as divine beings, so to ask for a king "like the other nations" would have been tantamount to requesting a new religious orientation. Concessions toward a monarchy were every bit as radical as concessions toward fertility religion. But the monarchy was established nevertheless. And the remarkable achievement was that Israel managed to adopt this new and plausible form of government without any loss of distinctiveness."[14] This was accomplished by transposing the Covenant tradition once again into a new mode of piety.

The nationalistic mode of Covenant piety is found expressed in the royal ideology undergirding the Davidic dynasty. According to this ideology, Yahweh had chosen Zion as his permanent dwelling place and had elected the House of David as his perpetual viceregency to govern Israel. Israel would now become a bona fide nation like its neighbors. To fix the new identity of Israel, Yahweh had established an eternal Covenant with David whereby David became Yahweh's declared son and "anointed one." This ideology effectively dispels any worry that choosing a king would violate the Covenant by asserting that a new Covenant was made directly with the king by Yahweh himself. To be sure, the Davidic monarchy was elevated well beyond the stature of the confederate judges, but there was no question that Yahweh remained sovereign:

> Israel's earthly kings are not divine in the sense that they represent incarnations of the holy God. They are divine in the sense that they share in the powers of the living God, king of the

universe, who uses these kings to effect order on earth and guarantee life and blessing to his people. The festival of covenant renewal certainly was changed when it became a festival presided over by kings ruling from Zion as God's adopted sons. But it did not lose its connection with the ancient covenant.[15]

Many biblical scholars have emphasized the discontinuity between the Davidic Covenant and the earlier Mosaic Covenant by suggesting that the Davidic Covenant represents an unconditional Covenant of eternal blessing: "This covenant is such that even wrongdoing cannot break it. The nation may suffer if the king is wicked, for God will chastise them as a father beats an erring son. But the oath of God will stand, even so! There could not be any clearer evidence of the great gulf that is fixed between this and the intention of the Sinai covenant, where the stress is on Israel's responsibility."[16]

This account is an exaggeration. There are marked differences between the Davidic Covenant and the Mosaic Covenant, but it is a distortion to say that the Davidic Covenant is uniformly unconditional and that its intention is other than to stress the responsibility of the people of Israel. Rather than viewing the Davidic Covenant as unconditional, we should regard it as *one*-conditional. The clear intention of this Covenant is to convey the message that as long as David and his heirs are on the throne the Covenant will be intact. The sovereignty of the Davidic dynasty is the singular condition of Israel's existence. Embedded in this condition is an admonition against deposing the king, for to do so would be to jeopardize the existence of Israel. The Davidic Covenant effects a displacement of responsibility, not its subduction. David is held accountable to Yahweh, and Israel is held accountable to David. Israel's responsibility is to respond with absolute obedience to David's authority, for David has been entrusted with God's authority: "The spirit of Yaweh speaks through me, his word is on my tongue" (I Samuel 23:2). And for his part, David's responsibility is to be a faithful and righteous servant of Yahweh (the term "servant" is applied to David sixty times), which means that he must rule Israel with justice and equity. David's righteousness was a condition of his election:

Your royal sceptre is a sceptre of integrity:
Virtue you love as much as you hate wickedness.
This is why God, your God, has anointed you
[Psalms 45:6]

David's righteousness is the presupposition but also the enduring condition of his kingship:

Yahweh swore to David
and will remain true to his word,
"I promise that your own son
shall succeed you on the throne.
If your sons observe my covenant,
the decrees that I have taught them,
their sons too shall succeed you
on the throne for evermore."
[Psalms 132:11–12]

What can we then say about the mode of piety characteristic of the Davidic Covenant? There remains the conviction that God is the source of existence. But the understnding of existence takes on a new dimension; now to exist means to exist *as a nation*. The cosmic dimension is still evident from the fact that the enthronement of Yahweh at Zion (and the enthronement of Davidic kings as his declared sons) is now reenacted in the New Year festival setting of the cosmic Covenant. But the emphasis rests upon Israel's new identity as a nation among nations. The promise of the Covenant is for Israel to continue forever as a prosperous state. The condition of existence is singular: to protect the sovereignty of the Davidic line by observing its divinely appointed authority. To be "in" the Covenant meant to comply with royal decrees and to support the house of David absolutely, for on David everything depended. As long as the Davidic house was secure, the cosmos and the nation were secure. The righteousness of Israel would be rewarded through the righteousness of David. And David's righteousness was the condition of God's favor upon him.

While the Covenant expressed in the royal ideology cannot be said to be uniformly unconditional, there is no question that it was excessively confident. Such is the style to which politicians are given; as long as there is one live soldier or one uncast vote, victory is at hand! And such was the style of the officials of the new sanctuary in Jerusalem who drafted the royal theology. But there was another side to the nationalistic mode of piety, a "minority opinion," as it were, to counterbalance the excesses of the royal ideology by emphasizing the contingency of Israel's nascent national existence. Across the aisle from the kings were the prophets, who also claimed to speak for God and were only too willing to unburden themselves whenever they perceived Israel's kings to be in violation of the "true" Covenant.

Two primary themes typified the prophetic tradition during the period of the monarchy, both having to do with concessions to the culture of Mesopotamia. One theme involved the institution of the monarchy, and the other involved the practice of fertility religion. We have seen already that a royal ideology had developed to suport the sovereignty of the Davidic dynasty. This particular ideology was rejected in the North following the division of the two kingdoms. But the northern kings, despite the rejection of royalist ideology, nevertheless tended to carry on in practically the same absolutist fashion as the Davidic kings. The kings of both Judah and Israel tended to have puffed-up images of their authority in line with the example of Mesopotamian rulers. This attitude of absolutism and the optimism and complacency associated with it elicited the rancor of the prophets, who were quick to remind the monarchs that Yahweh is king and that to Yahweh's justice even they must submit. The oracles of Amos represent a scathing indictment of the failure of Israel to recognize and obey the conditions of its existence. Amos broadsides the notion that Yahweh's Covenant is irrevocable. In fact, Yahweh has revoked it already, and the consequences are near at hand. There is an element of necessity in the Covenant, to be sure, but it is the necessity not of eternal security but of divine retribution. Amos understood Israel's existence in terms of nationhood, but its existence as a nation was not eternally fixed; it was as frail as a candle's flame, and it would now, of necessity, go out.

On the matter of religious practice the prophets were equally uncompromising. Canaanite culture and religion, we may recall, remained relatively undisturbed in the interstices of the tribal confederation. But this situation changed when the monarchy brought political unity to the entire region. Now the remaining pockets of Canaanite culture were flushed out into the open, where the inevitable face-off between Yahwism and Baalism would again become a hot issue. The kings of Judah and Israel, for the most part, took the line of tolerance toward the Canaanites. After all, they were subjects of the realm too and had to be appeased somewhat lest they rock the boat. This neutral policy permitted the free and open promotion of Baalism, sometimes in the context of the royal household. But the prophets would have none of this. Hosea represents Israel as a whore who has violated the terms of her marriage to consort with false gods. Her kings and priests are leading Israel down the road to certain destruction. The nation of Israel, the existence of Israel, is doomed:

> I mean to destroy you Israel;
> who can come to your help?
> Your king, where is he now, to save you,
> where are your leaders to champion you?
> Those to whom you used to say,
> "Give me a king and leaders."
> In my anger I gave you a king
> and in my wrath I take him away.
> [Hosea 13:9–11]

These two themes are well illustrated in Elijah's ministry during the reign of Ahab. In the story of Naboth's murder, Elijah attacks the king for abusing his power in taking the life and property of one of his subjects. On another occasion Elijah accuses Ahab of being the "scourge of Israel" for his tolerance of Baalism. But in the final analysis these two themes are not distinct. They appear to be more akin to foreign and domestic arms of the same underlying policy: absolute Yahwism.

Throughout the period of the monarchy, therefore, we find a fundamental juxtaposition between the royalist mode of piety and the more traditional prophetic mode. Both understood Israel's existence collectively, in terms of nationhood, and both recognized Yahweh as the source of that existence. But one focused with great confidence on the future glory of the nation, while the other trembled with the memory of Yahweh's admonitions of the past. We are reminded of the blending of anticipation and memory at Kadesh and the manner in which their integration produced the nucleus of the Covenant tradition. If we take a wide view of prophecy during the eighth and seventh centuries, we might see how these two emphases (promise and obligation) worked together again to produce a new prospect for the Covenant tradition.

In the prophets of the eighth and seventh centuries, we find the promissory elements of the Davidic Covenant combining with the obligatory elements of the Mosaic Covenant. This combination is evident in the developments toward individualizing the obligations of the Covenant and, at the same time, expressing the promise of a new form of Israel's existence in a Covenant of eternal blessing. The prophetic anticipation, inscrutable as it is, foreshadows another transposition of the Covenant tradition.

Before the period of the monarchy, Covenant responsibility was regarded as resting somehow vaguely on the whole community of Israel, but in the case of the Davidic Covenant an individual is charged with a responsibility to uphold the Covenant; Nathan and Elijah go straight to the king with their criticisms. In the prophetic careers of Amos and Hosea, it is true, we find oracles leveled at collective targets, but there is a decisively individual dimension in their emphasis upon traits of personal character. Amos rails against self-indulgence, deceit, greed, obstinence, imprudence, and shallowness. Hosea longs for fidelity, tenderness, honesty, contrition, and love. Being "in" the Covenant requires a personal integrity that is not identifiable with superficial adherence to conventional forms. But these are to be the personal qualities of some future Covenant, for both Amos and Hosea know that Israel's demise as a nation is impending. Yahweh is about to draw the blinds on Israel's past. Her existence may be restored again in the future, but this will not, strictly speaking, be a restoration, for the dynamic of history will itself be new.

The oracles of the prophet Micah have been extensively altered by later editors, but assuming the alterations were made by his admirers and the spirit of his ministry, we can see that

Micah, too, mixed the themes of personal obligation and Israel's destruction with the promise of a new order of peace and justice. In Isaiah and Jeremiah, however, we find the two themes most explicitly expressed. Isaiah's criticisms, like those of Amos, are made on the level of personal morality. He attacks the rich and the corrupt from whose actions social injustice stems. He also attacks the superficiality of worship. For these sins Yahweh will destroy his nation:

Yes, Jerusalem is falling into ruins
and Judah is in collapse,
since their words and their deeds affront the Lord,
insulting his glory.

[Isaiah 3:8]

But Yahweh will leave a remnant:

Those who are left of Zion
and remain of Jerusalem
shall be called holy
and those left in Jerusalem, noted down for survival

[Isaiah 4:3]

From this he will eventually restore the righteousness of David's rule:

A shoot springs from the stock of Jesse:
a scion thrusts from his roots:
on him the spirit of Yahweh rests,
a spirit of wisdom and insight,
a spirit of counsel and power,
a spirit of knowledge and the fear of Yahweh

[Isaiah 11:1–2]

In Jeremiah the belief that the old Covenant has passed and will eventually be restored under new conditions comes to its full height. Jeremiah looks for a new, individualized mode of piety:

See, the days are coming—it is Yahweh who speaks—when I will make a new covenant with the House of Judah (and the

House of Israel), but not a covenant like the one I made with their ancestors on the day I took them by the hand to bring them out of the land of Egypt. They broke that covenant of mine, so I had to show them who was master. It is Yahweh who speaks. No, this is the covenant I will make with the House of Israel when those days arrive—it is Yahweh who speaks. Deep within them I will plant my Law, writing it on their hearts. Then I will be their God and they shall be my people. There will be no further need for neighbor to try to teach neighbor, or brother to say to brother, "Learn to know Yahweh!" No, they will all know me, the least no less than the greatest—it is Yahweh who speaks—since I will forgive their iniquity and never call their sin to mind.

[Jeremiah 31:31–34]

One has the feeling that these prophets are struggling to say something entirely new about the nature and dynamics of Israel's existence, but they seem somehow lacking the adequate resources for articulating a new vision. It is clear to them that their existence will not be exactly what it has been in the past; Yahweh has seen to that already. But what existence will mean henceforth is still unclear. What they do feel certain of is that there will be some form of survival and that it will involve a mode of piety that will be individual in nature and everlasting in duration.

Legalistic Mode

In 587 B.C. Jerusalem was laid to ruins by Nebuchadnezzar's army, and its surviving literate population was carried off into exile in Babylon. It is difficult to see how one could exaggerate the significance of this defeat for the life of the Covenant community. The candle of Israel's national existence had indeed been extinguished, and Zion, the eternal abode of Yahweh, had been reduced to a hopeless pile of ashes. All that the Covenant community had believed about itself was empirically disproven. The dream of eternal existence as a nation had come to the reality of no existence. If ever the Covenant appeared implausible, it was in this moment of final despair. The Covenant of survival was now demonstrably false because in fact the nation of Israel had failed to survive. And yet this was not

134

to be the end of the Covenant community. What faced the community at this moment was another challenge to the plausibility of its myth, and it survived this challenge as a distinctive entity only because it managed, once again, to transpose the Covenant into a new mode of piety.

Not since Moses had the Covenant community had such an acute need for someone to reveal the meaning of its suffering and to articulate the conditions under which it might once again exist. This need was ultimately fulfilled by those who managed to keep alive the literary and prophetic traditions of the Covenant community. There can be little doubt that, if the exiles had not been allowed to preserve their literary heritage in material form, the Covenant tradition would have disappeared forever from the annals of history. We can speak of the survival of the Covenant tradition only because documents were saved and eventually rewritten and expanded to interpret the experience of the exile. The credit for this work goes to the prophets and priests of the exilic period, for these were the figures who managed to retell the narrative of God's people in such terms that the implausibility of the Covenant became its supreme vindication. On the basis of the exilic reinterpretation of national defeat there was kindled a hope of future restoration. The query posed by the contradiction of plausibility and distinctiveness ("How could we sing one of Yahweh's hymns in a pagan country?") drew its response from the likes of Ezekiel, Second Isaiah, and the priestly school. These figures inspired the promise of restoration and laid the foundations for a transposition of the Covenant to a new mode of piety.

As a result of the Deuteronomic reform carried out by Josiah (circa 622 B.C.), a new class of religious functionaries emerged in Judah: the teachers of the law. This group was responsible for the development of a case law tradition in the later period of the monarchy. These people were also the ones, no doubt, who had the inclination to drag along texts as the remnants of holocaust were taken into exile. In Babylon, under the conditions of exile, this class of teachers rose to the surface to become the principal leaders of the Covenant community. Their efforts kept the identity of the community alive. They organized a school, later to become the synagogue, which formed the nucleus of community life during the exile.[17] Worship life in the context of the priestly school included prayer, hymns, and homily. The homily amounted to a recitation of the events of Israel's history based on readings from the Deuteronomic documents and the writings of preexilic prophets. In this context the reinterpretation of history took place. Of chief importance to the priestly school were the prophets who had forecast the destruction of Israel's national existence, together with the laws whose violation had occasioned the destruction. The exile was viewed as Yahweh's sentence, justly imposed in retribution for Israel's crimes. The point was that this judgment might have been prevented if Israel had listened to the prophets and had complied more strictly with Yahweh's commands. This theme controlled the reassembly and editing of Israel's historic traditions. The work, started in the exilic period, finally emerged as the priestly narrative of the Pentateuch.

Under the conditions of exile, the Yahwists had few tangible symbols of their identity as a distinctive community; there was no king, no temple, no cult. The priestly school therefore emphasized such outward manifestations of the faith as could be found embedded in the tradition. This stress brought into prominence certain ritual observances that had previously been of limited significance. They included the observation of the sabbath, circumcision, and various ancient regulations governing diet and purification. The Covenant community could no longer be known by its king and its temple, but it could be known as a distinct entity by its strict adherence to these customs. The law, then, became the basis for a new mode of Covenant faith. It was in the priestly teaching concerning the law that the exiles were able to see the significance of their place in universal history. The law was the key to understanding the past and laying hold of the future. To the law they must cling, for it expressed the conditions of their existence:

> The important thing, therefore, was to return to Yahweh, because one might then have hope once more. But the possibility of once more attaining God's grace, which had been sealed by oath in the early history of Israel, was given through the law. After the catastrophe there still remained Yahweh's commandments and prohibitions, his regulations and ordinances. Because they had not been obeyed, disaster had struck; if they were now

finally obeyed, there was hope of deliverance. The law was the fixed and immobile rock to which one could cling in order to avoid being swept away by the tide of history.[18]

For the exiles, then, to exist meant to exist as a community *of the law*. To be "in" the Covenant had a special meaning for each individual: being in the Covenant meant being righteous before the law. And that involved a complete and total orientation of one's life around the law, including both inward attitude and outward behavior. This individual emphasis, anticipated by the preexilic prophets, was even more explicitly formulated by Ezekiel:

> See now: all life belongs to me; the father's life and the son's life, both alike belong to me. The man who has sinned, he is the one who shall die. The upright man is law-abiding and honest; he does not eat on the mountains or raise his eyes to the idols of the House of Israel, does not seduce his neighbor's wife or sleep with a woman during her periods. He oppresses no one, returns pledges, never steals, gives his own bread to the hungry, his clothes to the naked. He never charges usury on loans, takes no interest, abstains from evil, gives honest judgment between man and man, keeps my laws and sincerely respects my observances—such a man is truly upright. It is Yahweh who speaks.
>
> [Ezekiel 18:4–9]

For Ezekiel, Yahweh is the source of life, and life is given by virtue of righteousness before the law. The conditions of existence, the Covenant, are identified with the law. But "existence" is clearly understood by Ezekiel in individual terms; *each person* is declared alive or dead according to his or her performance: "He shall live because of the integrity he has practiced" (18:22). And it is on the basis of individual righteousness that the Covenant community has any hope of restoration. Ezekiel looks for a transformation of individuals through which Yahweh will save his people and restore them to the promised land:

> Then I am going to take you from among the nations and gather you together from all the foreign countries, and bring you home to your own land. I shall pour clean water over you and you will

be cleansed; I shall cleanse you of all your defilement and all
your idols. I shall give you a new heart, and put a new spirit in
you; I shall remove the heart of stone from your bodies and give
you a heart of flesh instead. I shall put my spirit in you, and
make you keep my laws and sincerely respect my observances.
You will live in the land which I gave your ancestors. You shall
be my people and I will be your God.

[Ezekiel 36:24–28]

There is a curious tension in Ezekiel between the obligatory
and promissory aspects of the Covenant. He is clear about the
obligations of the individual before the law, but when he is
speaking of the promise of salvation, his resources fail him and
he falls back upon visions of nationalistic glory.

We first encounter a transcendence of the nationalism typical of the prophetic tradition in the ministry of Second Isaiah.
Second Isaiah takes seriously the misgivings of the exilic community about the sovereignty of Yahweh. If he is truly a powerful God, then why do we, his people, suffer such indignity?
Second Isaiah explains that Yahweh is indeed the only God of
the universe, and in this the exiles may find comfort (Isaiah
44:6–8). Because Yahweh is the only God of all creation, and
because his Covenant with Israel is still intact, there is no cause
for despair. Salvation is immanent; the present plight of the
exiles is a temporary punishment, a second Exodus, which will
lead to a fulfillment of Yahweh's promises (Isaiah 43:6–7). But
the promise of salvation has a remarkably new dimension, for
Yahweh's salvation is not restricted to Israel. Yahweh will save
all humanity, and he will do so through the ministry of Israel:

It is not enough for you to be my servant,
to restore the tribes of Jacob and bring back the survivors of
Israel;
I will make you the light of the nations so that
my salvation may reach the ends of the earth.

[Isaiah 49:6]

Here we have a vision of an international Covenant. Second
Isaiah is the first of the eschatological prophets; he speaks of
a New Age which both continues and fulfills the past. He com-
bines several themes: comfort to Israel, responsibility to the

law, the universal sovereignty of Yahweh, the special election of Israel, and the promise of salvation to all humanity. And all throughout, his preaching is punctuated with grandiose images of cosmic history. The entire cosmos is being saved by Yahweh and delivered into a New Age characterized by his full revelation. This will be an age of "everlasting covenant" (55:3), "eternal salvation and justice" (51:6–8), "eternal love and peace" (54:8–10), and "everlasting joy and gladness" (51:11). The promissory element in this Covenant is raised well beyond anything envisioned by earlier prophets. Israel's existence is understood in a completely novel way. Israel will exist forever into the future, not simply as a nation, but as a nation with a unique role in inaugurating the New Age of Yahweh's kingdom. Second Isaiah understood these new elements to be the consequences of radical monotheism. But he, like Ezekiel, lacked the resources for making clear the cosmological details of the New Age. And so the true nature of Israel's future existence would remain obscure until the dawn of apocalypticism, when cosmological dualism would bring forth more explicit imagery.

The promises of Second Isaiah, inspiring as they were, were not realized upon the return of exiles to Palestine. The restoration in fact turned out to be a major disappointment. While the Jews were allowed to return to Jerusalem, their national existence was not restored, nor was it likely to be. There was no king and no cult. Even the rebuilding of the temple was delayed as the returned exiles struggled under severe political and economic conditions. From now on, the identity of the Covenant community would be that of a religion: Judaism. And far from discharging its new missionary task, "to lighten the Gentiles," the postexilic Jewish community tended to become rigidly isolationist. The self-possessing disposition of the priestly tradition gave way to outright suspicion of the external world as Judaism tightened itself around the law. The law now became an obsession that would dominate further developments in Judaism. The law was the lifeline of the Jews and came to be seen as fixed from eternity, never to be altered (Deuteronomy 12:32). This veneration for the law gave rise to some new developments in Judaism. Under the program of reconstruction initiated by Ezra and Nehemiah, the written law, Torah, became the final constitution of Judaism. From this time forth Judaism would be a religion based on written authority. The formal institution of the Torah gave rise to the task of determining the official canon of the legal corpus and also to traditions of interpretation and application to everyday life.

Throughout the period of postexilic Judaism there remained tension between isolationism and universalism, a tension which would eventually produce another crisis of plausibility and distinctiveness. On the one hand, Judaism was enjoined to safeguard the distinctive identity of the Covenant community by protecting the integrity of the law. To most Jews this stricture precluded any intermingling with Gentiles (thus the prohibition of intermarriages; Ezra, chap. 9). On the other hand, if the Jews were to take seriously the radical monotheism of Second Isaiah, they must exert themselves in the task of enlarging the boundaries of the Covenant community. Under the impact of Hellenism, this internal tension would become fractured into a spectrum of modes of Covenant piety.

Apocalyptic Mode

The irony of postexilic Judaism was that, even though many Jews returned to their promised land, they remained, practically speaking, in a foreign country. The international situation was one of great flux well into the Roman period. And all the while, except for a brief and unsatisfying interlude under the Hasmoneans, the Jews languished under the political dominion of external powers. When Cyrus of Persia conquered Babylon in 538 B.C., he displayed an attitude of tolerance toward the Jews and decreed that they should be allowed to return to Palestine and to rebuild their temple. He did not, however, grant them political independence, and the Covenant community therefore remained a vassal of the Persian Empire until the Alexandrian conquest in 333 B.C. The situation of the Jews during the Persian period is historically obscure, though we may assume from the displacement of Hebrew by the Aramaic dialect that Persian influence in their daily affairs was substantial. With Alexander, of course, came the ideal of unifying all humanity under the umbrella of Hellenistic culture. Cultural syncretism was systematically encouraged throughout the Alexandrian empire. While the personal rule of Alexander lasted for scarcely a decade, the ideal of "one world" became his legacy and was carried on by his successors. Following Alexander's death (323), Palestine was ruled for a century by the Ptolemies and then by Seleucid kings until the Roman conquest of Jerusalem in 63 B.C. As political wards during this entire period, the Jews could hardly have resisted the penetration of ideas from the thought worlds of Persia and Greece. Cultural syncretism was more evident, however, among the Jews who were living outside Palestine, and these were considerable in number; in fact, the Jews of the Diaspora greatly outnumbered those who had returned to Palestine.

What we find, then, are first Persian and then Greek cultural influences permeating the entire atmosphere during the formative period of Judaism. To resist their influence would have required enormous effort, an effort that some Jews were prepared to make and others not. Those Jews who actively resisted the influx of Persian and Hellenistic ideas had perfectly good reasons for doing so. After all, they had an obligation to preserve the integrity of the law and the distinctive identity of the Covenant community. And under the conditions of political dependency, the best strategy for this would appear to be that of constructing barriers to quarantine the law from contaminating influences. But there were also those who rushed out to embrace the new ideas, and they had their reasons too. There were undoubtedly many Jews to whom the experiences of the postexilic community disclosed a fundamental implausibility in the Covenant. And to those who felt the inadequacies of the faith, these new ideas would have come as welcome resources for achieving a more satisfying self-understanding.

The plain truth is that history had persisted too long in denying a place to the postexilic community. In fact, the entire Old Testament has been characterized as "a record of national failure."[19] This sense of historic failure became more evident as time passed. During the exile the prophetic themes of "just rewards," "suffering servants," "second exodus," and the like, were well taken by the Jews as they reviewed the sins of the past. And the prophetic vision of restoration in Palestine under some entirely new order might have been sufficiently inspirational—then! But *after* the restoration, when the promises of a new order remained unfulfilled and the horizons of history looked as bleak as ever—what *then* would become of the plausibility of the prophetic message?

The point is that the historical eschatology of the prophetic tradition lacked adequate resources for articulating a plausible vision of the future. It wanted to point the way toward a new historical order in which final judgment was somehow behind the Jews, but it could offer nothing concrete or intelligible beyond a restored national existence, a promise that was beginning to look like a fantasy. Nor was the theodicy of the tradition adequate to salve the continued indignity of postexilic vassalage. The Jews had always viewed Yahweh as the source of both good and evil, prosperity and adversity. But why would Yahweh allow them to suffer so long? The exile should have been enough! Perpetual failure in history predisposed many Jews to look for the consummation of Yahweh's purposes *beyond* history. And the ambiguity of their suffering predisposed them to look for sources of evil which opposed rather than served Yahweh's purposes. But the tradition failed the disillusioned Jew. It lacked adequate resources to formulate its own promise, and to that extent its myth was implausible. For some Jews the existence of a self-possessed theocracy in a pagan wilderness was sufficient. These people maintained a disciplined oblivion where the external world was concerned, and they delighted in meditating upon the law day and night (Psalms 1:2). But there were others to whom the Covenant appeared to promise more. And these people became predisposed to latch on to any new memes that might help them to envision their hopes *beyond* the realm of history. The thought worlds of Persia and Greece offered these memes, and with them came the resources for achieving another transposition of the Covenant tradition.

It would be misleading to create the impression that postexilic Judaism fell neatly into two camps divided by their opposing estimation of the intellectual milieu of the non-Jewish world. The reality of the situation was far more complex. We cannot avoid the conclusion, however, that the future existence of the Covenant community—its perceived nature and the strategies it called for—remained a live issue which generated divergence of opinion. And the divergence of opinion seems to have been further complicated by the varying degrees to which

Persian and Greek thought forms were appropriated. Gradually some Jews began to absorb features of cosmological and ethical dualism from Persian origins and to adapt them to the particulars of Yahwism. Thus angels and intermediaries began to appear in Jewish theology together with Satan in a new role as an adversary of Yahweh. Belief in resurrection and the afterlife, evident in Persian religion, had become fairly common among Jews by the second century. These features, grafted to the eschatology and theodicy of the prophetic tradition, led to the belief that individuals were tempted away from the law and into sin by Satan and that Yahweh would eventually impose his judgment upon the Jews. Rewards and punishments would subsequently be administered in the afterlife. It is impossible to trace the stages by which these features established themselves in various factions of Jewish thought, but they are clearly evident by the second century, when it becomes possible to identify a particularly Jewish form of apocalypticism.

Apocalypse means "revelation." Apocalyptic literature, which had considerable influence in Persian religion, is a genre characterized by pseudonymous secret revelations of catastrophic future events. The Book of Daniel falls into this category, as do several of the so-called "pseudepigraphal" books. Apocalypticism can be described as the worldview which underlies this form of literary expression. The apocalyptic worldview is both dualistic and deterministic. It describes world history as unfolding in epochs, according to a predetermined divine plan. World history, usually "this world" or "this eon," is contrasted with "the world to come" or "the eon to come."[20] The present age of history is dominated by the cosmic powers of sin and evil, but this age is being drawn toward a cataclysmic end, at which point God will intervene to conquer his foes (both celestial and terrestrial) and will establish a new eon beyond history. Central to apocalypticism is its ethical dualism. Humanity, living out the final throes of history, is offered the choice of moral alignment with either the forces of good or the forces of evil. At the point of divine intervention, there will take place a moral judgment of individuals. Those who stood with the powers of evil on that final day of judgment would be banished into eternal punishment along with Satan and his angels, but those who stood with the righteous would be raised from the dead and ushered into the new (suprahistoric) eon, an age of everlasting peace and righteousness.

This genre of literature would naturally become very appealing during historic moments of acute crisis, which was the case in Palestine near the middle of the second century B.C. At this time the Jews were under the dominion of Seleucid rulers who were set upon achieving solidarity among their subjects by a program of forced Hellenization. This program reached critical proportions for the Jews when, in 167 B.C., the practice of Judaism was prohibited and an Olympian cult was established in the temple of Yahweh. Armed rebellion of the Jews followed in what is known as the Maccabean Revolt. The Book of Daniel depicts these events in a series of portents that disclose the beginning of the end. God's judgment is near at hand, and the Jews are exhorted to follow Daniel's example of fidelity to the law so that they may be counted among the righteous. Some among them would no doubt be martyred, but these especially had the assurance of eternal reward in the life to come.

The Maccabean Revolt appears to have been a major turning point in the history of Judaism, for after this event Judaism begins to fracture into a variety of parties and sects and then to harden into the pattern that we find at the beginning of the New Testament period.

The mode of piety reflected in Jewish apocalyptic is much different from anything found before the exile. God is still regarded as the source of existence, the Covenant is still regarded as an expression of the conditions of existence, and humanity is still suspended between life and death. But the particulars have all been transposed into a new cosmological setting. Now "existence" has dual meaning; there is existence under the conditions of this eon and a new existence under the conditions of the eon to come. Existence as a nation seems to matter little, for it is merely a part of the old eon. What *matters* is the new existence, the eternal suprahistorical existence that will characterize the world to come. The Covenant expresses the conditions of this new life to come. By holding fast to the law on *this side* of judgment, one will have fulfilled the conditions for entry into the new form of existence. God's salvation is no longer viewed as a purification in history; it is salvation from the realm of history altogether. To be "in" the Covenant community means to be counted among those who will survive the denouement of history, that is, among those who will be judged righteous before the law on that final day.

Jewish apocalyptic had the effect of further elevating the importance of the law and also of intensifying its signficance for the individual. We should not be surprised that it had the effect of radicalizing individuals with respect to the law. Now it was clearer than ever that *any* offense of the law was a serious matter indeed. The impendency of judgment became oppressive to the individual whose eternal existence hung in the balance.

Apocalyptic was not universally recognized by the Jews. Some of the parties within post-Maccabean Judaism, namely the Sadducees, paid no mind to any of the features of cosmological and moral dualism. Their focus was on the realm of history, where their primary concern was to keep the temple cult intact, to sustain the status quo until Yahweh brought his historic plan another notch forward. The Pharisees apparently had mixed reactions to apocalyptic. Belief in resurrection was typical among the Pharisees, and strict adherence to the law was central in their teachings. But they appear not to have approved of the extremism of the apocalyptic movement. Others, however, became quite radical. The times were conducive to overreactions. The Hasmonean state was totally unacceptable to many Jews, and the Roman order which followed was even more so. Strongly held opinions about various religious and political issues brought forth intense rivalries within the Covenant community. Radical apocalyptic groups began to break away from center and isolate themselves into brotherhoods dedicated to various pietistic stratagems for coping with the last days. These included the Zealots, the Essenes, and the Christians.

Christological Mode

What can be known about Jesus of Nazareth as a historical personage is very little. That he was a Galilean Hasidic appears to be certain.[21] That he attracted followers by his effectiveness as a teacher is also beyond serious debate. It also seems certain that he appeared in Jerusalem, where his teachings were not particularly endearing to the Jewish establishment. He evidently became embroiled in controversy and was silenced by crucifixion at the hands of Roman authorities. Jesus' exhortations to the Jews were to repent and to obey the will of God. Just how radical were his views concerning the law and whether he had associations with the Essenes or the Zealots cannot be known. Nevertheless, his place in the larger context of Judaism appears to have been in the tradition of apocalyptic. But one thing that cannot reasonably be denied is that his ministry and the conditions of his execution were of decisive importance for a small group of Palestinian Jews who eventually saw in his career the resources for a new transposition of the Covenant.

The facts about Jesus' life and ministry, however, are far less significant for a survey of the Covenant tradition than is an understanding of the mode of Covenant piety which was generated by his followers. In the broadest view of Covenant history, the major significance of Christianity is that it took most seriously the exilic mission to extend the Covenant to all humanity. But the Christians realized that this mission could not be advanced if the Jews continued in their inflexible identification of the Covenant with the written and oral legal traditions. The law came to be viewed by the Christians in roughly the same manner that Amos, Hosea, and Isaiah regarded temple sacrifices: they were not essential for survival. The Christians came to see an element of implausibility in the law because it appeared to them to preclude the universal promise of the Covenant. Thus in the advent of Christianity we find a resurfacing of the postexilic tension which began with Second Isaiah, namely, the tension between the identity and the universality of the Covenant. What is unique about the Christians is the manner in which they joined elements of Jewish apocalyptic to the universal mission implicit in the radical monotheism of Second Isaiah to achieve a new mode of Covenant piety.

This combination of apocalyptic and universalism was as unique in Palestinian Judaism as it was in Diaspora Judaism but for precisely opposite reasons. In Palestinian Judaism apocalyptic was pervasive, but so too was the isolationism implicit in obsessive adherence to the law. But in Diaspora Judaism these elements were reversed. Jews of the Diaspora tended to be innocent of apocalyptic influences, but at the same time they were, by comparison, universalists who actively proselytized the Covenant in the Hellenistic environment. The combination of these elements together with their messianic claims gave the Christians a unique proclamation on both Palestinian and Hellenistic soil.

Paul Johnson has made a claim that the Council of Jerusalem in A.D. 49 is the starting point from which to reconstruct the origins of Christianity.[22] There is much to commend this view, for it is likely that this event was decisive for the universalism of the Jewish Christians. Accounts of this council are given in both Acts, chapter 15, and Galatians, chapter 2. It seems that Paul had come under intense criticism in Antioch for failing to insist upon circumcision among pagan converts. He apparently held fast to his practice, and a controversy ensued. It was finally agreed that Paul and a few companions would return to Jerusalem to sort matters out with the authorities of the church there. Paul's own account of the Council of Jerusalem suggests that this was a major showdown:

> I went there as the result of a revelation, and privately I laid before the leading men the Good News as I proclaim it among the pagans; I did so for fear the course I was adopting or had already adopted would not be allowed. And what happened? Even though Titus who had come with me is a Greek, he was not obliged to be circumcised. The question came up only because some who do not really belong to the brotherhood have furtively crept in to spy on the liberty we enjoy in Christ Jesus, and want to reduce us all to slavery. I was so determined to safeguard for you the true meaning of the Good News, that I refused even out of deference to yield to such people for one moment. As a result, these people who are acknowledged leaders . . . had nothing to add to the Good News as I preach it.
>
> [Galatians 2:2–6]

In brief, the result of the Council of Jerusalem was to recognize Paul's teaching concerning the law as normative for the Christian mission. If we look closely at Paul's teaching on the law, we can see the familiar tension between plausibility and distinctiveness which was to generate the Christological mode of Covenant piety. Some scholars have suggested that Paul's teaching on the law is entirely determined by his perspective as a Christian. This is misleading, for we must allow for some dissatisfaction with Judaism as a precondition for Paul's conversion to the Christian perspective. As Sandmel says, "It is not his Christian convictions which raise the Law as a problem for him, but rather it is his problem with the Law that brings him ultimately to his Christian convictions."[23] This approach encourages us to look for development in Paul's regard for the law. It is reasonable to suspect that Paul's attitude toward the law was both confirmed and deepened by his encounter with the Christians. As E. P. Sanders observes, "There may be more than one level of explanation for Paul's attitude toward the law."[24] The following reconstruction responds to Sanders's invitation to speculate on these matters.

First, Paul was probably an active participant in the efforts to proselytize Judaism in the Hellenistic environment. In his work as a Hellenistic Jew he would have become keenly aware of the practical obstacle presented by the law in the attempt to convert pagans. Non-Jews were especially, and quite understandably, put off by the prospect of circumcision. The law, then, would have been seen to stand in conflict with the principle of universalism. We may assume that Paul's dissatisfaction with the excessive demands of the law, which became a major issue in Antioch, was already evident before he became a Christian. As an active Pharisee we may also assume that Paul had experienced a certain amount of anxiety over the state of his own righteousness before the law. He might well have become convinced, as other Jews had, that, no matter how hard one tried, it was humanly impossible to comprehend, let alone fulfill, the whole law. The law had become so cumbersome by Paul's time that it was becoming oppressive. We might see here in Paul the same element of anxiety that Luther experienced in relation to the demands of the sacramental system in late medieval Christianity. This second level of dissatisfaction with the law was no doubt one of Paul's burdens before his conversion and, indeed, if the analogy with Luther is extended, may have been a contributing factor in his conversion. On practical grounds, therefore, Paul had probably come to see the implausibility of the legalistic Covenant even before his association with Christians. But Paul's pre-Christian critique of the law had probably also gone further than mere practical considerations. Just how much of the apocalyptic worldview Paul had absorbed before his conversion to Christianity cannot be precisely known, but we can assume that his Hellenistic environs (perhaps in addition to his own physical limitations) had convinced him that the world was under the influence of powerful evil forces of cosmic dimensions. It must have occurred to him that merely keeping the law was an inadequate bootstrap instrument of salvation against evil forces of cosmic magnitude. Clearing weeds out of the fields may be important for assuring a good crop, but how effective is even the most assiduous weeding against the forces of wind, hail, and fire? Even before he became a Christian, Paul must have come to believe that nothing short of a direct and decisive intervention of God could counteract the evil of this world.

These are the elements of Paul's religious quest on the eve of his conversion to Christianity. What is difficult to miss is his conviction of the implausibility, both practical and theoretical, of the law as an expression of the conditions of salvation. Yet Paul, like his contemporary Philo, was a *Jew* and could not fathom a satisfaction of his quest outside the distinctiveness of the Covenant community. Here we have, then, the elements of tension between plausibility and distinctiveness which were to generate a new mode of Covenant piety.

Paul found in the messianic claims of the Christians the direct intervention of God against the powers of evil that he had come to expect. In the crucifixion of Jesus the cosmic saving event had already taken place, and in his resurrection as the first fruit of the new order salvation had been achieved for all humanity (I Corinthians 15:12–28). After his conversion to this new perspective, Paul's estimation of the law moved to a new level of understanding: now the law takes on a Christological interpretation. In light of the Christ event, the inadequacy of the law is more clearly seen. The law is a reality of history, that is, it belongs properly *in the realm of history*, in the realm of flesh. But God's saving event in Christ has *ended* history. Now we live in the power of the Spirit, in the realm of the suprahistorical. The battle is over, the turning point is already behind us. Of what use, then, is the historical law in the posthistorical kingdom? The law is just fine, as laws go, but for Paul the domain of the law does not go beyond God's intervention in Christ, for in this act the domain of the Spirit has superseded history and its laws. Paul rejects the idea that the law is an adequate expression of the conditions for the eternal existence that God has promised to all humanity. The law has value only because the situation for Christians is still ambiguous. Christians have, as it were, one foot in history and one foot in eternity. God's final transformation of the cosmos must await Christ's return, and until then, as long as the historical flesh remains, the law should be respected as a guide. It is still God's law, but it is not an instrument of transcendence into the New Covenant of eternal survival: "He is the one who has given us the qualifications to be the administrators of this new covenant, which is not a covenant of written letters but of the Spirit: the written letters bring death, but the Spirit gives life" (II Corinthians 3:6).

The New Covenant, the new conditions of existence, are precisely the conditions of Christ's death and resurrection. And these very same conditions must be fulfilled in order for individuals to gain entrance into the kingdom of eternal salvation. The New Covenant community is the Body of Christ, and in order to be "in" the New Covenant, one must participate in Christ's death and resurrection through baptism: "You have been taught that when we were baptised in Christ Jesus we were baptised in his death; in other words, when we were baptised we went into the tomb with him and joined him in death, so that as Christ was raised from the dead by the Father's glory, we too might have a new life" (Romans 6:3–4).

What we have here is very clearly a transposition of the Covenant tradition from its legal foundations to baptismal foundations. The new mode of Covenant piety, the Christological mode, is also the baptismal mode. And as the following passage makes clear, the baptismal mode preserves the distinctiveness of the Covenant (that is, the posterity of Abraham) as well as advancing its universal promise for the salvation of all humanity:

> Before faith came, we were allowed no freedom by the Law; we were being looked after till faith was revealed. The Law was to

be our guardian until the Christ came and we could be justified by faith. Now that that time has come we are no longer under that guardian, and you are, all of you, sons of God through faith in Christ Jesus. All baptised in Christ, you have all clothed your-selves in Christ, and there are no more distinctions between Jew and Greek, slave and free, male and female, but all of you are one in Christ Jesus. Merely by belonging to Christ you are the posterity of Abraham, the heirs he was promised.

[Galatians 3:23–29]

Paul's rejection of the law as an adequate expression of the conditions for survival was an extraordinarily radical step. He followed this line because he was absolutely convinced that new conditions for existence prevailed. But Paul was not the first radical in the Covenant tradition. With Paul, as with previous transpositions, the continuity of the tradition invests itself in a radical departure from the conventions of the past.

The Christological mode of Covenant piety extends the dualism and the determinism of apocalyptic, but it rejects the legalistic method of atonement typical of Jewish apocalyptic. Instead, it proclaims a new logic of salvation. God is still the source of existence, and he still promises survival of the old eon to the faithful but under new conditions. God had intervened in history in a final way to defeat his foes through the death and resurrection of his Son. This death and resurrection mark the beginning of the new eon, with the final transformation to follow shortly. Meanwhile, Jesus has already entered into the eternal kingdom and may be followed there by those who join in his death and resurrection through baptism.

Dogmatic Mode

Despite Paul's disparaging remarks about the "covenant of written letters," the Christian church soon found itself pressed by circumstances into a course of development toward its own form of legalism. By the end of the second century, the core of Christian piety would shift from the baptismal experience to emphasize more explicitly its cognitive and moral implications. These developments took place as the Christian proclamation adjusted itself to the demands of its Hellenistic environment.

With the passing of time Christians became increasingly aware that their own interpretation of the Covenant tradition could not be reconciled with mainstream Judaism. Tensions between Christian and non-Christian Jews increased steadily until the Roman destruction of Jerusalem in A.D. 70. By this time the Christians were already sufficiently aloof from establishment Judaism to remain neutral throughout the struggle with Rome. After this point the Christian position in Palestine was severely impaired, and efforts were thereafter concentrated in the Diaspora. But Jewish-Christian relations did not improve. Scarcely a decade after the destruction of the Jerusalem temple, Christianity was declared a heresy in synagogue liturgy: "May the Nazarenes and the heretics be suddenly destroyed and removed from the book of life."[25] By the end of the century the heresy had been fixed by the Academy at Jamnia.[26] And for their part, the Christians found themselves declaring that they were the true heirs to the ancient Covenant (compare Matthew, Hebrews) and that Jews who were not also Christians would be forsaken by God. Certainly by A.D. 135, when Bar Kochba led a Jewish revolt against Roman legions, there was little to salvage in the relations between Christians and Jews. Christianity was now, in the minds of Roman officials, Jewish authorities, and Christians themselves, a separate entity.

The year A.D. 135 represents a turning point of a different order as well. It marks the effective demise of apocalyptic as a genre of literature among both Jews and Christians. Jewish nationalistic hopes, sustained by apocalyptic, had now been vitiated. And Christian hopes for the return of Jesus, also sustained by apocalyptic enthusiasm, were increasingly questioned in the Gentile communities. The parting of the ways with Judaism coincided with demands that the Christian proclamation be made more plausible to its Hellenistic audience. Thus, as the church struggled to fix its identity, both negatively against Judaism and positively against the Hellenistic background, it was drawn more deeply into the thought forms of the Greco-Roman world.

As the Christian church extended its proclamation throughout the Hellenistic environment, it encountered both external and internal challenges that would produce a prolonged crisis of plausibility and distinctiveness. In the context of this crisis the identity of the church was finally worked out, bringing the Covenant community to a new mode of piety.

Some historians believe that Christianity was first declared illegal during the reign of Nero (A.D. 54–68). Tradition has it that Nero accused Christians of arson to displace blame for the burning of Rome from his own shoulders. Whether or not this is true, there were several executions of Christians before the end of the first century. The general policy of Roman officials was not to search out all Christians and put them to the sword, but rather to persecute only those who somehow attracted public attention. Christians were regarded by many Romans as "haters of the human race" because they did not participate fully in the public life of the Empire and because they obstinately refused to recognize Roman gods. Their blasphemy was taken as a threat to Rome because it might offend the gods and bring their wrath upon the Roman state. Christians were no different from Jews on this score, but they were becoming more visible as a result of their aggressive missionary efforts. Christians, then, were held to be atheists by their external critics, but they were suspected of other offenses as well, including gross superstition, incest, cannibalism, infanticide, and conspiracy. Opposition seems to have been especially keen among Roman elites. We must bear in mind that cultured Romans were highly chauvinistic about their culture, so that a foreign religion of the lower classes that happened also to be a derivative of Judaism would have been subject to a fair amount of prejudice. But the Greco-Roman criticism of Christianity was not entirely prejudicial. As Christianity became more visible, there began to appear a few intellectual critiques from pagans who had taken the time to investigate the claims of Christians and to evaluate their plausibility.

In response to the criticisms of the pagan world, both prejudicial and reasoned, a tradition of Christian apologetics began to emerge in the second century. There were by this time several Christians who were sophisticated enough in Hellenistic letters to meet the critics on their own intellectual turf to argue for the rational defense of the faith. The stakes were high for these pioneers of the tradition of Christian theology; Christians were being martyred for the faith, and as a result there was much to be gained by a demonstration of its plausibility.

The most famous of the second-century apologists was Justin the Martyr. In many ways Justin set the tone for a new Christian attitude toward classical culture. He argued that Christianity was the "true philosophy," and he fixed upon the Greek concept of *logos* to show that in Christianity there is encountered a full disclosure of what the best Greek philosophers had already apprehended in part. Justin's arguments worked both ways. He set out to demonstrate that pagans should find nothing distasteful in the Christian proclamation, but as his works were also (primarily!) read by Christians, his arguments had a secondary impact in their suggestion that Christians should find little objectionable in classical culture. But Justin's conciliatory stance toward Hellenistic thought was not universally shared among Christians. Indeed, his own student, Tatian, and later Tertullian, emphasized the radical contrasts between Christianity and pagan culture. Yet these efforts to drive a wedge between Athens and Jerusalem were not unambiguously successful, for they deepened the commitment of Christian apologists to resolving theological issues by using the language and thought forms of Hellenistic culture, and therefore they further advanced the process of syncretism.

While there remained considerable external challenges to the plausibility of Christianity, these were no more threatening to the church's integrity than the challenge of internal diversity. As the Christian mission moved forward, it was inevitable that variations on its teaching would emerge, and as variations appeared, the church developed theological and administrative measures to control them. At the opening of the second century, we might say, the church found itself in a position not unlike that of the Covenant community at Kadesh; as the community grew larger and more varied, it was pressured to produce standards of order and measures of enforcement.

Of particular alarm to many early Christians was the persistence with which Gnostic tendencies remained in the church. Gnosticism is an extraordinarily complex phenomenon whose details cannot detain us here. It will do to describe Gnosticism as a form of speculative mysticism whose origins appear to be as much psychological as historical. Gnosticism presents individuals with a scheme for salvation based on the disclosure of secret knowledge (gnosis). Gnostic cosmology and anthropology are radically dualistic; evil matter (body) is opposed to benign spirit (soul). The soul of an individual becomes imprisoned by matter and finds its release by apprehending specially revealed knowledge from the spirit world. This knowledge is brought by a messenger who appears in human form but who, in reality, is a celestial being. When grafted to Christianity, Gnosticism produced distortions in the doctrines of creation, sin, resurrection, and Christology—creation became an event of great evil, sin became a lack of saving knowledge, resurrection of the body was denied, and Christ became nonhuman.

As the church struggled against Gnostic heresies throughout the second and third centuries, it continued in the direction of a more systematic articulation of orthodox teachings, a process of theological refinement which was characterized by increased reliance upon the intellectual resources of Hellenistic culture. Thus, internal challenges to the distinctive Christian proclamation actually pushed forward the program of hellenizing Christianity. But the challenge of Gnosticism was only one factor in the church's struggle to maintain its integrity against a relentless barrage of questions. There were questions about correct teachings regarding the nature of Jesus and his relations with God, questions about Jesus' failure to return as promised, questions about the proper conduct of worship, questions about morality, questions about the status of those committing sins after baptism, and questions about many more issues. These questions had to be answered, and the more successful the Christian mission was, the more frequent and varied the questions became. And so it became necessary to define and legitimate the structures of authority which could speak to these various questions in a unified voice. If the church failed in this challenge, its unity would be lost. But it did not fail. In the process of drawing distinctions between orthodoxy and heresy, the church also achieved a new self-understanding; a doctrine of the church itself became a necessary correlate to doctrines concerning God, creation, Jesus, sin, and so forth.

Early in the second century, Ignatius had established the authority of church leaders: "Similarly are all to respect the deacons as Jesus Christ and the bishops as a copy of the Father and the presbyters as the council of God and the band of the apostles. For apart from these no group can be called a church."[27]

Later in the same century, Irenaeus linked the authority of the bishops to the authority of the apostles to create the doctrine of apostolic succession. Those bishops, therefore, who stand in a line of succession from the apostles reign as supreme arbiters over the church's doctrine and discipline. Christ entrusted the faith to his apostles, and these apostles had transmitted this deposit of faith to the bishops of the churches they founded. The authority of the bishops was therefore the authority of Christ himself. It was the bishops who had the power to answer any and all questions; the bishops *were* the church and the church *was* Christ. Outside the church there was no salvation, for to be outside the church was to be disunited from Christ. It was also in the authority of the bishops to declare which scriptures would be authentic and which formulations of faith would be orthodox. The bishops were becoming the principal agents of meme selection.

By the end of the second century, then, the structures of ecclesiastical authority were in place. Although there would continue to be modifications of detail, the church came into the third century, the century of expansion, equipped with the elements it would need to manage even greater diversity. These elements of authority were the apostolic bishops, a canon of scriptures authorized and interpreted by them, and a formula of faith (baptismal creed), also authorized by them. These elements carried the force of standards by which theological expression and moral behavior would be judged. They were brought into being because of the need to enforce conformity of thought and behavior, a need exposed by tendencies toward divergence in the church. Thus the church, already in the second century, was rapidly developing a system for "laying down the law."

The church was also developing the means for enforcing its orthodoxy: the penitential system. By the mid-second century the practice of penance was well established in the church as a manner of dealing with postbaptismal sin. The sacrament of baptism was understood to remove the consequences of all previous sin as one entered into the New Covenant, but as it happened, Christians continued to commit sins after their baptism and, as one's baptism could not be repeated, there emerged the sacrament of penance. This took place through a public confession of sin and expression of repentance, after which the penitent was excluded from communion in the church for a specified period of time. Exactly which sins required the redress of this ceremony and how long the period of excommunication was to endure were considered to be pastoral problems. Initially, it seems, the practice of penance was applied to acts of moral wrongdoing, but as intellectual diversity increased in the church, sins of heresy were added. If schismatics did not repent, they were eventually considered apostates, and apostasy was a sin which it was beyond the power of the church to forgive. The choice of unrepentant heretics was a choice for death, for outside the church and its teachings there was no hope of life eternal.

By the and of the second century, the framework of Christian doctrine had come far enough beyond the Pauline teachings to warrant its description as a new mode of Covenant piety. External criticism and internal diversity created new tensions between the plausibility and the distinctiveness of the Christian proclamation, and the church availed itself of the intellectual resources of Hellenistic culture as useful tools on both fronts. Apologetic foreign policy and dogmatic home policy eventually merged to produce the Christian tradition of systematic theology, the new bearer of Covenant piety. The baptismal faith of the Pauline era had given way to the baptismal dogma of the Patristic era. The New Covenant of the Spirit was transposed to a New Covenant of "written letters"; the authority of the Cross became the authority of bishops, scriptures, and creeds. The spontaneous relationship of believer to God would now have to check out theologically before salvation was declared. The dogmatic mode of Covenant piety does not, however, displace the essential features of the Covenant. God is still the source of existence, even though he is apprehended now in the unity of three persons. The meaning of existence remains basically what it was under the terms of the apocalyptic and Christological covenants, that is, existence means the survival of this life and the attainment of eternal life. But the conditions of existence are expressed differently.

To be "in" the Covenant now means to hold the right thoughts, to do the right things, to conform to the teachings of the right books and the right men. To satisfy the conditions of existence means to satisfy the conditions of the church.

I do not mean to imply that the dogmatic tradition which has prevailed in Christian thought since the Patristic age represents a *distortion* of the faith; it represents merely another transposition of the Covenant tradition. If the church had not laid hold of Hellenistic thought forms to develop a consistent and defensible framework of orthodox teachings, it undoubtedly would have been consumed by history after the fashion of the Essenes, Gnostics, and mystery religions.

Summary

The ultimate aim of this book is to point in the direction of reestablishing the conditions of personal wholeness and social coherence in Western culture, and I have argued that this project requires the restoration of myth. I have argued further that any efforts to regenerate myth must of necessity observe the limits of plausibility imposed by the contemporary environment and the limits of distinctiveness imposed by the tradition. This chapter set out to survey the latter. The survey is incomplete, for by breaking off at the end of the second century I ignore many subsequent attempts to transpose the Covenant tradition. A complete survey would include later Judaism, post-Reformation Christianity, and, of course, Islam. But I have attempted not to provide an exhaustive history of the tradition but rather to survey a few of its most critical periods. From this survey several conclusions appear to be justified.

1. The general approach I am following in this book, that is, to reconcile plausibility and distinctiveness, is a salient characteristic of the tradition itself, so that the task at hand may be seen as the very same one taken up by all those who have wanted to "preserve the faith" of the Judaeo-Christian tradition.

2. The distinctive feature or "essence" of the Judaeo-Christian tradition has been, from its inception, the notion of Covenant as an expression of the conditions of existence.

3. In its efforts to maintain essential continuity with its distinctive tradition, the Covenant community has, as circumstances demanded, taken radical departures from the conventions of its past. We have called these turning points "transpositions of Covenant piety."

4. A survey of these transpositions shows that they are responses to environmental changes (social, political, and intellectual) which occasion new understandings of one or more of the following variables:
   a. the source of existence
   b. the meaning of existence
   c. the conditions under which existence is achievable.

5. The one feature that remains fixed in these transpositions is the preoccupation of the Covenant community with survival, or continued existence. This feature is evident from the ultimate stress laid upon:
   a. awareness of the conditions of existence
   b. commitment to fulfilling these conditions.

At the end of the World War II, Dietrich Bonhoeffer sowed a whole crop of theological activity with a single question. He asked, "Who is Christ for a world come of age?"[28] The question provoked response because it was clearly focused upon contemporary tensions between plausibility and distinctiveness. Bonhoeffer wanted to preserve the distinctiveness of the Christian proclamation in terms that would be plausible to the modern world. I think it must now be seen that, with all due respect to Bonhoeffer, he had the question dead wrong. His question is wrong because he mistook the skin for the wine. The task of preserving the Covenant tradition is to preserve not the distinctiveness of a particular *mode* of Covenant piety but to preserve the *Covenant*. The central question must therefore be: *what is the Covenant for a world come of age?* That is, what can existence mean for us? What are the conditions for achieving existence? How can we effectively elicit commitments to achieving existence? Only by responding to these questions can we claim to be the true heirs of Abraham.

5

The Limits of
Plausibility

The Church disowned, the tower overthrown, the bells up-
turned, what have we to do
But stand with empty hands and palms turned upwards
In an age which advances progressively backwards?
—*T. S. Eliot, "The Rock"*

The tone of this book is about to change. Thus far I have
been trying to "read" the intellectual history of Western culture from the standpoint of a natural historian of culture. But
henceforth I aim to speak with more personal engagement. If
the reader is unprepared to make allowances for occasional
excesses, then this may be a good point to part company. Yet
I hope the reader will stay, for in these remaining chapters the
foregoing discussion is brought to bear upon the contemporary
crisis of amythia. At this point the voice of the natural history
of culture shifts to the voice of philosophy. If the natural historian of culture describes the differential survival of meanings
(memes) in a cultural tradition, then the philosopher evaluates
the memes and attempts to influence their selection. In fact,
I would define the vocation of philosophy in terms of this as-
piration to influence the fundamental meanings in a tradition.
The vocation of philosophy is to countervail amythia—that is,
to strive toward establishing the cognitive conditions for personal wholeness and social coherence by advancing reasoned
arguments in support of some meanings and in opposition to
others. The careful reader will not have been fooled by the thin
veil concealing this rather bumptious ambition to declare the
standards of acceptable meaning for Western culture. But now
my motives are fully disclosed, and in their defense I offer only

160

the assertion that they are inherent in the vocation of philosophy.

There is no longer any point in being mealymouthed about it; the personal metaphor of God is dead. To continue to talk as if our world were in the caring hands of a transcendent intelligence takes us well beyond the acceptable limits of plausibility in contemporary culture. This is a serious matter, as I hope is clear from the previous discussion of amythia. But serious as it is, I see no reason for not taking the death of God completely in stride. There is nothing to be gained by overreaction to the death of the personal metaphor. A generation ago when the death of God was making headlines those who accepted the idea typically responded in one of two ways.[1] Some found cause for great melancholy—now that God is dead, the full weight of responsibility for the world falls upon human shoulders. Others leapt for joy—now that God is dead, we are free at last to create our own destiny. Both reactions reveal a dim historical perspective on the death of God; both see the event way out of historical proportion, as if there were something absolutely unique about it. I do not want to play down the importance of the event for the Judaeo-Christian tradition, but neither do I want to suggest that it is *the* decisive turning point in the history of the Covenant community.

As strange, challenging, and ambiguous as our moment in history is, we should be able to recognize its features. We have been here before. We of the Covenant community—I am using "we" in a broadly inclusive sense here, to represent all who have been directly or indirectly shaped by the Covenant tradition—we of the Covenant community know this moment from our memory of the wilderness when it was suicidal to turn back and utterly hopeless to press on. We know this moment from our memory of being newcomers in the land of Canaan when we wondered how to make crops grow and how to keep terrifying cosmic forces in harmony. We know this moment from our memory of the lawlessness in the last days of the confederacy when we longed for a new order of government. We know this moment in history because we remember how it was to try to carry on singing when the temple lay in ashes. We remember our ambivalence when we returned to a hopelessly reconstructed homeland. We have been here before with our brother Saul, the Pharisee, who languished with us under a leviathan system of legal constraints. And we recall our frustration when Jesus failed to return to us and when the Romans ridiculed us.

This is a rare moment in history; there is nothing routine about it. But it is not unique. We have lost our bearings before. God's death is nothing to be sad *or* happy about. His was a good life, and he died full of years and honors. But the Covenant tradition does not have to die with him. Did the tradition die when the temple burned? When it burned again? We can still recover our bearings—not necessarily, to be sure, but if we poise ourselves once again between memory and anticipation, between distinctiveness and plausibility, between the corpses of the past and the embryos of the future, and if we quicken our senses, there is a good chance.

A brief reminder is called for here. This book pretends to specify not a new mode of Covenant piety but only the limits or coordinates within which a new expression of the faith might stand a chance of capturing the modern imagination and thereby restoring the conditions of myth. Again, the object is to *commission* a new mythopoetic venture, not to engage in the process of mythmaking itself. We might think of the task in terms of commissioning an architectural firm to build a home for us. The architects will need a few things to go on, a few suggestions, if the home is to meet our needs and likes. They will have to know something about the building site, the interests, activities, and aesthetic proclivities of the occupants, the financial parameters, and so on. In the last chapter we surveyed the Covenant tradition to give our mythmakers some idea of how the tradition has developed. In terms of the analogy, we showed the architects through the houses we have occupied in the past to point out what features we liked and disliked about them, why we moved from one to the next, and so on. What was learned in this visit will be useful to the architects in laying out specific features for the "next in a series." In the present chapter we are making a kind of site visit to determine the limits which the contemporary intellectual landscape will impose on the work.

Our question is, if not simple, at least straightforward: How can we continue to affirm the Covenant under the conditions of the death of God? When the Psalmist asked, "How can we sing one of Yahweh's hymns in a pagan country?" he was really asking the same question. And the response of the Covenant community was then to reassess the meaning of its existence. Not a bad place to start.

The Meaning of Existence

We have seen that the meaning of existence has been a variable in the Covenant tradition. Early in the tradition to exist meant to live safely in the promised land, to have children and food, and to have them with assurance and abundance. It was modest but sufficient. Later on in the tradition, existence came to have a larger meaning. In the period of the monarchy, to exist meant to exist as a nation, as a significant historical entity. And later still, when the nation was destroyed, existence was defined in terms of fulfilling a universal historic mission. There were no positive expectations of an afterlife beyond historical existence. When an individual died, he/she was removed to what scholars like to call the "shadowy existence" of Sheol. To exist after death in Sheol was not really to exist. Existence was to live in history. But then, under the influence of Persian culture, existence came to mean a form of life beyond history. And then gradually the meaning of existence was further individualized and expressed in terms of surviving the death of the body to live forever in an eternal realm. This body, this history, this life were insignificant by comparison with the real, transhistorical, spiritual life of God's kingdom. This most recent variation on the theme of existence is the one still promised in the dogmatic mode of Covenant piety. Our task is not to pick through the history of the Covenant tradition to determine which of its former meanings best suits the contemporary cognitive landscape. This landscape has its own features which tell us what "existing" can and cannot mean. We are, of course, primarily concerned with what it can and cannot mean for human beings to exist.

Leaving aside epistemological problems for the moment, we can say that among scientists something very close to a consensus prevails, namely, that reality consists of a hierarchy of natural systems.[2] That is to say, matter is organized into various levels of complexity which can be described as levels of existence. This hierarchy of natural systems becomes a bit murky at the extreme macro and micro levels of understanding, but insofar as human beings are concerned, we can say without any fear of contradiction that it is pure unacceptable nonsense to speak of human existence outside the context of natural systems, biological systems in particular. Human existence, in every intelligible sense, is a part of nature. One of the "givens" of the contemporary cognitive landscape is that there is no intelligible realm beyond nature. Here is exposed the central feature of implausibility inherent in the dogmatic mode of Covenant piety. In this mode "true" existence is imagined to be beyond nature. "Spirit" is imagined to be something that can exist independently of any natural systems of organized matter. But to the contemporary mind any talk of transcending nature is implausible and will therefore not find a place in an acceptable expression of faith. This statement does *not* mean, however, that we may no longer speak of transcendence; it means only that transcendence must be seen as a natural phenomenon. To speak of intranatural transcendence is intelligible (for example, "the existence of a dog transcends the existence of a stone"), but to speak of transcendence into some supernatural and nonmaterial realm of existence is wildly fantastic to the modern mind.

What must be clearly understood about the hierarchy of biological systems is that "higher" levels of organization and function depend absolutely upon "lower" levels. Thus, to choose a quaint example, it would be odd to speak of the possibility of the intricate breathing techniques of a yogi apart from a respiratory system. To speak of breathing independent of a respiratory system is unintelligible nonsense. In the same way, it makes no sense to the modern mind to speak of the higher functions of human existence, say, intelligence, as taking place apart from lower levels of organization. There can be no cognitive experience whatsoever apart from a living brain. This statement has decisive implications for the traditional doctrine of subjective immortality. The dogmatic mode of Covenant piety asks us to believe that when an individual dies biologically he or she will go on having experiences. This is pure fantasy. When I die my brain will cease to function, and my experiences at that point will be indistinguishable from those of a year before my birth, that is, there will not be any. There is no individual psychological or spiritual existence after death. The individual or subjective survival of biological death is not something which can be included in a plausible understanding of existence.

Even when the doctrine of subjective immortality is shown to be doubtful on theoretical grounds, there remain those who defend it on practical grounds. The assumption is that without the expectation of an afterlife there can be no source of hope in this life. To this line of defense it must be objected, first, that it denies genuine hope among the many generations of the Covenant community who lived before the doctrine of immortality appeared. And second, it assumes a correlation between hopefulness and expectation of a life after death. I seriously doubt that any such correlation can be demonstrated. Hope is as evident and as durable among agnostics as it is among traditional Christians. But it might also be suggested that the practical territory belongs to those who dispute the doctrine of immortality. Here one might argue that expectations of a life after death are conducive to attitudes of depreciation toward *this* life. If the "other side" is all that really matters, then whence comes the motivation to exert oneself for the improvement of conditions on "this side"? The end point in this argument is to declare that belief in a life after death is a dangerously maladaptive meme, for it displaces energies away from those activities which are conducive to survival in the natural environment.

Architects of the New Covenant should be well advised that the test of plausibility cannot be passed by expressing the meaning of human existence in terms that include the subjective survival of death. It fails because it violates the limits of plausibility set forth in the biological infradiscipline. But there is no need to stop here. The doctrine of subjective immortality is just one strand in a much larger fabric of thought about human existence. The controlling meme for much of our thinking about human existence has been the idea of individuality itself. The idea of a subjective survival of death is merely an extension of our emphasis upon subjectivity before death. Visions of life after death are expressions of a desire to extend life as we know it here and now. And we know our existence here and now in terms of its individuality. We normally do not think of our bodies in terms of a congress of biological systems. We regard the body as a unit, an individual thing; my body *has* a heart, lungs, and so forth. And the same principle holds for our perception of ourselves as persons; we define ourselves not by incorporation but rather by distinction, by autobiography rather than by history. The self—that is, the subject—is an individual, a discrete unit, an atom. We even attribute philosophically ancient atomic properties to the self: indivisible, indestructible, eternal, complete and unique; relations with others are accidental, not constitutive.

The subjective definition of human existence is an old one which entered the Judaeo-Christian tradition by the process of Hellenization and was thence folded into the dogmatic mode of Covenant piety. And it has been with us ever since, deeply embedded in the psychology of Western culture through its religious, artistic, political, economic, and social expressions. This ideal of individuality, I suggest, is a less soluble meme in Western consciousness than the idea of God. Perhaps this is already proven by the fact that atheism is now a common condition among us, but its anthropological equivalent is virtually unknown; we do not even have a word for it (anindividualist?).

Because of the ultimate importance of individualism throughout Western culture, we might regard it as a "given" in the landscape of modern mentality. If so, then any attempt at a plausible rendition of the Covenant tradition would necessarily involve the notion of individuality in its expression of what it means to exist as a human being. Are we so thoroughly conditioned to identify our existence with individual subjectivity that an alternative definition of existence would appear unintelligible and therefore implausible? I wonder. Might it rather be that we already feel the implausibility of individualism but find ourselves unable to do anything about it; that we presently languish under the tyranny of subjectively defined existence and continue to do so only because we lack the resources to express existence otherwise? There is something to this notion. We now experience our subjectivity as a burden. This is a symptom of amythia. Cut off from the public network of shared commitments and objective values, we find ourselves alienated in a universe of oppressive privacy, in a kind of self-enslavement.

Have we not been here before, we of the Covenant community? When the temple in Jerusalem was destroyed and the Jews were hauled off to Babylon, they lacked the resources for expressing the meaning of their existence: how can we sing . . . ? So what did they do? They drilled themselves deep into the only thing left, the law, and applied themselves feverishly in an attempt to satisfy its every demand. How is it different with us? When God died and took objectivity and "his image" with him, we were left without adequate resources for a new expression of existence, and so we turned toward the self in a feverish attempt to satisfy its every demand. The contemporary tyranny of the self is no different from the ancient tyranny of the law. Eventually, of course, the early Christians found the resources for a new definition of existence. But here the similarities end, for we are still waiting, "with empty hands and palms turned upwards." Here we fall speechless and turn with hollow anticipation to the architects of the New Covenant. Perhaps they can find the resources.

The implausibility of individualism is not something that comes to us entirely as a vague suspicion. We have learned from the social sciences that the self is not atomic at all but rather a socially constructed fiction. My "self," the character of my thoughts and attitudes, the substance of my subjective experience, is never free of social influences. In fact, apart from social influences, we find little that we might want to call a self. What we know about feral children (and it is mercifully little) suggests that they are not human at all except in the minimal sense of physiology. To exist as a human being, then, is to exist in a community of human beings. Radical individuality can be at best a "shadowy existence," not something to be hoped for in the New Covenant.

I have been attempting to argue here that any attempt to transpose the Covenant tradition must, if it hopes to make sense to the contemporary mind, avoid expressing the human condition in terms that will involve supernaturalism and individualism. A contemporary Covenant will have currency only if it defines what human existence is and can be in the context of natural systems and social relations. The limits of plausibility require, therefore, that the New Covenant be *monistic* and *communal* in form. At this point it will be useful to digress momentarily to clarify these formal features further.

All living organisms make their livelihood in transactions with an external environment, which is to say that survival is a bipolar proposition. This vital polarity is universal; that is, wherever there is a living organism, there is an opposing environment. The biological terms for describing this vital polarity are *crisis* and *homeostasis*; when a life need (for example, fear, hunger) is experienced, the organism is found in a state of crisis, whereupon it seeks to achieve a state of homeostasis (equilibrium), either by eliminating a threat posed by the environment or by appropriating and converting resources from the environment. This fundamental distinction between crisis and homeostasis is undoubtedly the ultimate biological foundation for all human notions of good and evil. And it is also, I suggest, the biological source of all schemes of salvation. Schemes of salvation (and every myth has one) present humanity with some generalized polarity of terms which are the structural equivalents of crisis and homeostasis. Familiar examples would include sin/grace, bondage/freedom, inauthentic/authentic, oppression/liberation, ignorance/ knowledge, lost/found, and so forth. And every scheme of salvation expresses a way of moving from one state of existence to the other. Thus one is moved from a state of sin to a state of grace or from a state of bondage to a state of freedom, and so forth, by some activity that is specified in the myth. It is by virtue of this bipolar symbolism that myth holds such profound attraction for human beings for in these symbols, and in the process of transcending from one state to the other, there is expressed the logic of the life process itself. In a very direct way, then, participation in the logic of a myth brings forth a recognition of the meaning of life, but it also grants an endowment of hope vis-à-vis the environment. The biological payoff in the logic of myth is a sense of confidence for enduring all states of crisis.

Having seen the deep structure of all religious thought, we now look at variations in forms of participation. There are two sets of variables here. A particular scheme of salvation may be either individualistic or communal, and it may be either monistic or dualistic. We have seen examples of each of these formal options in our survey of the Covenant tradition. These options relate to the movement from a state of deficiency (crisis) to a state of wholeness (homeostasis). In the individual form of participation, the transcendence from one state to another is individualized, that is, the deficient state is defined in terms of a personal deficiency to be overcome by some form of personal transformation. Thus, for example, in the Christological mode of piety, the individual is transformed by baptism from a state of sin to a state of grace. In contrast, the tribal mode of piety involves a transformation of the entire community from a state of bondage and homelessness to a state of freedom and dwelling upon the land. In the nationalistic mode, too, the transformation from one state of existence (no nation) to another (nationhood) is a communal transformation. The direction that is taken on the individual-communal option will reveal how the salvation scheme defines what it means to exist as a human being. The individual option stresses the subjectivity of human existence, while the communal option stresses our social character. In saying that individualism is implausible, we are saying that the New Covenant must address the contemporary situation by defining human existence collectively. In particular, this will mean that the focus of morality in the New Covenant will stress social responsibility by transmitting memes by which we see ourselves first and foremost as members and *then only* as individuals.

Salvation schemes also express themselves in dualistic or monistic terms. Monistic schemes view the movement from the state of deficiency to the state of wholeness in terms of a continuum, while dualistic schemes view the movement in terms of transcendence from one ontological realm to another. In both cases the perceived environmental threats to existence are removed, but the process of removal is fundamentally different. In a monistic scheme the deficiency is removed by activities which *reduce* threats. Thus in the cosmic mode of piety, the danger of chaos is removed and the abundance of the earth is assured by enacting a ritual. In a sense this process strives to achieve a purification or a perfection of the present order. In the national mode the threat of the present order is reduced (and the future forever secured) by God's promise to keep David in his favor. Alternatively, dualistic schemes symbolize the movement from crisis to homeostasis by a process of *escape* from one order to take up a secure future in an entirely different order. Thus in the apocalyptic mode of piety the threats of this eon will be transcended and the next eon will be free of all evil. Here too, the particular option that is taken on the monistic-dualistic choice will reveal how human existence is defined by the salvation scheme, and further, the choice will be determined by the cosmological resources that mythmakers have at their disposal. In my survey of the Covenant tradition I observed that the salvation scheme shifted from monistic to dualistic under the influence of Persian cosmology. It has already been suggested that contemporary limits of plausibility rule out dualism as an option for the New Covenant, and this is the case because contemporary cosmology defines human existence entirely in the context of natural systems.

We are now in a position to see some of the general features that will accompany a contemporary transposition of the Covenant tradition. The Covenant will be transposed *from* conventions which include the metaphor of God as person and a scheme of salvation which is dualistic and individual *to* conventions whereby God is not a person and salvation is achieved in the context of natural systems and social relations.

There is no ground for complaining that a transposition of this sort will entail any loss whatever to the distinctiveness of the Covenant tradition. It is demonstrably false that the tradition has limited itself exclusively to either the individual form or the dualistic form of salvation. These forms are variables which can be emphasized or de-emphasized at will to suit the limits of plausibility that press upon the Covenant tradition. In our suggestions to the architects of the New Covenant, we are advising against individualism and dualism because they are implausible options. If these options are emphasized, the Covenant will not capture the imagination of contemporary culture, and amythia will continue.

In making these points I have settled on the position that human existence cannot mean more or less than is allowed by natural and social systems of organized matter. And on this point many will jump forth to complain that this is mere reductionism; the doctrine of humanity is hereby reduced to *mere* biological and social limits. The possibility of human transcendence appears to be ruled out; hope of a radically restored creation is extinguished, and salvation is denied. But is it? Earlier I mentioned intranatural transcendence as a way of speaking to the question of hope. It is true that a plausible Covenant can no longer speak of humanity as the kind of being that can transcend biological and social limitations, but nowhere does this view suggest that biological and social limitations are themselves immutable. In fact, we now know that biological and social limitations can be changed radically to make way for a new humanity.[3] We cannot, as individuals, live eternally, but we can make significant progress toward the extension of life both temporally and spatially. It may one day be common for individuals to live on the order of 150 years, and it is conceivable that humans might one day occupy planets of their own making. If we continue to think only in terms of what is possible in our own individual lifetimes, these prospects look thin and science fictional, but when we think of the future primarily as members of a historic community, they begin to appear rich and realistic. In spite of all our problems, the present material welfare of most contemporaries is infinitely superior to that of medieval feudal society. A description of contemporary life would no doubt fall on the ears of wretched medieval serfs as a wild fantasy. And what about the human community? What are its limits? Perhaps under the conditions of a New Covenant, it will again be possible to speak of the universal promise of the Covenant in concrete historical terms. The urgency of the moment challenges us to envision a universal order of opportunity and justice, perhaps a common language, perhaps the prohibition of war, perhaps more efficient and democratic forms of government. Let the architects consider these and even greater possibilities.

By now there are more than a few smirks on readers' faces; shades of innocent Enlightenment optimism and all that. The dogmatic mode of piety may look positively inspiring by comparison to the claptrap that materialist futurists can generate. Well, perhaps, but I assure the reader that I can imagine gloom as easily as I can glory in the future of the human community, and the difference I see is that a Covenant which defines human destiny in exclusively natural and social dimensions is infinitely superior to the supernaturalism of the past for one simple yet powerful reason: it represents a vision of existence which places our hopes where our efforts can make a difference.

Conditions of Existence

We locate human existence in the context of natural systems and social relations. These are merely the coordinates of our nature, and it cannot be said that we have defined human existence and destiny except in the most general way. The specific images and metaphors (memes) to define what we are and what we can be will be left to the invention of the architects of the New Covenant. Because our discussion of human existence has been on a general level, we are restricted in what we can say about the conditions of existence, the actual terms of the Covenant. Still, we are left with a fair amount to think about. We can address the question "What are the conditions beyond which there is no promise of natural and social existence?" Or perhaps we can put the question more positively: what conditions must be fulfilled in order to preserve and enhance natural systems and social relations? With this question before us, on the two tablets of nature and society, we might say, we can begin to see some of the general characteristics of the New Covenant.

First let us consider the table of natural systems. Any longterm hope of sustaining and enhancing human life will obviously have to observe the conditions for a stable environment. The New Covenant will have to find memes for representing the biosphere in sacramental terms. It might even propose special rites that would function to reinforce the solidarity of humanity with natural systems. Population control is another obvious requirement of the New Covenant. This is a delicate matter, since the ultimate commitment of the Covenant community to life cannot easily be reconciled with negative memes concerning human generativity. At the same time the limits of the earth to bear humanity must be obeyed. A possible compromise might be to formally recognize voluntary sterilization and other birth control strategies as the equivalents of sacrifice. The current interest in proper nutrition and physical fitness will continue to be affirmed but somehow apart from the present preoccupation with self-image. Care for the body is an essential condition of existence, and it would not be inappropriate to find ways to reinforce it religiously. Free and adequate health care to all is an absolute prerequisite; to profit from health care will be an offense to the New Covenant as much as the medieval sale of indulgences was to the Gospel. The conquest of disease is an obvious condition of existence. If the New Covenant continues some practice equivalent to the recognition of saints, then chief among them should be those whose efforts have resulted in techniques for the extension of life. Another major condition of existence is the eradication of technologies that threaten the stability of natural systems. Nuclear technology is one that comes directly to mind. If there is an equivalent to heresy in the New Covenant, then certainly those who promote life-threatening technologies should be identified.

What are some examples of social commandments that might be appropriate for the New Covenant? First, much more stress must be laid upon education. Knowledge under the New Covenant should have the glow of righteousness about it. The ultimate importance of education follows from the stress in the tradition laid upon awareness of the Covenant. We take seriously Konrad Lorenz's point that "life is an eminently active enterprise aimed at acquiring both a fund of energy and a stock of knowledge."[4] Education, like health care, is nothing less than a means to life and should be free for all. Another condition of existence is economic equality. Unequal distribution of wealth is a constant source of social and political strife and must therefore constantly be opposed. "Life isn't always fair" is a shibboleth of opportunism. Economically speaking, life is precisely as fair as we will it to be. The community of the New Covenant will affirm this ideal as clearly as the primitive Christian church did. The New Covenant will also take seriously the universal scope of its mission and will therefore dare to envision a day of world order and justice. This is a very long-range goal indeed but one that is within the realm of the plausible. The New Covenant will work toward this goal by subverting nationalism, not by political interference, but by promoting international humanism.

I offer these general characteristics here in the spirit of tentative speculation. These are just some of the features that appear to me to follow from a monistic and communal understanding of human existence. None of these ideals is new; the only novelty here may be the suggestion that they should be elevated to the status of religious doctrine. Each one of these conditions of existence has been legitimated at one point or another by reference to religious principles, but the New Covenant will seek to affirm them as religious principles in themselves. It would therefore not be inappropriate for variations on these themes to appear in creedal form. They will be the girders and the joists of the New Covenant. But their precise character awaits the elaboration of a new root metaphor.

The Source of Existence

Modes of Covenant piety, as I have repeatedly observed, include specific notions about the source of existence as well as the meaning and conditions of existence. These three things, the source, meaning, and conditions of existence, require a high level of internal consistency if the faith they express is to be intelligible. We are now in a position to consider the limits of plausibility which bear upon expressions of the source of existence. I have already offered a critique of the personal metaphor as a way of comprehending God's nature in a previous chapter, and I will not repeat it here. My conclusion was that the personal metaphor has become impotent as a vehicle for transmitting culture because it has lost its power of explanation. But I have also argued here that the task of revitalizing Western culture calls for a transposition of the tradition to a new root metaphor. If not personality, then what? Is some metaphor available to us that can integrate cosmology and morality with sufficient power to elicit the commitment and the sacrificial behavior of individuals?

Before taking up this question directly, it will be useful to ask whether there is any ground for rejecting God talk out of hand, for if so, then to search for new metaphors would be a waste of time. If by the term "God" we understand ourselves to be referring to the source of existence, then it would appear that we are at least justified in the assertion that God exists. If God is the source of existence, and if existence, no matter how defined, is undeniable, then it might be concluded that "God exists" follows necessarily. But does it? Certainly it is meaningful to speak of something that exists without binding ourselves to the claim that its ultimate source exists. All we are compelled to accept is that the source once existed or once emitted existence. If I observe light rays from a distant star, I am justified in positing the erstwhile existence of the star, but as to its present existence, there remains doubt. Even if we find ourselves forced to accept the notion that the source of existence always exists, then we might further inquire about the source of this "existing" source. The standard reply to this query has been that God's existence is its own source. But then, we ask, if a logical twist of this order can be employed when speaking of God, why not use it one step earlier to say that the existence of the world as we know it is its own source? These are all arguments at which philosophical theologians have chipped away since the synthesis of biblical religion and Greek philosophy early in the Christian era. While they may have an arcane attraction as intellectual exercises, all the arguments both for and against the existence of God are notoriously inconclusive and no longer particularly interesting beyond the confines of introductory courses in the philosophy of religion.

The logical confusions which result from attempts to speak meaningfully and positively about the source of existence should be telling us something. Some say what we learn here is that God's existence is the substance of faith; there is no way to demonstrate the existence of God, so we must therefore accept it with the uncritical innocence of a child. This is not merely begging the question but involves us in a totally unacceptable conception of the meaning of faith. The faith of the Covenant community has always meant commitment to fulfilling the conditions of existence, and it must not be reduced to a mere suspension of intellectual faculties. No, the confusions we encounter when speaking of God's existence are telling us something else. They are telling us that we have come to the end of the metaphysical line, that we may no longer use the language of existence to talk about the ultimate source of existence. The trouble is, we do not have nonexistential resources for talking about the source of existence. And when we use our existential language to speak of preexistential realities, we open the floodgates to all sorts of wild fantasies over which we have no reasonable means of control. As Wittgenstein has taught us, we are better off restricting our language to the uses for which it evolved.

But if this line of reasoning is correct, and I believe it is, then we are forced into a corner of profound silence about matters that relate to the existence and nature of God. And if we are compelled to be agnostic about the source of existence, then the task of revitalizing Western culture by transposing the Covenant tradition to a new root metaphor appears forever doomed to failure. Does agnosticism, regardless of how reverent it might be, leave us without license to seek a root metaphor to integrate cosmology and morality? Not necessarily. I accept the fact that contemporary limits of plausibility preclude intelligible discourse about God's existence and nature, but I do not see how this prevents us from discussing God's activity. The New Covenant might be called an agnostic mode of piety, a mode in which there are no metaphors for discourse about God apart from metaphors about creation and history. There is good biblical precedent for this agnostic mode of Covenant piety. We have already seen that the divine name YHWH was not regarded by early Hebrews as expressive of God's nature; his nature was not at their disposal. Yahweh was known only by his works. The Hebrews enforced this "agnosticism" by strictly limiting the very utterance of the divine name. And while the tradition did use the personal metaphor for the source of existence, it was restrained by a refusal to attribute sexuality and other anthropomorphisms to God. There is nothing distinctive in the tradition that is lost by a refusal to speak of God's existence and nature.

We can now return to our original question and ask it in terms of God's activity. Is there a root metaphor of activity that will integrate cosmology and morality? There is, and here I can see no superior alternative to the metaphor of *evolution* itself. Evolution as a metaphor adequately encompasses all aspects of creation; it is not narrowly biological. In the early chapters of this book, we saw how it provided an adequate framework for discussing the prebiotic development of matter as well as the development of living organisms. And we saw that the concept of memes made it possible to speak of cultural evolution as well. Evolution is a plausible way of speaking of both natural systems and social relations. Once we have heard the last of speculation concerning the existence and nature of God, we are left with the metaphor of evolution as the most appropriate way of speaking about the source of existence. It is difficult to imagine a more compelling manifestation of transcendence than that presented to us by the reality of evolution.

Now we are at one of those rare and wonderful points at which philosophers, theologians and scientists all come bounding in together with the same objection: does the metaphor of evolution *really* integrate cosmology and morality? Well, let us see. Evolutionary theory gives us a vision of what is true about the world (cosmology), and it gives us some ideas about how to behave in the world (morality). In this way it presents itself as an adequate root metaphor for myth. To be more precise, evolution tells us how human life came to be on this planet, and it discloses to us the fact that human life has survived by virtue of its awareness of the conditions of its existence and by acting to achieve these conditions. But this reasoning will not stop the critics. They will complain that all the evolutionary theory in the world cannot tell us that human survival is a *good* thing. Evolution may show us what facts and what values were instrumental in bringing about the human life form, but it cannot show us objectively why we ought to behave in such ways as to preserve and enhance human life. It can only do so by adding in the moral assumption that "human life is good." But such an assumption is not a part of evolutionary theory, nor is it a fact. It is a value that is asserted by faith or by authority.

Very well then, I concede that the metaphor of evolution does not conclusively demonstrate the objective value of human survival, but it does demonstrate that human beings are, as a matter of *fact*, biased in the direction of valuing their own survival. It is, in other words, a biological fact that we humans value human existence. And it is also the case, I believe, that this value (that is, "humans ought to survive") is a factual precondition of all values, for it is manifestly clear that brains (organs which evaluate) would never have evolved to the point of moral judgment except by the influence of a principle which can be expressed in the value, "humans ought to survive."

Therefore the moral judgment "humans ought not to survive" can be shown to presuppose its own denial.

So much for logic chopping. There is ultimately no need to refute the naturalistic fallacy in order to restore the perceived objectivity of human values. And perceived objectivity is what counts in averting amythia. What finally matters is getting people to put their lives in the service of common ideals; getting them to see their private concerns as part of something larger and more significant; getting them to sacrifice willingly, to say, "relative to me *this* is more important. . . . to *this* I have no option but to submit." I believe the metaphor of evolution has the potential for capturing the modern imagination in this way, precisely because, in the most general way, it satisfies the demands of both distinctiveness and plausibility. When artfully presented, when fitted with its implications for hope and its call to service, the metaphor of evolution can restore Western culture to its bearings in nature and in history. When artfully presented, evolution can take its place as a controlling meme at the center of the Western intellectual and moral tradition. The logic of human salvation generated from this root metaphor would then become the substance of the religious life, and the conditions of existence that are implicit would become the provender of political discourse. Such a view can restore to Western culture its bearings and its responsibility as a selective agency. A universally shared standard of truth—that is, truth as adaptivity—might emerge to guide Western culture to a new character, as was the case in the formative period of Christian unity. When artfully presented, the root metaphor of evolution can begin a centripetal movement toward a reunification of Western culture and the restoration of personal wholeness and social coherence.

I say again: *when artfully presented*. I have no illusions that anyone reading these chapters or textbooks on evolution might be stirred to the point of self-transcendence and life reorientation. Such inspiration is a task for mythmakers. The ideas presented in the last two chapters have no more force than a finger pointed in the direction of traditional and contemporary resources upon which the architects of the New Covenant are called to reflect. The resources for distinctiveness are seen in the formal character of the Covenant tradition, and the resources for plausibility are seen in the modern scientific world-view. The architects of the New Covenant are challenged to bring these resources to bear upon one another under the threat of amythia and to bring forth the conventions of a new mode of piety.

One additional resource will be required, and that is the courage to reclaim the promised land. The architects of the New Covenant are those many intelligent, informed, and moral men and women who have been estranged from their cultural heritage by its attachment to implausible conventions. Theirs is the task of reentering the churches and synagogues with a radical proposal for transposing the Covenant tradition. Theirs is the task of calling out the Babylonian captors of the Covenant and holding them accountable to the standard of adaptivity. There will be trouble, to be sure, but they will be encouraged by the knowledge that they are the children of the promise.

6

Reclaiming the
Promised Land

Not all those who descend from Israel are Israel; not all the descendants of Abraham are his true children. Remember: It is through Isaac that your name will be carried on, which means it is not physical descent that decides who are the children of God; it is only the children of the promise who will count as the true descendants.

[*Romans 9:7–8*]

In 1799, Friedrich Schleiermacher published a book entitled *On Religion: Speeches to Its Cultured Despisers*. The intended audience of that book included Schleiermacher's own friends, many of whom were disillusioned with the religious life because it appeared to them overly preoccupied with rational dogmatism and moralism. These friends of Schleiermacher, the "cultured despisers" of religion, were heavily influenced by the romantic movement. They were fed up with the arid intellectualism of the Enlightenment. In the *Speeches* Schleiermacher sets out to convince his friends that they are more religious than they suspect. True religion, he says, is not intellectualized dogma, nor is it a collection of moral rules, but true religion can be found only in the deepest experience of the individual. Truly religious people are characterized not by their knowing or their doing but by their *feeling*. Schleiermacher was trying to convince his romantic friends that in their misunderstanding of the religious life they failed to see that they were *themselves* truly religious.

The aim of this chapter, and in a sense the entire book, is consistent with the aim of Schleiermacher's *Speeches*. I want to appeal to all you contemporary men and women who no

180

longer identify with the Judaeo-Christian tradition and to challenge you with the suggestion that you are the true heirs to the Covenant. Some of you are still nominally in the church, but you sometimes think you have no good reason for being there, for much of what the church teaches seems like nonsense to you. Still, maybe all your friends are there, or maybe you think your children ought to be there, or maybe you occasionally resonate to a sermon about starvation in Africa or about the need for disarmament. So you stay. But others of you have left the church completely, some only recently and others perhaps a generation or more ago. Some of you call yourselves atheists and some agnostics, but most of you (and you are vast in numbers) just simply do not think about what the church is saying, or has said, or might say. Your memories of church are memories of stories about events that took place long, long ago, before electricity and radar and space flights and penicillin. You remember warnings and promises about what would happen to you when you died and why it was important for you to be nice to strangers, especially the ones who had been beaten up by robbers and left in a ditch. Maybe you remember some of the best things, like how it felt to hear the organ play and to stand in a crowd and sing great and powerful songs. Or do you remember how the church hall smelled of coffee and good things to eat while the adults visited together and the children chased about having as much fun as possible without spoiling their clothes?

But that was a long time ago. You don't go there anymore; it is too uncomfortable. They get you to say that you believe in things you do not believe in: "God the Father Almighty," "maker of heaven and earth," "his only son our Lord," "born of the virgin Mary," "ascended into heaven," "resurrection of the body," "and life everlasting, Amen." And so you quit going. For some of you it was a conscious decision; you found yourselves glancing about the congregation during a prayer or a hymn, looking at the faces and saying to yourself, "I don't belong with these people anymore. They think differently from me. They live in a totally different world." Some of you were not deliberate about it at all. You just trickled out bit by bit until you discovered one day that you were no longer churchgoers. And oddly, you did not miss it at all—or perhaps what you missed you had found missing long before you quit going. Anyway, deliberate or not, you do not think of yourselves as religious persons anymore. That is, when you get sick you do not think that God is punishing you, and when you do not have a job you do not think that praying about it will do any good, and when you see a picture of Marx or Freud or Darwin, you do not automatically think of the devil. Religious people, you suppose, are okay. That is, they might be quite harmless and well meaning. It is just that they are different; they live in their world and you live in yours.

It really is quite a shame that so many people like your-selves—intelligent, informed, moral men and women—have left the church and for no good reason. Not believing in a personal God is no good reason; not believing in the reality of the devil or the promise of immortality or in the efficacy of prayer are not good reasons for leaving the church. These things have nothing to do with what the church is really about. They are no more essential to the church's true mission than gothic arches and stained glass windows.

Let me make a serious proposal to you. I propose that you go back into the church and take an active role in its future. Yes, I am serious. I say it is your church and that you shirked your responsibility by leaving it in the first place. The church is your inheritance and your responsibility. Think of it this way: suppose a millionaire dies and leaves all his money to a niece named Jane Smith, and when the estate is settled, two women, both named Jane Smith, show up to claim the money. To which would you give it? You would say that the money should go to the niece, to the one who has the best claim, and of course there are ways of checking these things out. Now suppose I tell you that you have a better claim to be the church than all those people you decided you did not belong with? Let us check out your claim. Do you feel that there is something mysterious and wonderful about the fact that something exists rather than nothing at all? If you do, then I ask, do you believe that human life should survive with dignity on this planet? And if you do, then is it your conviction that the future of the human community depends upon awareness of and commit-ment to behaving in a manner consonant with the conditions of its existence? If so, do you profess a commitment to behaving in this manner? If you answer yes to each of these questions, then I say no one has a better claim to be in the church than you have. You are hereby the children of the promise.

You might think this sounds rather minimal. Yes, it is minimal. Moments of radical historical change are often just that, a time for simplification and clear focus. Most of the great moments in our religious history have been moments when the faith has been simplified. The invention of monotheism was a simplification of polytheism, the invention of Christianity was a simplification of Judaism, the Reformation was a simplification of the medieval sacramental system, and so forth. A simplification of the sort I present to you is long overdue.

Have you considered the misfortune that will befall the church if everyone like you were to leave? If all the intelligent, informed, and moral men and women were to leave the church, then the church would fall into the hands of stupid, ignorant, and immoral people. Is this not already happening? Some of you left the church because its view of reality is not sympathetic with the scientific worldview. Now, if everyone did this, then how much sympathy for science would remain in the church? For every person like you who leaves the church, the church moves closer toward an antiintellectual and antiscientific identity. I say that science is no enemy to the church. On the contrary, the scientific worldview is probably the most valuable single resource at the church's disposal. Remember, the faith of the Covenant community is to observe and obey the conditions of human existence, and what better source of this knowledge do we have?

Have you considered the cultural disinheritance that comes with leaving the church? Do you know that whole generations of kids are growing up who will be unable to appreciate Shakespeare and Dante and Milton and Eliot because they do not know the Bible well enough to understand literary allusions to biblical stories? The situation is better in Europe, where religion is studied in the schools, but in America the signs of illiteracy are already clear. The long-term effect of leaving the church is to cut yourselves off from your own past. Think of the American black population for a moment, cut off from their culture and dragged into a situation where they were denied a collective memory. It is a great danger, I say, this unpremeditated rejection of your past. Nothing good can come of it.

But you complain that you do not believe it anymore, so why stay? Again, I say that not believing all that the church teaches is no reason for leaving it. How many scientists left science because they quit believing in ether and phlogiston? You do not have to believe it all in order to accept it. There's a difference. I may not admire my grandfather, but I would not on that account change my surname, nor would I obscure the details of his life from my children. It is their birthright. I cannot name a single black friend of mine who would consider moving back to Africa, but they are all dead serious about recovering what they can of their lost culture. If you did not believe what the church professed, then why did you not make some noise about it? Why did you not say, "Hey, that stuff about the virgin birth isn't true. Let's quit saying it is!"? Why did you not say that instead of pulling out and letting the church go on saying foolish things? You must know enough about church history to see that the church *is* what the church *says* it is, but if people like yourselves just leave instead of forcing it to say sensible things, then who is to blame for its foolishness? The church has consistently maintained that its proclamation has been truthful. Now, there are two ways to lay claim to the truth. One is to prove what you are saying is true, and the other is to say what has been proven true. The church has followed both methods, but it will not follow the latter without pressure. The sad thing is that too many people like yourselves found it easier just to leave.

I seriously want you to consider going back, not just because it is your birthright and because you embody the essence of Covenant faith. You should go back because the church is really the best place to start the work of revitalizing Western culture. There is no better place for engineering a transposition of Covenant piety than in the Covenant community. The church is the repository of traditional resources for a new myth, and you, my friends, represent the contemporary resources. It is unlikely that Western culture can find its bearings unless we bring these resources together. Oh, there will be trouble enough, for sure. But we can hope that from the friction of plausibility and distinctiveness there might arise the elements of a new adaptive mode of piety.

It is especially important for scientists, artists, and politicians to involve themselves in reclaiming the promised land. How many scientists still go to church? What occasions do they have to explore the impact of their work on the natural history of culture? How many talented artists, poets, novelists, filmmakers, and songwriters find themselves in a church regularly? What resources presently inform the work of these meme crafters? Where are the politicians? Do they ever converse with nonpoliticians? Where do the conversations take place between scientists, artists, and politicians? How can we hope for an integration of cosmos, ethos, and pathos before creating the social conditions for their interaction? These conversations might take place in the universities, but even so they amount to only a small and elite fraction of the interaction that must take place if Western culture stands a chance of revitalization. Let us consider the task in larger terms. Why not see in the church an opportunity for reintegration? There is a church within walking distance of every town and city dweller in Western civilization. What a network! What are the possibilities for revitalizing Western culture if in each one of these churches there were a lively and sustained conversation about the meaning and the conditions of human existence? Of course, this is what the church is for! But presently it is still fixed upon implausible conventions of understanding.

What we are really talking about here is finding an effective way of *institutionalizing* the scientific worldview. The scientific worldview is widely accepted, of course, and it is partly institutionalized by virtue of its central position in the educational system. But it has never been fully integrated into the myth of Western culture in the way the Platonic or Aristotelian worldviews were. One might say that the scientific worldview has penetrated all aspects of the myth of Western culture except its salvation scheme. The salvation scheme of our myth is still tied to an ancient cosmology. I say that it is time to get on with the business of changing this situation. It is time to take evolution seriously enough to make it the root metaphor of our culture and the substance of our salvation scheme. To institutionalize evolution in this way is probably the only realistic chance we have for regenerating the conditions for personal wholeness and social coherence. And the way to achieve this goal is to bring the limits of plausibility right square into the church and to apply them diligently. Then see what results.

Think back for a moment to what I had to say in chapter 2 about the function of the worship service. There it was said that the worship service was the principal instrument for instilling the memes of a myth in the biochemistry of the brain where they can shape behavior. Worship, as it were, translates principles into chemicals. The *only* problem with the church is that it has the principles wrong. It keeps talking about supernatural and individual salvation. Your role as architects of the New Covenant will be to help the church update its principles with a monistic and communal understanding of human existence. How will you achieve this? By going back into the churches armed with the metaphor of evolution and the hermeneutic of adaptivity and by applying these to the proclamation. In the process there will follow a new venture in mythopoesis. Do not worry about having all the particular elements of a new myth fully worked out; they will develop. Remember the early Christians. When they brought their messianic claims, minimal as these were, into the synagogues, they did not have all the particular images and metaphors worked out. Images and metaphors developed in the heat of interaction, that is, as the Christological hermeneutic was applied to the tradition. And eventually there emerged stories, letters, creeds, sermons, songs, pictures, statues, liturgies, and all the rest of the mechanics for transmitting a cultural tradition. It all started with a small core of assertions, and it started in the sanctuaries of the established religion. And it started because a few courageous people had a better idea about human existence and its conditions.

You will be called heretics. Never mind that; so were the early Christians. But they endured, and so will you, for you know that you are the true children of the promise. Remember also that for each one like yourselves who leaves the church the promise grows weaker, and for each one who returns the promise is strengthened.

It remains for me to make a few suggestions about the strategy and tactics of reclamation. The strategy is, again, to force the tension of plausibility and distinctiveness by reentering the churches and holding their teachings and practices accountable to the metaphor of evolution and the hermeneutic of adaptivity. In general the process will resemble the pattern of previous transpositions—that is, existing institutional forms will be reinterpreted within the new limits of plausibility. The cosmology of Mesopotamia became institutionalized in the worship life of ancient Israel as a result of an agricultural reinterpretation of Yahwism. And when the monarchy came to replace the confederacy, it adapted forms that were already in place. The same is true of the Christological reinterpretation of the Old Testament material. In the program at hand, the Covenant will be transposed by an evolutionary reinterpretation of traditional forms together with the invention of new forms.

It would take us far beyond the purpose of this book to actually carry out this program—this work falls to you—but it might at least be interesting to illustrate the approach by applying the limits of plausibility to the figure of Christ. This is the beginning point for a new departure from prevailing conventions. The earliest Christians maintained that Jesus of Nazareth was the Messiah, God's anointed one who was understood to be carrying out God's plan to bring an end to the old eon. Later in the tradition, under greater Hellenistic influences, Jesus came to be seen as the Son of God. Greek categories required that the significance of Jesus be expressed in terms of his nature and his metaphysical relation to God, and not simply in terms of his historic function. But it was of little importance whether Jesus' significance was put forth in functional or ontological terms; what was essential in the Christology of the early church from the very beginning was the insistence upon *identifying* Jesus with God. On one level of understanding, the essential claim of the Christian church was its assertion to be the true Covenant community, but on another level the distinctiveness of Christianity lay in the identification of the Christ with God: *Jesus is Lord.* Any reinterpretation of the Christ figure must preserve this identity, as it is the central claim of Christianity. So now we ask, what can be made of this Christological claim in light of the metaphor of evolution and the hermeneutic of adaptivity?

To begin, we would have to say that it is inappropriate to identify the Christ figure with the nature of God, since, as we have seen, there are no plausible means of speaking of God's nature. The Christological claim must therefore be made with reference to God's activity, that is, with reference to evolution. And here we might say that in the Christ figure we find revealed in a powerful way the logic (logos) of human evolution, that is, the logic of self-sacrifice. In the Christ figure we find revealed the paradox that in self-sacrifice there is found the promise of human life. In chapter 2 the point was made that self-sacrifice is a precondition for the specifically human form of adaptation, that is, culture. Without self-sacrifice there can be no authentically human life.

Under this interpretation of the Christ figure there is nothing at all implausible in the assertion that God was in Christ, if by that we mean to say that the Christ figure embodies the process by which we come to exist as human beings. This interpretation should not be seen as a piece of shallow reductionism, for in truth the Christ figure has never been available to us as anything more than the incarnation of a process. If a charge of reductionism is to be made, then it must be directed at those who transformed the Jesus of history into the Christ of faith. Nor is the ultimacy of the Christological claim lost under this interpretation, for the principle of self-sacrifice, revealed in the Christ figure, is not something without which human beings can possibly live; its recognition and realization are central to our salvation. To be a Christian is to confess, "It is in the Christ figure that I have come to see self-sacrificial behavior as non-optional."

This truth about our existence can be learned otherwise, however, so there is no basis for the claim that the Christ figure is unique. In fact, any claim to uniqueness must be rejected as implausible because it obstructs achievement of the universal promise of the Covenant. The uniqueness of the Christ figure works against the universal Covenant in the same way that circumcision did under the legalistic mode of piety. The true source of our salvation must finally be seen in the translation of the principle of self-sacrifice into the biochemistry of behavior, that is, *we too* must embody the process that is revealed to us in the Christ figure. This is what being *in Christ* can mean for us. And we should be prepared to accept the fact that the effectiveness of this translation in a contemporary setting may be enhanced by an aggressive denial of the uniqueness of the Christ figure. I am suggesting that the power of the Christ figure can actually be released by presenting the Christ as one of many occasions for recognizing the adaptive value of self-sacrifice. And here I am encouraging you to be shameless in your mythmaking. Feel free to borrow and create new forms of expression to supplement your reinterpretation of the Christ figure. Let your objective be your only guide, that is, to bring this generation to a commitment to serving the conditions of human existence.

The tactics of reclamation will vary according to the particular settings in which you find yourselves as well as according to your sense of style. The only useful advice is to encourage experimentation. Find a church and sit in. As you become involved in the life of the church, you may be surprised to find that quite a few others of like mind still attend. They will be especially pleased with your homecoming. Elect each other to whatever governing bodies prevail in the church, volunteer to teach Sunday school, join the choir, join the ancillary organizations, attend adult education programs, entertain the pastor in your home. Do not worry about not belonging there; it is *your* church. Remember that the church is what the church says it is, and *you* are the church. Never mind the creeds and prayers and hymns. They are really just archaic forms of affirming life. So join in. But at the same time you might add to the tradition. A tradition that abhors addition is moribund. You poets, write new verses for some of those spectacular hymns and request that they be sung by the congregation. Work up some alternative articles for a new creed, and ask for a discussion of their propriety in the adult education program. Try your hand at ten new commandments. Suggest to the pastor that he/she preach with more specificity about *this* life and what might be hoped for in a monistic cosmology. Send the pastor some books and articles that might be useful. Read the Bible in light of the hermeneutic of adaptivity, then gently challenge

189

the pastor's biblical interpretation. Encourage the most talented young people you know to consider the ministry as a profession. Find out how to influence the education of the clergy. Cultivate the view that the ministry is practical ecology. Find a way to engage your congregation in Jewish-Christian dialogue. Jews and Christians should discover together what brought about a parting of the ways and should then discuss together what the Covenant can mean in a world come of age.

In general, help the church to find new and adaptive ways to do and to say everything. Help the church to see that truth, goodness, and beauty are, of necessity, expressions of adaptivity. Help the church to see that its ultimate concern has always been for our survival. Let the church become a place for reflection upon the meaning and conditions of human existence. Let it become a place for assessing our performance and confessing our failures to fulfill these conditions. And let it become a place for renewing our commitments to recognize and obey these conditions. If the church cannot fulfill these functions within contemporary limits of plausibility, then it is, quite simply, no longer heir to the Covenant.

I have, for about a dozen years now, sustained a conversation with a colleague about the possibility that the church might be an effective force in the revitalization of Western culture. He says no—the church is too old, too bulky, too committed to dead metaphors. Hear him:

> I don't expect the church to haul itself heavily up on another Mount Nebo and catch a sudden vision of another promised land. It didn't happen that way the first time, either. Moses may have caught a glimpse of something dim in the distance, but the people drifted in for centuries. In a general direction. It is not reasonable to expect the church to do anything suddenly. It is too large, too old for amazing agility. Faced with poverty, we should expect the institution to form a committee and eventually decide to sell a crown or print brochures. It cannot do much else. The sudden changes are the province of sects. By definition, they wish for some different direction for things, and give it a try. They give up, go outside, and try something unusual.[1]

Perhaps. But it is too soon to give up and go outside. The trouble is that most of you gave up and went outside without having forced the church into a serious encounter with the scientific worldview. You left even before you amounted to a sect with a clear vision of an alternative for the church's future. All I am proposing is that we try it again. But this time, let us use all the artifice at our disposal to present a transposed and compelling Covenant to the modern mind.

Notes

Foreword

1. Friedrich Nietzsche, *The Birth of Tragedy*, trans. Hausmann (Edinburgh, Scotland: Foulis, 1910), p. 175.
2. William Barrett, *Time of Need: Forms of Imagination in the Twentieth Century* (New York: Harper, 1972), p. 339.

1. Nature and Culture

1. Richard Dawkins, *The Selfish Gene* (New York: Oxford University Press, 1976), p. 13.
2. Konrad Lorenz, *Behind the Mirror: A Search for a Natural History of Human Knowledge* (New York: Harcourt Brace Jovanovich, 1977), p. 27.
3. Mary Midgley, *Beast and Man: The Roots of Human Nature* (London: Methuen, 1980), pp. 306–17.
4. Lorenz, p. 113ff.
5. Carl Sagan, *The Dragons of Eden* (New York: Random House, 1977), p. 43.
6. See C. P. Snow, *The Two Cultures: and a Second Look* (New York: Cambridge University Press, 1959).
7. Michael Polanyi, *The Tacit Dimension* (New York: Doubleday, 1967); and *Personal Knowledge: Towards a Post-Critical Philosophy* (New York: Harper and Row, 1958).
8. Perhaps the best introduction to the controversies surrounding sociobiology is Michael Ruse's *Sociobiology: Sense or Nonsense?* (Dordrecht, Holland: D Reidel, 1979).
9. E. O. Wilson and Charles Lumsden, *Genes, Mind, and Culture* (Cambridge, Mass.: Harvard University Press, 1981), p.1.
10. Dawkins, p. 206.
11. Ibid.

2. Myth and Culture

1. Some of the issues discussed in this chapter relate to the new discipline called *evolutionary epistemology*. For a general introduction to the field, see H. C. Plotkin, ed., *Learning, Development, and Culture: Essays in Evolutionary Epistemology* (New York: John Wiley and Sons, 1982).

2. Paul MacLean, *A Triune Concept of the Brain and Behavior* (Toronto: University of Toronto Press, 1973).

3. Robert Isaacson, *The Limbic System* (New York: Plenum Press, 1974), p. 221.

4. Ibid., p. 243.

5. Leslie Hart, *Human Brain and Human Learning* (New York: Longman, 1983), p. 108.

6. Ibid., p. 106.

7. Michael Gazzaniga and Joseph LeDoux, *The Integrated Mind* (New York: Plenum Press, 1978), p. 137.

8. Helen Keller, *The Story of My Life* (New York: Doubleday-Page, 1903), pp. 23–24.

9. John R. Anderson, *Cognitive Psychology and Its Implications* (San Francisco: W. H. Freeman, 1980), chap. 4.

10. David Barash, *Sociobiology and Behavior* (New York: Elsevier, 1982), p. 256.

11. The scholarly literature on myth is vast, and I shall make no attempt here to survey the field. For a comprehensive view of major schools of interpretation, see William G. Doty, *Mythography: The Study of Myths and Rituals* (Tuscaloosa, Ala.: University of Alabama Press, 1986). See also Joseph Campbell, ed., *Myths, Dreams, and Religion* (New York: E. P. Dutton, 1970).

12. Stephen Pepper. *World Hypotheses* (Berkeley: University of California Press, 1942), p. 91.

13. Thomas S. Kuhn, *The Structure of Scientific Revolutions*, 2d ed. (Chicago: University of Chicago Press, 1962), p. 24.

14. See Joseph Campbell, "Mythological Themes in Creative Literature and Art," in *Myths, Dreams, and Religion*, pp. 138ff.

15. See Ira Progoff, "Waking Dream and Living Myth," in Campbell, *Myth, Dreams, and Religion*, p. 178.

3. The Crisis in Contemporary Culture

1. Christopher Dawson *The Dividing of Christendom* (Garden City, N. Y.: Image Books, 1967), p. 25.

2. Frederick Copleston, *A History of Philosophy*, vol. 2, pt. 1 (Garden City, N. Y.: Image Books, 1962), p. 120.

3. H. E. Barnes, *An Intellectual and Cultural History of the Western World* (New York: Dover, 1965), vol. 1, p. 334.

4. H. O. Taylor, *The Medieval Mind* (New York: Macmillan, 1927), vol. 2, pp. 76–77.

5. Ibid., p. 73.

6. For a summary of church history in the later Middle Ages, see Williston Walker, *A History of the Christian Church*, 4th ed., (New York: Charles Scribner's Sons, 1985), especially pp. 283–415.

7. Dawson, *The Dividing of Christendom*, p. 22.

8. David Maland, *Europe at War, 1600–1650* (London: Macmillan, 1980), p. 187.

9. Niccolo Machiavelli from *The Discourses* book 3, chap. 41, in *Michiavelli*, ed. John Plamenatz (London: Fontana/Collins, 1972), p. 302.

10. John Milton, *Aeropagitica and Other Prose Works* (London: J. M. Dent and Sons, 1927), pp. 36–37.

11. Peter Berger, *The Sacred Canopy* (Garden City, N. Y.: Anchor Books, 1967), p. 48.

12. See. A. J. Ayer, *Language, Truth, and Logic*, 2d ed. (London: Gollancz, 1946).

13. Benedict Spinoza from *The Ethics*, in *The Chief Works*, trans. R. H. M. Elwes (New York: Dover, 1951), vol. 2, p. 78.

14. Archibald MacLeish, "Hypocrite Auteur," in *Collected Poems, 1917–1952* (Boston: Houghton Mifflin, 1952), pp. 173–174.

15. Victor Frankl, *The Unheard Cry for Meaning* (London: Hodder and Stoughton, 1978), p. 26.

16. Robert Bellah, *Habits of the Heart: Individualism and Commitment in American Life* (Berkeley: University of California Press, 1985), p. 76.

17. *The American Freshman: National Norms for Fall 1987* (Los Angeles: Cooperative Institutional Research Program, 1987). This report has been published annually since 1966. See especially issues from 1975 to 1985.

18. I have seen no studies of the coincidence of decline of religion with the proliferation of political parties in Europe, though I suspect they might be revealing.

19. R. M. MacIver, *The Ramparts We Guard* (New York: Macmillan, 1950), p. 76.

4. The Limits of Distinctiveness

1. In the task of identifying divergent modes of piety, I have been influenced by E. P. Sanders's concept of "patterns of religion." See

Sanders, *Paul and Palestinian Judaism* (London: SCM Press, 1977), pp. 12–24.

2. The Bible seldom uses abstract terms such as "existence." The absence of such terms does not mean, however, that biblical authors were not mindful of existence and its conditions; it means only that we must look for their expression in more concrete images. For our purposes, "existence" finds its equivalent in the biblical use of "life." God, as the Giver of Life, is the source of existence. For a more complete account of the biblical use of "life," see G. W. Buchanan, *The Consequences of the Covenant* (Leiden: E. J. Brill, 1970), chap. 4.

3. For a portrayal of the patriarchs, see John Bright, *A History of Israel* (London: SCM Press, 1972), chap. 2.

4. Helmer Ringgren, *Israelite Religion*, trans. David Green (London: Society for Promoting Christian Knowledge, 1966), p. 27.

5. See Bright, *A History of Israel*, chap. 3, for a first-rate attempt to reconstruct this period on the basis of biblical and archaeological evidence.

6. So argues Bright, *A History of Israel*, p. 125.

7. W. J. Dumbrell, *Covenant and Creation* (Exeter. Paternoster Press, 1984), pp. 83–84.

8. Delbert Hillers, *Covenant: The History of a Biblical Idea* (Baltimore: John Hopkins University Press, 1969), pp. 25–45.

9. Norman K. Gottwald, *The Tribes of Yahweh: A Sociology of the Religion of Liberated Israel, 1250–1050 B. C. E.* (Maryknoll, N. Y.: Orbis Books, 1979), pp. 210–219.

10. Georg Fohrer, *A History of Israelite Religion*, trans. David Green (London: Society for Promoting Christian Knowledge, 1973), p. 47.

11. Bright, *A History of Israel*, p. 164.

12. This reconstruction is based on Robert Murray, "The Cosmic Covenant," paper delivered before the department of theology at Durham University, October 1985.

13. Ringgren, *Israelite Religion*, pp. 189–190.

14. The monarchy was not universally approved and remained a subject of criticism for its duration. Some critics continued to believe that a monarchy implied apostasy. See Fohrer, *A History of Israelite Religion*, pp. 149–50.

15. Walter Harrelson, *From Fertility Cult to Worship* (Garden City, N. Y.: Doubleday, 1969), p. 94.

16. Hillers, *Covenant: The History of a Biblical Idea*, p. 112.

17. Fohrer, *History of Israelite Religion*, p. 311.

18. Ibid., p. 313.

19. Dumbrell, *Covenant and Creation*, p. 206.

20. Ringgren, *Israelite Religion*, p. 335.

21. Geza Vermes, *Jesus and the World of Judaism* (London: SCM Press, 1983), p. 11.

22. Paul Johnson, *A History of Christianity* (New York: Atheneum, 1980), p. 3.

23. Samuel Sandmel, *The First Century in Judaism and Christianity* (New York: Oxford University Press, 1969), p. 28.

24. E. P. Sanders, *Paul, the Law, and the Jewish People* (Philadelphia: Fortress Press, 1983), p. 48.

25. Quoted in Johnson, *A History of Christianity*, p. 43.

26. W. H. C. Frend, *The Early Church* (Philadelphia: J. B. Lippincott, 1966), p. 46.

27. Quoted in J. L. Gonzalez, *A History of Christian Thought* (Nashville: Abingdon Press, 1970), vol. 1, p. 76.

28. Dietrich Bonhoeffer, *Letters and Papers from Prison*, ed. Eberhard Bethge, trans. Reginald Fuller (New York: Macmillan, 1967).

5. The Limits of Plausibility

1. For an overview of the controversy, see Bernard Murchland, ed., *The Meaning of the Death of God* (New York: Vintage Books, 1967).

2. A. R. Peacocke, *Creation and the World of Science* (Oxford: Clarendon Press, 1979), p. 113.

3. See Brian Stableford and David Langford, *The Third Millennium* (London: Sidgwick and Jackson, 1985), for an occasionally dreamy forecast of the future of biotechnology.

4. Konrad Lorenz, *Behind the Mirror*, p. 27.

6. Reclaiming the Promised Land

1. Conrad Røyksund, "An Urge to Harmonize." Luther College, Decorah, Iowa, 1984.

Selected Bibliography

Allison, Henry E. *Benedict de Spinoza*. Boston: Twayne, N.J.: 1975.

Alston, William P. *Philosophy of Language*. Englewood Cliffs, Prentice-Hall, 1964.

Anderson, John R. *Cognitive Psychology and Its Implications*. San Francisco: W. H. Freeman, 1980.

Arbib, Caplan, and John Marshall, eds. *Neural Models of Language Processes*. New York: Academic Press, 1982.

Arbib, Michael A. *The Metaphorical Brain*. New York: Wiley-Interscience, 1972.

Ayer, A. J. *Language, Truth, and Logic*. London: Gollancz, 1946.

Bainton, Roland. *The Horizon History of Christianity*. New York: Avon Books, 1966.

Barash, David. *Sociobiology and Behavior*. 2nd ed. New York: Elsevier, 1982.

———. *The Whisperings Within*. New York: Harper & Row, 1979.

Barbour, Ian. *Myths, Models, and Paradigms*. New York: Harper & Row, 1974.

Barnes, H. E. *An Intellectual and Cultural History of the Western World*. 3 vols. New York: Dover, 1965.

Bell, Clive. *Art*. New York: Capricorn Books, 1958.

Bellah, Robert N., et al. *Habits of the Heart: Individualism and Commitment in American Life*. Berkeley: University of California Press, 1985.

Benedict, Ruth. *Patterns of Culture*. Boston: Houghton Mifflin, 1934.

Berger, Peter L. *The Sacred Canopy*. Garden City, N.Y.: Anchor, 1969.

Black, Max. *Models and Metaphors: Studies in Language and Philosophy*. Ithaca, N.Y.: Cornell University Press, 1962.

Bloom, Alan. *The Closing of the American Mind*. New York: Simon and Schuster, 1987.

Bonhoeffer, Dietrich. *Letters and Papers from Prison*. Trans. Reginald Fuller. Ed. Eberhard Bethge. New York: Macmillan, 1967.

Bright, John. *A History of Israel*. 2nd ed. London: SCM Press, 1972.

Buchanan, G. W. *The Consequences of the Covenant*. Leiden: E. J. Brill, 1970.

Butter, Charles M. *Neuropsychology: The Study of Brain and Behavior*. Belmont. Calif.: Wadsworth, 1968.

Campbell, Joseph. *Myths to Live By*. New York: Viking Press, 1972.

Campbell, Joseph, ed. *Myths, Dreams, and Religion*. New York: E. P. Dutton, 1970.

Cassirer, Ernst. *Language and Myth*. Trans. Susanne K. Langer. New York: Harpers, 1946.

Cavalli-Storze, L. L., and Feldman, M. W. *Cultural Transmission and Evolution*. Princeton: Princeton University Press, 1981.

Chadwick, Henry. *The Early Church*. Middlesex: Penguin Books, 1967.

Chagnon, Napoleon A., and Irons, William, eds. *Evolutionary Biology and Human Social Behavior*. North Sichuate, Mass.: Duxbury Press, 1979.

Changeux, Jean-Pierre. *Neuronal Man: The Biology of Mind*. Trans. Laurence Garey. New York: Oxford University Press, 1985.

Chomsky, Noam. *Language and Mind*. New York: Harcourt, Brace & World, 1968.

Clements, R. E. *Prophecy and Tradition*. Oxford: Basil Blackwell, 1975.

Clinard, Marshall B., ed. *Anomie and Deviant Behavior*. Glencoe, Ill.: Free Press, 1964.

Conway, Flo, and James Siegelman. *Snapping*. New York: Delta, 1978.

Copleston, Frederick. *A History of Philosophy*, 9 vols. Garden City, N.Y.: Image Books, 1963.

Corning, Peter A. *The Synergism Hypothesis*. New York: McGraw-Hill, 1983.

Cranfield, C. E. B. *Romans: A Shorter Commentary*. Edinburgh: T. & T. Clark, 1985.

Cupitt, Don. *Only Human*. London: SCM Press, 1985.

Daly, Martin, and Margo Wilson. *Sex, Evolution, and Behavior*. 2nd ed. Boston: Willard Grant Press, 1983.

Davies, J. G. *The Early Christian Church*. London: Weidenfeld & Nicolson, 1965.

Dawkins, Richard. *The Selfish Gene*. New York: Oxford University Press, 1976.

Dawson, Christopher. *The Dividing of Christendom*. Garden City, N.Y.: Image Books, 1967.

————. *The Formation of Christendom*. New York: Sheed & Ward, 1967.

De Grazia, Sebastian. *The Political Community: A Study of Anomie*. Chicago: University of Chicago Press, 1948.

Despland, Michel. *The Education of Desire*. Toronto: University of Toronto Press, 1985.

Doty, William G. *Mythography: The Study of Myths and Rituals*. Tuscaloosa: University of Alabama Press, 1986.

Dumbrell, W. J. *Covenant and Creation*. Exeter: Paternoster Press, 1984.

Eibl-Eibesfeldt, Irenaus. *The Biology of Peace and War*. New York: Viking Press, 1979.

Eichrodt, Walther. *Theology of the Old Testament*. 2 vols. London: SCM Press, 1967.

Embler, Weller. *Metaphor and Meaning*. Jacksonville, Fla.: Everett/Edwards, 1966.

Feldman, Edmund B. *The Artist*. Englewood Cliffs, N.J.: Prentice-Hall, 1982.

Festinger, Leon. *A Theory of Cognitive Dissonance*. London: Tavistock Publications, 1957.

Fohrer, Georg. *History of Israelite Religion*. London: S.P.C.K., 1973.

Frankl, Victor. *The Unheard Cry for Meaning*. London: Hodder & Stoughton, 1978.

Frend, W. H. C. *The Early Church*. Philadelphia: J. B. Lippincott, 1966.

Gager, John G. *Kingdom and Community*. Englewood Cliffs, N.J.: Prentice-Hall, 1975.

Gans, Eric. *The Origin of Language*. Berkeley: University of California Press, 1981.

Garforth, F. W. *Education and Social Purpose*. London: Oldbourne Book, 1962.

Gazzaniga, Michael S., and Colin Blakemore, eds. *Handbook of Psychobiology*. New York: Academic Press, 1975.

Gazzaniga, Michael S., and Joseph E. LeDoux. *The Integrated Mind*. New York: Plenum Press, 1978.

Geertz, Clifford. *The Interpretation of Cultures*. New York: Basic Books, 1973.

Glover, Willis B. *Biblical Origins of Modern Secular Culture*. Macon, Ga.: Mercer University Press, 1984.

Gonzalez, Justo L. *A History of Christian Thought*. 3 vols. Nashville: Abingdon Press, 1970.

———. *The Story of Christianity*. 2 vols. San Francisco: Harper & Row, 1984.

Gottwald, Norman K. *The Tribes of Yahweh*. Maryknoll, N.Y.: Orbis Books, 1979.

Grant, Michael. *Saint Paul*. London: Weidenfeld & Nicolson, 1976.

Grant, R. M. *Gnosticism and Early Christianity*. New York: Harper & Row, 1966.

Gray, John. *The Canaanites*. London: Thames & Hudson, 1964.

Gregory, Silvers, and Diane Sutch. *Sociobiology and Human Nature*. San Francisco: Jossey-Bass, 1978.

Harrelson, Walter. *From Fertility Cult to Worship*. Garden City, N.Y.: Doubleday, 1969.

Hart, Leslie A. *Human Brain and Human Learning*. New York: Longman, 1983.

Hawkes, Terence. *Metaphor*. London: Methuen, 1972.

Hewstone, Miles, ed. *Attribution Theory: Social and Functional Extensions*. Oxford: Basil Blackwell, 1983.

Hillers, Delbert. *Covenant: The History of a Biblical Idea*. Baltimore: John Hopkins University Press, 1969.

Isaacson, Robert I. *The Limbic System*. New York: Plenum Press, 1974.

Jerison, Harry J. *Evolution of the Brain and Intelligence*. New York: Academic Press, 1973.

Johnson, Paul. *A History of Christianity*. New York: Atheneum, 1980.

Keller, Helen. *The Story of My Life*. New York: Doubleday-Page, 1903.

Kelly, J. N. D. *Early Christian Doctrines*. London: Adam & Charles Black, 1977.

Kirk, Ursula, ed. *Neuropsychology of Language, Reading, and Spelling*. New York: Academic Press, 1983.

Klopf, A. Harry. *The Hedonistic Neuron*. New York: Hemisphere, 1982.

Kneller, George F. *Educational Anthropology: An Introduction*. London: John Wiley & Sons, 1965.

Kris, Ernst, and Otto Kurz. *Legend, Myth, and Magic in the Image of the Artist*. New Haven: Yale University Press, 1979.

Kuhn, Thomas S. *The Structure of Scientific Revolutions*. Chicago: University of Chicago Press, 1962.

Küng, Hans. *Art and the Question of Meaning*. New York: Crossroad Publishing, 1981.

Langer, Suzanne. *Philosophy in a New Key*. Cambridge, Mass.: Harvard University Press, 1960.

Lenneberg, E. H. *Biological Foundations of Language*. New York: Wiley, 1967.

Levitt, Eugene E. *The Psychology of Anxiety*. 2nd ed. Hillsdale, N.J: Lawrence Erlbaum Associates, 1980.

Lightfoot, David. *The Language Lottery*. Cambridge, Mass.: MIT Press, 1982.

Lindbeck, George A. *The Nature of Doctrine*. Philadelphia: Westminster Press, 1984.

Lippard, Lucy R. *Overlay: Contemporary Art and the Art of Prehistory*. New York: Pantheon Books, 1983.

Loew, Cornelius. *Myth, Sacred History, and Philosophy.* New York: Harcourt, Brace & World, 1967.

Lorenz, Konrad. *Behind the Mirror: A Search for a Natural History of Knowledge.* New York: Harcourt Brace Jovanovich, 1977.

Lubar, Joel F., ed. *A First Reader in Physiological Psychology.* New York: Harper & Row, 1972.

McCleary, Robert A., and Robert Y. Moore. *Subcortical Mechanisms of Behavior.* New York: Basic Books, 1965.

MacIntyre, Alistair. *After Virtue.* Notre Dame, Ind.: University of Notre Dame Press, 1981.

MacIver, R. M. *The Ramparts We Guard.* New York: Macmillan, 1950.

McKay, John. *Religion in Judah under the Assyrians.* London: SCM Press, 1973.

MacLean, Paul. *A Triune Concept of the Brain and Behavior.* Toronto: University of Toronto Press, 1973.

Maland, David. *Europe at War, 1600–1650.* London: Macmillan, 1980.

Manis, Melvin. *Cognitive Processes.* Belmont, Calif.: Wadsworth, 1966.

Martland, Thomas R. *Religion as Art: An Interpretation.* Albany: State University of New York Press, 1981.

Maxwell, Mary. *Human Evolution: A Philosophical Anthropology.* New York: Columbia University Press, 1984.

Mayes, A. D. N. *Israel in the Period of the Judges.* London: SCM Press, 1974.

Merton, Robert K. *Social Theory and Social Structure.* New York: Free Press, 1968.

————. *Sociological Ambivalence and Other Essays.* New York: Free Press, 1976.

Midgley, Mary. *Beast and Man: The Roots of Human Nature.* London: Methuen, 1980.

Miller, George A., and Elizabeth Lenneberg, eds. *Psychology and Biology of Language and Thought.* New York: Academic Press, 1978.

Milton, John. *Aeropagitica and Other Prose Works.* London: J. M. Dent & Sons, 1927.

Murchland, Bernard, ed. *The Meaning of the Death of God.* New York: Vintage Books, 1967.

Musgrave, P. W. *The Sociology of Education.* 3rd ed. London: Methuen, 1979.

Oatley, Keith. *Perceptions and Representations.* New York: Free Press, 1978.

Ornstein, Robert, and Richard F. Thompson. *The Amazing Brain.* Boston: Houghton Mifflin, 1984.

Ottaway, A. K. C. *Education and Society.* London: Routledge & Kegan Paul, 1953.

Paivio, Allan. *Imagery and Verbal Processes*. New York: Holt, Rinehart & Winston, 1971.

———. "Mental Imagery in Associative Learning and Memory." *Psychological Review*, vol. 76, no. 3 (May 1969), pp. 241–263.

Peacocke, A. R. *Creation and the World of Science*. Oxford: Clarendon Press, 1979.

Pelikan, Jaroslav. *Historical Theology: Continuity and Change in Christian Doctrine*. New York: Corpus, 1971.

Pepper, Stephen C. *World Hypotheses*. Berkeley: University of California Press, 1942.

Phares, E. Jerry. *Locus of Control in Personality*. Morristown, N.J.: General Learning Press: 1976.

Piaget, Jean. *The Origin of Intelligence in the Child*. Originally published 1936. London: Penguin, 1977.

Plamenatz, John, ed. *Machiavelli*. London: Fontana/Collins, 1972.

Plotkin, H. C. *Learning, Development, and Culture: Essays in Evolutionary Epistemology*. New York: John Wiley & Sons, 1982.

Polanyi, Michael. *Personal Knowledge: Towards a Post-Critical Philosophy*. New York: Harper & Row, 1958.

———. *The Tacit Dimension*. New York: Doubleday, 1967.

Prestige, G. L. *Fathers and Heretics*. London: S.P.C.K., 1977.

Restak, Richard M. *The Brain: The Last Frontier*. New York: Warner Books, 1979.

Ricoeur, Paul. *The Rule of Metaphor*. Toronto: University of Toronto Press, 1977.

Ringgren, Helmer. *Israelite Religion*. Trans. David Green. London: S.P.C.K., 1966.

Rorty, Richard. *The Consequences of Pragmatism*. Minneapolis: University of Minnesota Press, 1982.

Rose, Steven. *The Conscious Brain*. New York: Vintage Books, 1976.

Rowley, H. H. *Worship in Ancient Israel*. London: S.P.C.K., 1976.

Rurtenbeek, Hendrik M. *The Individual and the Crowd*. New York: Mentor Books, 1964.

Ruse, Michael. *Sociobiology: Sense or Nonsense*. Dordrecht: D. Reidel, 1979.

Sagan, Carl. *The Dragons of Eden*. New York: Ballantine, 1978.

Sanders, E. P. *Paul, the Law, and the Jewish People*. Philadelphia: Fortress Press, 1983.

———. *Paul and Palestinian Judaism*. London: SCM Press, 1977.

Sandmel, Samuel. *The First Century in Judaism and Christianity*. New York: Oxford University Press, 1969.

———. *The Genius of Paul*. New York: Schocken Books, 1970.

Sewell, Elizabeth. *The Human Metaphor.* Notre Dame, Ind.: University of Notre Dame Press, 1964.

Shils, Edward. *Tradition.* Chicago: University of Chicago Press, 1981.

Smith, Curtis, G. *Ancestral Voices: Language and the Evolution of Human Consciousness.* Englewood Cliffs, N.J.: Prentice-Hall, 1985.

Snow, C. P. *The Two Cultures: And a Second Look.* New York: Cambridge University Press, 1959.

Spinoza, Benedict. *The Chief Works.* Trans. R.H.M. Elwes. 2 vols. New York: Dover Publications, 1951.

Spitz, Lewis W. *The Renaissance and Reformation Movements.* Chicago: Rand McNally, 1971.

Stableford, Brian, and David Langford. *The Third Millennium.* London: Sidgwick & Jackson, 1985.

Tapper, Ted. *Young People and Society.* London: Faber & Faber, 1971.

Taylor, H. O. *The Medieval Mind.* 2 vols. New York: Macmillan, 1927.

Trivers, Robert. *Social Evolution.* Menlo Park, Calif.: Benjamin/Cummings, 1985.

Vermes, Geza. *Jesus and the World of Judaism.* London: SCM Press, 1983.

Walker, Williston. *A History of the Christian Church.* New York: Charles Scribner's Sons, 1985.

Wheelwright, Philip. *The Burning Fountain: A Study in the Language of Symbolism.* Bloomington: Indiana University Press, 1968.

———. *Metaphor and Reality.* Bloomington: Indiana University Press, 1962.

White, Robert W., and Norman F. Watt. *The Abnormal Personality.* 5th ed. New York: John Wiley & Sons, 1981.

Whorf, Benjamin Lee. *Language, Thought, and Reality.* Cambridge, Mass.: MIT Press, 1956.

Wiles, Maurice. *The Christian Fathers.* London: SCM Press, 1966.

Williams, Robin M. *American Society: A Sociological Interpretation.* New York: Alfred Knopf, 1964.

Wilson E. O. *On Human Nature.* New York: Bantam Books, 1979.

———. *Sociobiology: The New Synthesis.* Cambridge, Mass.: Belknap Press, 1975.

Wilson, E. O., and Charles Lumsden. *Genes, Mind, and Culture.* Cambridge, Mass.: Harvard University Press, 1981.

———. *Promethean Fire.* Cambridge, Mass.: Harvard University Press, 1983.

Wolf, Eric. *Anthropology.* Englewood Cliffs, N.J.: Prentice-Hall, 1964.

Young, J. Z. *Programs of the Brain.* Oxford: Oxford University Press, 1978.

Index

About the Author

Loyal D. Rue is Associate Professor, Department of Religion and Philosophy, Luther College, Iowa.